VIEW OF THE GROUNDS

D0098580

AMERICAN SPACE

John Brinckerhoff Jackson

AMERICAN SPACE

The Centennial Years
1865-1876

W·W·NORTON & COMPANY·INC·
New York

Copyright © 1972 by W. W. Norton & Company, Inc.
FIRST EDITION

Library of Congress Cataloging in Publication Data
Jackson, John Brinckerhoff, 1909–
    American space.

    Bibliography: p.
    1. United States—Description and travel—
1865–1900.   2. United States—History—1865–1898.
I. Title.
E168.J24   917.3'03'8   72-5266
ISBN 0-393-06321-6

PRINTED IN THE UNITED STATES OF AMERICA

1 2 3 4 5 6 7 8 9 0

TO
W . G . J .

Contents

Contents

Illustrations

AMERICAN SPACE

CHAPTER ONE

USA

1. AFTER THE WAR

The coffee-table book—large, handsomely bound and illustrated, with a modicum of text—has long been a familiar feature of the American home. The current fashion is for colored reproductions of obscure works of art, and for sensitive photographs of untouched nature, also in color; the remote, the primitive appear to have the greatest appeal. But a hundred years ago popular taste preferred familiar subjects. Book after enormous book was published to show by means of pictures what a remarkable people we were and what a remarkable country we lived in.

This was not hard to do, for in the 1870s there seemed to be many reasons for optimism and national self-satisfaction. After a ruinous civil war the Republic was reunited, more prosperous, more vigorous than ever. The completion in 1869 of the Union Pacific had revealed to us some of the promise of the West, and as the public well knew, within a few years' time the hundredth anniversary of our independence was to be celebrated by an immense international fair. What could have been more natural than for us to remind ourselves of our accomplishments as a nation, and to seek to learn more about the vast new regions extending to the Pacific? We were aware of our social and cultural shortcomings, but the progress we had made during the first century of our existence was a topic few Americans could fail to find inspiring.

It was in response to this sentiment that a great number of books depicting America and its triumphs made their appearance in the decade after the war. As literature, as history, as reliable description, few of them deserve praise. More often than not the accompanying text made much of our small beginnings and boastfully told of how far we had come since Jamestown and Plymouth, and of how in many ways we now excelled the rest of mankind. "Foreigners," said the editor of *Our Country and Its Resources*—a book with more than 260 illustrations—"have often given us credit for being the only religious nation in the world." He noted that Americans bathed more often and were possessed of more refinement. Still, it was for the pictures that the books were bought, and it was to them that the possessor quickly turned.

Innumerable woodcuts and engravings, many of them crude, some of them works of art, gave glimpses of our past and of our scenery: Indians lurking in the forest, bearded farmers riding on sulky plows, frontiersmen chopping down trees, tremendous waterfalls; Paul Revere galloping through the spring night, battles in the recent war, and many panoramas of towns of brick and slate, plumes of smoke coming from factory chimneys. For all their distortion and irrelevant detail, they still call back to life episodes in our history with a vividness few photographs can rival.

The tendency to take stock, to contrast the present with the past, was not confined to commercial publishers. In 1874 the United States government produced its own version of the coffee-table book: an enormous atlas, sixteen by twenty-eight inches, based on the census of 1870. Much of its text, as well as many of its charts and maps, dealt with the growth of the population and its expansion since the first census of 1790. It was intended, so the foreword said, "to promote the kind of political education which has hitherto been so greatly neglected in this country." So the five thousand copies of the atlas were mostly distributed to colleges and schools.

By modern standards of graphics or cartography the publication was far from perfect; but for its time it was innovative in
several ways. The superintendent of the ninth census (and the
compiler of the atlas) was Francis Amasa Walker, professor of
political economy at Yale, later to be president of M.I.T., and an
economist of international reputation. It was he who was largely
responsible for making the national census what it is now: a
comprehensive statistical survey of the economic and demographic
growth of the nation during the previous decade; until his time
it had been little more than an elaborate head count. It was also
Walker who in this atlas introduced to America the official use
of what is now known as thematic cartography—the inclusion of
other than topographic and political information on maps. Maps
with superimposed symbols and colors are now of course very
common, but it was not until the middle of the nineteenth century that they came into general use. The great expositions, beginning with that of London in 1851, had been faced with the
task of presenting statistics in a manner easily understood by the
public, and a variety of now familiar signs and symbols were
devised. Many of these were used by Walker in his atlas and
others were invented—notably the "pie," or as it was then called,
"the clock with several hands." Walker himself undertook to illustrate certain population statistics from the census by means
of varying intensity of color on maps. His efforts were shown at
a meeting of the American Geographical Society in 1871, where
they aroused such interest that the Secretary of the Interior was
persuaded to authorize a special atlas where both of these novel
techniques were used: shades of a color, and symbols.

There were maps of the physical features of the United States
—rivers and forests and geological formations and rainfall; and
then there were maps illustrating population distribution and
industry and vital statistics. There were maps of the incidence
of deaf mutes and intestinal diseases, of foreign-born, of illiteracy
—not only by state but by county—all in varying intensities of
one color. To us there is nothing unusual in the procedure; but
Walker was the first American to try to show the spatial dimen-
sion of social and economic facts, to relate social problems to
their physical setting and thereby throw a new light on them.

How was America to be understood by its citizens unless they
learned to perceive the relation between men and their environment? And this they could do (Walker suggested in his foreword)
by comparing the physiographic maps with those devoted to
population and industry. "The compiler trusts . . . that this juxtaposition of the two orders of facts will afford the true explanation of a vast number of phenomena seeming most strange and
contradictory . . . that an illustration, so large and varied, of the
effects of physical influences upon the progress of population and
the condition of society, may even serve to suggest to the physical
geographer some possible modification of his own generaliza-
tions."

Almost all of the maps show the existence in 1870 of a clear-
cut western boundary to the area of continuous settlement—
which to Walker meant an area where there were at least two
persons to the square mile. At that date the population of the
United States was about 38,500,000. Of this number perhaps a
million lived west of that line of continuous settlement—in California, Oregon, Utah, Colorado, and New Mexico. Walker further
included among these exiles "the solitary ranchman, the trapper,
and fisherman, the small mining party, and the lumbering camp
at the sources of the streams that find their later way into the
more populous regions." But where precisely was this line of continuous settlement, east of which lived the overwhelming majority of Americans? Roughly speaking, it followed the 97th meridian, which runs due north and south some fifty miles west of the
Minnesota–North Dakota line, passes near Wichita, Kansas, and
again some miles west of Fort Worth, it divides the United States
into two almost equal parts—which is to say that a hundred years
ago more than half of the country was without continuous settlement as we understand it.

In reality the line was not so neatly drawn. A westward bulge
of the line in Texas included San Antonio. Along the Platte
and Missouri rivers long thin fingers of settlement reached into
the otherwise empty plain, and all the way from Laramie, Wyoming, down into the Rio Grande Valley, there was a narrow
but continuous settled area, just as there was the length of Utah.
On the other hand, much of northern Minnesota and Wisconsin

lay outside the line. So, for political reasons, did Oklahoma, then known as the Indian Territory. Furthermore, in 1870 there was a sizable piece of northern Michigan where not even two people lived in each square mile of forest. The southern half of Florida, as well as the Adirondacks, was beyond the pale. Finally, a large fragment of northern Maine had lost population during the previous decade and had in a sense reverted to wilderness. This was the one region of the United States where the population had significantly decreased, and Walker ascribed the change to casualties in the war, emigration to the West, and the collapse of the shipbuilding industry.

The density of population varied considerably. It was highest in New England and the Middle Atlantic States—74 persons to the square mile. (It is now more than 350.) But another region of high density extended from south of Chicago up the western shore of Lake Superior to Green Bay, Wisconsin. It consisted chiefly of Americans of German descent. As might be expected, the lowest density was to be found in the frontier lands of Kansas and Nebraska, though coastal Georgia and northern Florida were also scantily populated.

Walker had his own way of defining cities: to him they were communities (no matter what they chose to call themselves) with more than 8000 inhabitants. Even by this generous definition only about a fifth of the American population could be called urban; all the rest lived in villages or on farms. During the previous ten years there had been a sensational increase in the number of large cities—those between 250,000 and 500,000 inhabitants. In 1860 New York had been the only one; in 1870 there were five: New York, Philadelphia, Brooklyn, St. Louis, and Chicago, in the order of their size.

The black population was still largely concentrated in the area of the onetime Confederacy; it was most numerous in the lowlands of Mississippi and in the Black Belt of Alabama—so called because of its rich soil; and in South Carolina blacks outnumbered whites. Already there were black communities in most of the northern cities, and blacks were part of the frontier populations of Kansas and Texas. Every other American in those days was either a Methodist or a Baptist; more Americans were engaged in agriculture than in any other occupation, except in industrialized New England and the Middle Atlantic States, and in California and Nevada where mining was favored.

The modern American who examines the atlas is likely to be struck by the great number of very distinct demographic areas that existed in the country a hundred years ago: areas where there were more men than women, where incomes were either extraordinarily high or extraordinarily low; where there were concentrations of foreign-born or illiterates, or where the per-capita public indebtedness was unusually high. Walker and his contemporaries no doubt perceived these spots of intense color as clearly as we would; but he made no comment on them. Apparently he was content to define the regions of the United States, except for the East Coast, in terms not of social characteristics but in terms of river basins; and in itself this kind of definition marked a great advance in recognition of environmental factors over the traditional definition in terms of states. Perhaps one reason for Walker's refusal to define these regions demographically was that it would have been contrary to the temper of the times to give formal recognition to spaces which had neither well-defined legal or topographical boundaries: spaces whose content was very much in transition and which would be eliminated by what he termed the "imperial sweep" of the growing nation.

2. EXPANSION

In the decade after the Civil War there could not have been many persons left to remember the early years of the Republic. They would have belonged to that fortunate generation which rediscovered and first celebrated the wonders of the still half-wild landscape of America. Niagara Falls, the Valley of the Hudson, the White Mountains, the North Forest had moved and inspired them all when they were young. Yet sometimes it had been as if they were strangers admiring alien works of art; neither history nor daily association had as yet had time to create a bond between them and the surrounding splendor; they did not yet belong together. If as Americans they speculated about the relationship it was to hope that the natural scenery would have an edifying effect on the people living in its midst.

The younger generation saw the national environment in a different light. Perhaps they knew it better, for they had traveled more. Though they inherited without questioning their parents' belief in the superiority of America over all other nations, they had a belief of their own that the country belonged to them by right of conquest as well as by right of inheritance: it was theirs to do with as they pleased. Unlike their fathers they saw themselves not merely as inhabitants but as owners, and with an owner's instinct they sought to find out the value of the patrimony.

That is why, during the postwar years, the relationship between Americans and their environment began to change. The relationship had no less of love and pride, but it had less emotion and more of calculation. We had acquired new needs, and we looked to the landscape to satisfy them. Reverence for the past and for the beauties of unblemished nature was certainly a virtue; but there were practical matters to take into account. Simply to admire the richness of the land was no longer enough.

In terms of everyday work, the generation of the postwar years undertook to reorganize the national landscape and bring it up-to-date. With what objective in mind? Growth: but growth of an unheard-of sort, geometric and without discernible limits. It was clear to all and welcome to most that the United States was about to embark on a period of extraordinary expansion, and Berkeley's lines on the course of empire were quoted as a prophecy soon to be fulfilled. Who could doubt that in the half century to come the nation would outgrow its present boundaries? One statistician confidently foretold a population in 1960 of 3 billion; others, more cautious, calculated that by 1900 there would be 300 million Americans, the majority west of the Mississippi; F. A. Walker suspected that even 90 million was an optimistic figure. More room, in any event, would be needed. Cuba, alternating between period of ominous discontent and even more ominous quiet, was to be had for the taking; it was only a matter of time before Canada became part of the Union. Mexico would inevitably become an American charge, though not (so it was widely hoped) until its people had learned better civic behavior. California, in the seventies still a frontier community but already foreseeing the time when it would be the most heavily populated state in the Union, made friendly gestures toward the Sandwich Islands, as Hawaii was then called. The purchase of Alaska in 1867 was thus a sensible precaution. Worthless for the time being, it belonged to the Western Empire of the future.

State after western state estimated its future growth: Kansas with a little more than 300,000 inhabitants in 1870 saw itself with 30 million a half century later. Fortunately the new states and territories had generous dimensions; textbooks and editorials tirelessly repeated the familiar comparisons between the New West and the Old East: Colorado was twelve times the size of Massachusetts, Arizona was the size of all New England, with New York and New Jersey added for good measure; every mountain cascade was shown to be somehow superior to Niagara, every plain exceeded Mt. Washington in height. "These are marvelous boundaries," exclaimed one writer on the lands beyond the Mississippi, "and they represent the grand scale upon which our new Western countryside is laid out . . . Nothing is done there in a small way. Human plans are as large as the states."

But the East felt the need for expansion too; dissatisfaction with existing boundaries, whether of the farm, the village, the city, was general, and there was scarcely a large center that had not, to its own gratified amazement, expanded during the previous decade well beyond its established political boundaries. Although Manhattan Island still contained patches of wilderness, New York City had started to invade the mainland in Westchester County, and Brooklyn was reaching out into rural Long Island. Along the lines of the horse-drawn streetcars, and in the seventies along the lines of the cable cars and elevated railways, cities stretched tentacles into the neighboring farmlands. Small-time contractors built rows of detached dwellings on speculation, encouraged by the eagerness of city officials to extend roads and waterlines out beyond the built-up areas. "New York and Philadelphia," observed an architectural journal in 1870, "have been the scene of extensive operations in real estate within the last few years. In the neighborhood of both these cities, farms without number have been purchased by speculators and divided up into lots, which have been sold to another class of buyers, also speculators." The density of the city population—save in the oldest and poorest sections—declined, but the city itself spread wider and wider. "We are confronted with the appalling prospect of a place of business ten miles long," a New York editor complained, "with twenty-five or thirty miles of wharfage and shipping on three sides. What must be the scale of expenses when such monstrous distances must be traveled in the transactions of business?" A flurry of speculation about the city of the future appeared in magazines and newspapers after the Chicago Fire of 1871; all agreed that more space, more spaciousness was urgently needed: but upward or outward—which way was the city to expand? The New York *World* offered "the ideal city of the nineteenth century" to its readers; a city with a downtown business section of broad streets and ample public transportation. Surrounding it was to be "a broad area . . . where every house could have a goodly expanse of ground about it filled with trees and shrubbery . . . There is no reason why a man should not spend his days in the din and turmoil of the wharves and exchanges, and walk in the close of the evening amid the trees and vines of a rural home." Alluring though the vision was, it had its detractors: flight to the suburbs meant the evisceration of the city. Already in the early seventies there were lamentations that New York was increasingly the home of the very poor and the very rich; the substantial middle class was fleeing it in increasing numbers. "A rich, specific, and magnificent life arises from the compactness of settlement in cities," the editor of a monthly magazine declared, "which diffusion and distribution would more or less impair. . . . The 'ideal city' would be prone to divide the interest, weaken the intercourse, and abridge the pleasures of the people." The writer then proposed his own solution: the expansion of the American city upward into the air space. The development of the steam-powered elevator justified thinking of great residential towers, ten stories high or higher. Roof gardens would substitute for suburban greenery.

More space was always the answer; less space, or space confined within irrational limits was seen as the source of many environmental evils. Every attempt to design larger and more humane tenements in the seventies seemed to founder on the obsolete dimensions of the average city lot. What could be built on a piece of land with a street frontage of 25 feet and a depth of 100? This was not the only reason tenement design showed little improvement, certainly; but more and more architects clamored for some reorganization of urban space and dreamt of limitless room as the only true solution of urban problems.

Horizontal growth, swift, unplanned expansion over the countryside, was what prevailed in the smaller cities and towns, whether factory towns in the East or new railroad towns in the West. No longer limited in size by dependence on a finite source of power—falling water—the steam-powered factories which began to multiply in the seventies stretched their brick lengths parallel to the railroad tracks, mile after mile: inexhaustible supplies of coal meant limitless growth. Whereas in former times the workers had lived in a cluster near the factory, now they moved away (when they could) into the newer, more spacious flats and duplex houses provided by speculative builders on the outskirts of town, leaving their former dwellings to the poorer, more recently arrived immigrants. If at first it was the factory which promoted the sprawling growth of towns, the railroad, particularly in the metropolitan East, contributed its share. "It is curious to observe," wrote an architect in the seventies of the new towns growing up around Philadelphia, "that as they hug the railroads they almost invariably succeed." In the Midwest and in the Plains States, the landscape architect Horace Cleveland in the seventies noted how every whistle-stop confidently looked forward to becoming, at no very distant date, an important city. Its unpaved, untraveled streets were appropriately broad, the rows of stakes marking the still unsold lots extended for miles. It was another landscape architect, Morris Copeland, who in the same years advised the small towns in the East to think and plan for future expansion. "New towns," he said, "may grow to be a Chicago or St. Louis, and each should have its maturity foreseen and provided for in its infancy." He advised farmers living near towns to plant their hedges and lay out their roads with future residential developments in mind.

As always the city dweller fancied that the rural landscape

was a place of unchanging harmony, to be cherished and protected, but in fact no part of the environment was less wedded to the established spatial order. "The country is full of rural improvements," the editor of a farm journal announced in the late sixties—and then went on to suggest many more for the future.

The size of farms was increasing, and the further west one traveled, the larger they became. In the forties a farm of 80 acres had been held to be of manageable size for the new farmer in a new region, but the homestead of 1862, of 160 acres, was none too large in the Midwest, and the farmer venturing into the Great Plains soon wanted another quarter section. Expansion of the farm not being everywhere possible, next best was expansion in the size of the fields. A generation earlier the policy had been to have many small fields; fields of ten acres, square in shape, each surrounded by a stout fence; but in the sixties, fields four times as extensive were becoming general, and a farming expert in Illinois urged the planting of hedges or the building of fences around every 80 acres of a farm. The reasons for the expansion in the size of fields were obvious: mechanized farming equipment called for more space for maneuvering, and the tendency to raise one or two commercial crops—wheat or corn or hay—instead of a variety of crops for home consumption made the former fragmentation unnecessary and highly inconvenient. Moreover the increasing cost of fencing irritated many farmers. To the vexatious problem of how to provide space with effective boundaries a number of solutions were proposed: hedges of various kinds, portable fences, trenches and walls of sod, strands of wire. The invention in 1874 of an effective barbed wire provided the perfect answer: fences became flexible, easy to erect, and inexpensive. They also became all but invisible, to the dismay of the first generation of livestock to brush against them.

The final effect of all these changes—increase in the size of farms, consolidation of fields, introduction of the barbed-wire fence—was to give the rural landscape of America, beginning in the seventies, a new spaciousness, a larger scale. Nowhere was the search for a more efficient organization of space more noticeable than in the new type of barn that became common throughout the United States in the years after the war. "It was a former practice," wrote the editor of the *Country Gentleman* in 1876, "to place barn buildings in the form of a hollow square, surrounding and sheltering the cattle and manure yard. The practice is now becoming more common and approved to group all the accommodations in one building, as it is more compact, less expensive in erection, is warmer in winter, and saves much labor in attendance by placing everything near at hand." Like many other contemporaneous developments, the new barn represented the solution of a number of distinct problems, economic, social, and technological, all requiring a new organization of space. The invention of the balloon frame in the 1830s and its immediate popularity in the Midwest permitted the rapid construction of houses by relatively unskilled persons, using light, milled members of standard sizes, nailed together rather than joined. The balloon frame possessed other advantages over the traditional type of timber construction: it allowed of greater interior spaces without interruption, and it was relatively easy to modify or add to. It was therefore ideally suited for the building of barns for the storage of large amounts of hay and cumbersome machinery, and for indoor work calling for room. Such in fact were the needs of an increasing number of American farmers: those who raised dairy cattle or fed beef cattle found that the storage of hay and the preparation of feed called for ample storage and work space; and the new farm machinery had to be kept indoors. Balloon frame construction did little more than suggest possibilities; but the possibilities were thoroughly exploited: every farmer became an innovator in the designing and building of large, free interior spaces; ingenious and frequently daring experiments in planning and construction became commonplace on the farms of America for the next half century.

Whatever may be the accepted theory in such matters, vernacular architecture in the United States of a century ago showed itself to be no less resourceful than architecture of a more formal kind. Unpretentious dwellings, utilitarian structures on the farm or in town, factories and warehouses designed by contractors, engineers, carpenters, gifted amateurs, often incorporated on an appropriate scale the open plan, the centralized utilities, the concern for light and flexibility that more celebrated architects were introducing into their projects. And in every instance the measure of success was the creation of a new spaciousness. If Goethe's "more light" epitomized the ideal of his generation, "more space" was what America a century ago was demanding in a score of different ways.

3. ENVIRONMENTS

The tendency of certain forms and spaces to increase in size, either by expansion or consolidation, accounted for many of the changes in the American landscape in the postwar years. Another tendency, closely related to it but distinct in origin, was also at work: the defining (or redefining) of spaces in terms of "natural" boundaries. It manifested itself in two widely separated fields of spatial organization: in the design of parks and gardens and suburbs, and in the layout of farms and ranches in the West.

The preference for "natural" boundaries ran counter to the well-established American tradition of artificial or man-made boundaries. West of the Appalachians almost every boundary had been determined by the grid: that pattern of sections, townships, ranges imposed by the Land Survey of 1785. The great majority of the states, territories, counties, and townships—to say nothing of individual holdings—were defined by survey lines running due north and south, east and west. A map of any large section of the United States, even today, resembles an immense composition of squares and rectangles, regardless of the nature of the terrain or the type of exploitation.

The grid system of land subdivision is unpopular with many contemporary Americans, chiefly for esthetic reasons; yet it possessed and still possesses important virtues, political as well as economic, and in the early years of Western (and Midwestern) settlement it served the nation well; it expressed very clearly the general belief in equality of opportunity, and in the possession of land as one of the bases of citizenship. But that was in the day of the independent, more or less self-sufficient farm, and as settlement after the Civil War pushed into the Great Plains and beyond, and as farming became more of a commercial enterprise, the disregard of topography, the assumption that all pieces of land of the same size had the same value, became totally unrealistic.

This was especially true when farming invaded the relatively dry and treeless region west of the 100th meridian, which cuts through the western half of the Dakotas, Nebraska, and Kansas. Beyond that fateful line the climate changes radically; land without the presence or availability of surface water to supplement rainfall is unfit for agriculture, and the possession of a homestead as such means nothing. The square of 160 acres, so reassuring in the more humid East, has no fixed value on the Plains; often it does not suffice to feed a half dozen cows.

So it was water in one form or another that determined the size and location of a viable unit, whatever Washington supposed; it was topography that made land profitable or worthless. In the seventies a number of "colonies," of which Greeley was the largest and most successful, established themselves in eastern Colorado. The location which each of them chose was in a valley with a river, where irrigation could be practiced. The communities adapted themselves to the terrain, leaving the higher surrounding plains, in Horace Greeley's words, "to the half-savage herdsmen who rear cattle and sheep." They were defining their holdings in terms of physical characteristics, that is to say; and where those characteristics ceased, there they fixed their line of demarcation. Instead of all spaces being potentially equal, they fell into classifications based on natural features and natural boundaries.

Cattlemen defined their holdings in the same manner. A writer on Colorado as a prospective home for settlers in the 1870s explained the word "ranch" as "a term for a spring of water and some rude buildings, and an indefinite amount of grazing land."

So obvious was it that the old system of land subdivision did not suit the West that even the government began to see the need for classifying land in a different, more topographical way. It no longer served any useful purpose to lump all (or most) of the public domain under the heading of agricultural land, to be divided into rectangular holdings of 160 acres. Tentatively, and even reluctantly, Washington, beginning in 1866, undertook to classify lands according to physical characteristics, in terms of suitability for mining, farming, grazing, and so on.

It was not until 1909—more than a half century later—that a Land Classification Board was established, with the Geological Survey doing the field work. But the intervening steps, ineffectual though they may have been, serve to illustrate the growth of what was then a new concept of how to organize space. First it was the mining lands which were officially recognized as possessing distinct characteristics of their own; then it was land suited to irrigation, then forests, until much of the American landscape became a composition not only of political units but of natural environments. And was it not this new kind of definition of land that inspired the creation in 1872 of Yellowstone National Park? It was an environment with spectacular natural characteristics, and for that reason Congress set it aside as "a public park or pleasuring ground for the benefit and enjoyment of the people."

The man who most clearly formulated the new doctrine was Major John Wesley Powell. The first white man to descend the Colorado River, he was recognized as an authority on the geography of the desert Southwest and the culture of its Indian inhabitants. In 1870 he was commissioned by the Department of the Interior to undertake a Geographical and Geological Survey of the Rocky Mountain Region, and for the next seven years he and his small party explored and mapped the little-known Plateau region surrounding the Grand Canyon. In 1878 he finally submitted his report. Despite the fact that all the recommendations it contained were rejected by Congress and that many of his judgments were bitterly resented by Western publishers and politicians, Powell's *Report on the Arid Region of the United States* remains a document of exceptional importance, and it has been called "one of the most significant and seminal books ever written about the West."

It is neither long nor impressively erudite; it is a straightforward discussion of the climatic peculiarities of the desert Southwest and of the possibilities for agriculture in the region. Nowhere does Powell express any interest in its natural beauties or their preservation. Agriculture would be possible, he declared, under certain very restricted conditions: that the inhabitants practice a combination of ranching and irrigation farming on a limited scale, that they organize irrigation districts and form small communities or neighborhoods, and that they organize for the communal use of the range. He further stipulated that every rancher-farmer possess at least 2560 acres—or four square miles— most of which would be part of the community pasturelands.

The details of Powell's proposal—how the irrigation and "pasturage" districts would be organized, how the rangeland would be chosen from the public domain—need not detain us. What matters is the nature of the land units he suggested. He rejected not only the traditional homestead of 160 acres but the rectilinear survey as well. The holdings were to be defined by the physical characteristics of the land: by the availability of water and range. Two points were repeatedly made: "The division of these lands should be controlled by topographic features," and "The people settling on these lands . . . should not be hampered with the present arbitrary system of dividing lands into rectangular tracts."

A minor point in Powell's proposals but an interesting one was his aversion to fencing the communal pastureland, on the somewhat implausible ground that it would cost too much. But Powell after all belonged to his generation, and along with many contemporaries he undoubtedly objected to the artificial boundary, the man-made definition of space. Across the continent, among the farmers of the Midwest and East, the same desire for innovation in the layout of fields was already apparent: mechanization had not only eliminated many walls and fences, it was also demanding its own special terrain. "The general use of the mowing machine," observed a contributor to *Rural Affairs* in 1865, "will, we trust, make for a great improvement in the external appearance of farms. Stumps, bushes, stone heaps, and obtruding rocks must disappear." And so they did in the course of time, setting the smooth mowed fields apart from the hillsides with their rocks and stumps; and with the planting of trees on the rough terrain the contrast between the physical characteristics of the various sections of the farm became all the greater.

The effect of a landscape of fields all conforming to the topography of the farm, none of them rigidly confined within straight lines, struck many as a great improvement over the former system of rectangular divisions. Somewhat diffidently a landscape architect suggested to the readers of a rural magazine that farms be laid out in an ornamental, not to say picturesque, manner: fields of an irregular shape, bounded by hedges or rows of trees, with gently curving carriage roads leading to the house and its neighboring barn. But the farm had to evolve in its own way, without benefit of advice from landscape architects. A countryside far more hospitable to their ideas was the new suburb. The challenge here was unmistakable: the average developer laid out the land in rectangular, more or less uniform lots with a grid pattern of streets. To transform this depressing spatial artificiality into a series of "natural" environments called for art and ingenuity. The first traditional element to be eliminated from the plan of the suburban property was the fence or wall; both had fallen into great disfavor among landscape architects and their prosperous clients. In the 1840s Emerson had quoted with approval the old New England dictum that good fences made good neighbors. A generation later the wall was seen not only as distinctly *un*-neighborly but even un-Christian. The most cherished feature of the suburban domain was not (as with the farm) its crops, but its privacy, its integrity as a domestic environment. Fences therefore played a different role: polite indications that a property line existed and was not to be casually crossed. "That kind of fence," said one landscape architect, "is best which is least seen and best seen through"—but which still suggested exclusion.

Frank Scott, who described himself as a friend and student of A. J. Downing, wrote a book on *Suburban Home Grounds* in 1870, in which he discussed the landscaping problems of the commuter, "the man who must leave his home after an early breakfast to attend to his office or store business," and who had built a home on a suburban lot. Urging the suburbanite to eschew all pretensions of having a parklike estate with a vegetable garden, Scott offered as the ideal a composition of trees and lawn—trees as a tactful and natural-appearing boundary, lawn as a private and sheltered environment. Jacob Weidenmann, a onetime associate of Olmsted, achieved a national reputation in the seventies as a designer of "picturesque" lawns, and published an expensive folio of his work, and Eugene Baumann, a New Jersey landscape architect of the period, also tackled the problem of converting the small, rectilinear suburban holding into a natural, esthetically self-contained environment. All expressed the growing dissatisfaction with the conventional-size lot: "The speculative habit of cutting up suburban lands into narrow city lots 25 x 100 feet," Scott declared, "or but little more, destroys all chance of making true suburban improvements. Such lots will only sell to citizens who are either too poor, too cockneyish, or too ignorant of their own needs to insist on something more."

The spatial reorganization underway on the farms and ranches of America, and proposed by Powell, was impressive because of the vast dimensions involved and the struggle for survival on the part of the hard-pressed men who urged it. By contrast the contribution of landscape architects, fussily detailed and inevitably influenced by fashion, seemed trivial. Nevertheless the new American landscape was the creation of many elements in society: farmers, ranchers, engineers; architects and landscape architects; and innumerable men and women working for urban and rural improvement. The spirit behind the new kind of space— expansive, free of the past, more and more involved with the transformation of the natural environment—derived from workaday America, but it was the artist who gave it form and meaning.

4. REFORMERS

It was the spectacle of America bursting out of its historic confines and taking possession of untrammeled space that engrossed the attention of the journalists and the compilers of promotional picture books. To be doing something where it had never been done before and in an altogether new manner—this was worth recording and celebrating. *Why* it was done and what the consequences were likely to be were questions never answered and presumably never asked.

But many Americans in every walk of life watched the changes in the landscape and realized with dismay that more than simple growth and expansion was taking place. What gave them pause was not so much the reckless waste of natural resources as it was the decay of the community, the breakdown in the old relationship between men and that fraction of the world they lived and worked in. Disruption was just as evident in the established countrysides of the East and South as in the settlers' and homesteaders' West; in the brand-new railroad towns of Nebraska and Kansas as in the factory cities of New England; all parts of the country were threatened by incoherent change. An influential element, including not a few architects and landscape architects, confessed their inability to deal with a raw and turbulent way of life, and withdrew from it, but there were others who undertook to bring a new kind of beauty and order to the evolving landscape. They came from various callings—engineers, journalists, landscape architects, farmers. What roused them to action was less the prospect of power or professional renown than a sense of responsibility for the country. None of them succeeded in carrying out his projects for improvement, but all of them left some trace of their efforts.

Horace Cleveland, the Boston landscape architect who left a flourishing practice to move to Chicago in 1869, developed over the years an even larger practice in the Midwest; but unlike most of his Eastern colleagues he found himself involved in the far from glamorous problems of the newly settled West. Whenever the railroad invaded the High Plains, new towns followed. Crude and graceless, they failed as communities; their new inhabitants suffered from loneliness and isolation. As a designer primarily interested in the harmonious and efficient division of land for human needs, Cleveland discovered a new challenge in the railroad towns of the West. Laid out by railroad engineers, the pattern of their streets and lots was an inflexible grid that destroyed or hid all topographical beauty, produced inaccessible building sites, and often made easy communication and assembly next to impossible. Protest and criticism were the beginning of his crusade, but he continued by giving advice and help, suggesting how to take advantage of the terrain, how to introduce variety in the location of houses, how to plant trees and modify the rectilinear streets. For the Midwestern public he wrote on how to plant groves of trees in the immense landscape of Kansas and Nebraska, not merely to provide lumber for the railroads and the farmers, but also to create a softer beauty.

His former partner, Morris Copeland, remained in the East. Until his death in 1874 he worked to improve the rural landscape by means of good planting and good siting. Writing for farmers and the inhabitants of small towns, he told how to lay out gardens and farms, and he said that country roads need not be straight and bleak and exposed to the sun and wind; that they could be made attractive and refreshing features of the landscape. Copeland wrote mainly on the everyday problems of country living, but his plan for the city of Boston showed how wide his interests were, and how he had developed a consistent philosophy of large-scale urban design at a time when Americans still thought in terms of fragmentary improvements.

George Waring, Jr., was still another advocate of new communities and a revitalized landscape. By profession an engineer who had worked for three years on the restructuring of the terrain of Central Park, he devoted himself in the years after the war to the predicament of the Eastern farmer and villager. He lectured to groups of farmers in Vermont and Maine about soil chemistry and scientific farming. He took over a derelict farm in Rhode Island, and in a widely read series of weekly letters to the *American Agriculturist*, told of his experiments with new farming techniques, and of his day-by-day successes and failures. He designed model barns, designed model sewerage systems for small New England villages, told how to build parks and streets. He was a graceful and versatile writer; the *Atlantic* published his reminiscences of life as a cavalry officer during the war, his accounts of European travel, as well as his discussions of the plight of the Eastern farmer. What seemed to be his main concern was how to bring some element of sociability and relaxation to the average Eastern farmer who in the course of recent agricultural changes had lost contact with the community. His recommendation that farmers take up fox hunting to relieve the lonely monotony of their life made no impression; he was undoubtedly more in earnest when he outlined in 1875 a plan for creating farm villages or small centers of community life throughout the United States. For the rectilinear West and Midwest he proposed that every township (an area of 36 square miles) be divided into nine "settlements," in each of which there was to be a small compact village of some 300, living around a small common with a church, a school, a store, and a "public house." The farmlands were to extend back of the dwellings. In the East a different kind of farm village was called for, resembling the old villages Waring had admired in the Connecticut Valley. In New England the new community was to result from the consolidation of existing farms and the laying-out of a new village somewhere near the center of an area of four square miles; it was to be a tree-lined street, in keeping with the Eastern tradition, and with those amenities which would in time foster community life. He saw two merits in the plan: first, the farmer and his family would enjoy easy sociability with their neighbors; second, the farmer would be able, at the end of the work day, to leave the scene of his labors—something which every other working American could do. The scheme, he remarked, promised "what seems the easiest, if not the only relief from the dullness and desolation of living which makes American farming loathsome to many who ought to glory in its pursuit, but who now are only bound to it by commanding necessity."

How many of Waring's proposals for rural reform derived from Horace Greeley it is hard to say. Waring had been the manager of Greeley's model farm at Chappaqua before the war, and the two men shared a belief in the future of scientific agriculture; and though Greeley's book, *What I Know of Farming*, published in 1870, caused some merriment among experts, it contained many sound suggestions which Waring might well have inspired. In any case, Waring's farm villages strongly resembled in layout the community founded in Colorado in 1870 later named Greeley in honor of its chief promoter. If the designers of suburbs had as yet no very clear concept of how to produce a community as distinguished from a collection of isolated residences, there existed a hundred years ago in America an active search for new and better rural societies, and it is likely that Powell's suggestions for relatively compact irrigation communities were influenced by the writings of Greeley and Waring.

Nor was there any lack of men to tell Americans that there was a new way of perceiving and understanding the natural world around them; that the lyrical and romantic approach should be abandoned in favor of a kind of affectionate appraisal based on knowledge. Although his reputation now rests on his many volumes of nature essays, John Burroughs in the sixties and seventies wrote much about farm life; from early training he knew it well. The farmer, he said, was to be envied not only for his intimacy with nature, but for "his trees, the satisfaction in his growing crops, in his improved fields." And as the Eastern countryside lapsed into wilderness Burroughs became the explorer and chronicler of the deserted farm, the untraveled country road, the meadow grown into a small jungle. For a generation of Americans he served as a guide to a landscape in retreat. To perceive the environment was to know it and possess it; turning it to some account, if only an emotional one.

No American of the period better illustrated that pragmatic approach than Nathaniel Southgate Shaler. When at Harvard in the fifties he was the favorite pupil of Agassiz, and he remained at Harvard for the rest of his life, first as lecturer and professor of geology and then as Dean of the Scientific School. By all accounts he was a dynamic and popular teacher, a firm believer in strenuous fieldwork and exploration. His early accounts of travels in New England and the East revealed the extent of his interest in the environment; an excursion on foot from Cambridge to Pittsfield produced observations on farming, forestry, the impact of industrialization, the decline of the early New England stock, as well as on geology and geography. His energy as a writer seemed boundless: he produced and published books and essays on whales, earthquakes, the silver question, a park system for Boston, photography, the moon; and in his less didactic intervals he found time to compose five volumes of romantic dramas in blank verse. It was Shaler who first undertook to study highways and highway construction and who introduced highway engineering into the college curriculum; it was likewise he who wrote one of the most informative descriptions of the natural resources of the country. And finally it was Shaler who in 1875 first proposed a detailed topographical survey of the state. "How to get the most out of this dear old earth in our time and for our time," he remarked, "this is the ever-present question of all ages." Once such a survey had been made, it would provide "a perfect basis for all the great operations of the engineer. Is a railroad to be constructed . . . are mill-powers to be improved, drainage works undertaken, or cities supplied with water"; the survey would prove invaluable. "Every township, village or city has endless questions of sewerage, road building, taxation, questions concerning the placing of public buildings etc., in everyone of which such a map is a matter of the utmost importance."

What Shaler and many of his generation implicitly believed was that it was the natural environment, not tradition or art, which determined the form of the landscape; and for that reason it was often advisable to transform the environment in a drastic and permanent manner. The greater the zeal Shaler and others felt for improving the lot of their compatriots the more determined they were to alter the environment to serve the needs of the economy. Powell proposed the systematic exploitation of the forests of the Arid Region, and advocated an extensive system of dams throughout the West. In the preface to his *Report* he dwelt on the desirability of draining "the coast swamps of the South Atlantic and Gulf slopes, the Everglade lands . . . the flood plain lands of the great rivers of the south . . . and the lake swamp lands found about the head waters of the Mississippi." Cleveland's interest in planting forests in the treeless plains derived in large part from his belief that the climate could be thereby changed; Shaler himself proposed moderating the climate of the northern tier of states by deepening Behring Strait to allow the warmer waters of the Pacific to enter the Arctic Ocean, and Waring's subsequent career was inspired by the success of the man-made landscape of the Dutch Polders. We sometimes call that postwar generation the one which discovered conservation, but it would be more accurate to call it the one which abandoned ancient attitudes toward the environment and began to transform it and redesign it to suit the needs and conveniences of men.

How many lesser figures of whom we now know little or nothing were also influential in propagating the then revolutionary environmental approach to design? There were those like Catherine Beecher and her sister Harriet Beecher Stowe, and the writer-architect E. C. Gardner, who advocated the radical reform of the American home, not merely as an institution where the woman of the house was burdened with heavy routine work, but as a physical environment. "I can think of but one use for houses," declared a character in Gardner's *Illustrated Homes,* written in 1875, "and that is to prolong life. . . . Everybody knows there isn't a well person in America and it's all because of our miserable houses. They are not half warmed or ventilated. They are damp and dark, very well contrived to kill people, but not at all adapted to keep us alive." She added: "Health is everything . . . and if I am really to give you a handful of advice, it will be that you show the construction of houses that should minister to health."

And if the city was subject to little constructive analysis, its component elements were scrutinized and redesigned both as more wholesome environments and as better organizations of space. Samuel Sloan, the Philadelphia architect, introduced to America the concept of the hospital as a therapeutic environment instead of merely an institution; an essential part of the patient's treatment and recovery. H. P. Bowditch, a Boston doctor, first proposed in the late sixties the design of healthy as well as inexpensive housing for the urban poor. We remain largely ignorant of the architects and educators who, inspired by the example of Henry Barnard, revolutionized the design of school buildings by introducing scientific criteria of light and ventilation and indirect heat. Aside from the writings of the economist Edward Atkinson and of C. J. H. Woodbury, the literature on the design of factories in the postwar decades is scanty; yet it was then that radical changes in industrial architecture were taking place: the introduction of such environmental factors as lighting and ventilation and fire prevention, and most significantly, of the concept of a micro-climate.

The innumerable Village or Rural Improvement Societies, organized to beautify American towns and villages and elevate the quality of life in rural communities can be discussed later; but mention should be made of some of the men who helped formulate and direct the movement. B. G. Northrop, a clergyman and later a member of the Connecticut Board of Education, was known as the "Father of the Village Improvement Society"; it was he who in the seventies promoted the tree-planting and beautification programs that transformed the towns of Barre, Great Barrington, Lenox, Litchfield, New Milford, Norfolk, Connecticut, and Geneseo, New York, into models of village landscaping, and it was also he who made Arbor Day—the creation in 1874 of Governor Norton of Nebraska—a national observance. Northrop, Donald Mitchell, whose writings on rural matters, particularly *My Farm of Edgewood,* enjoyed immense popularity in the sixties, as well as Horace Bushnell, the theologian, did much to arouse interest in the neglected beauties of the Eastern rural and village landscape, and theirs was the proposal, widely adopted throughout the East, to celebrate the Centennial in 1876 by the planting of "Centennial" trees and groves, and the adorning of parks and school grounds. It is to the efforts of these men and these organizations that we owe those characteristic American landscape compositions of unfenced lawns and rows of uniform trees flanking a thousand small town residential streets and country roads. These survive to remind us of a nationwide movement to create a new kind of communal space, a more natural, a more open environment: each was an anonymous testimonial of love for the American landscape.

Our neglect of those earnest figures, deeply concerned with improving the nineteenth-century environment, urban as well as rural, has inevitably distorted our interpretation of one aspect of our past. In an age like our own where sensitivity to environmental factors has been exalted to the status of a virtue there are doubtless many features of those attempted reforms which we find uncongenial: a reliance on mechanical solutions, a tendency to subdue nature rather than cooperate with it, an un-awareness of interaction instead of opposition between man and the world surrounding him. Nevertheless that was the generation of Americans which more than any other energetically established a national environmental policy; our growing disenchantment with this heritage, inevitable though it may be, still has far to go before it achieves an equally coherent—and equally satisfactory—landscape ideal.

CHAPTER TWO

The Northwest

1. PIONEERING

A hundred years ago when Americans spoke of the Northwest as the new Eldorado, the Land of Promise, it was Minnesota and Nebraska and Dakota that they meant. Especially Minnesota; still part of the traditional wooded landscape, less remote than the others, it had an almost legendary appeal. What child of that generation had not heard Longfellow's tale of the deeds of Hiawatha in the land of the Dacotahs? The Falls of Minnehaha were little more than a mile from Minneapolis, and many tourists visited them. It had been George Catlin, the artist of the American Indian, who first called attention in 1835 to the scenic beauties of the upper Mississippi. He had, in fact, proposed a "fashionable tour" by steamer from Rock Island, Illinois, to the Falls of St. Anthony near Minneapolis. Two years later the tour was already popular, given an early prestige by the voyage of the eighty-year-old widow of Alexander Hamilton, traveling west to see her son William. Many foreigners made the tour in subsequent years, and their enthusiastic accounts (in which they often compared the upper valley of the Mississippi to the Rhine) spread the fame of the Minnesota Territory. More than one artist painted and exhibited a panorama of the river; that of Henry

Lewis, completed in 1849, was more than 1200 yards long and 12 feet high. Another panorama of the same landscape displayed real smoke coming from the Indian tepees along the riverbank, and the steamboats produced real steam. It was such a panorama (along with a daguerreotype of Minnehaha Falls) which, we are told, inspired Longfellow to choose the Northwest as the locale of his poem.

But all of the Northwest eventually became known, at least from reading and hearsay. The governments of the several states and territories had early begun to turn out quantities of promotional literature; maps, and pamphlets in four languages, including Welsh. Agents were dispatched to buttonhole likely immigrants at the New York and Boston docksides, and all the way to Norway and Germany and Sweden, where they proclaimed the many advantages of the region: the soil was fertile, the land cheap, the economy expanding; the climate was justly celebrated for its invigorating qualities ("cold, but a *dry* cold"). What better testimony to its virtues could there have been than the long career of a Wisconsin man who died, "the oldest man in the world," in 1867 at the age of 141? Among those seduced by the descriptions of the climate was Thoreau. In 1861, vainly seeking a cure for the tuberculosis which was to carry him off a year later, he journeyed by steamboat up the Mississippi to St. Paul. Botanically the countryside held many charms, but the rigors of pioneer life and the Southern sympathies of a group of St. Paul residents were more than he could bear. After a few months he returned to Concord.

No less intense was the propaganda of the railroad companies, understandably eager to promote the settlement of the region, possessing as they did immense amounts of land, granted them by Congress to help finance the costs of construction. They urged settlers to come, singly or in groups, foreign or American; buy land, raise crops and ship them by rail to market. Horsecars in the larger Eastern cities bore bright advertisements of the marvelous Northwest on their sides. Excursion trains were organized for prospective buyers, and special hotels or "immigrant houses" were hastily built for the settlers when they arrived in Minnesota. An added inducement was the promise that the railroads would lay out towns along their lines. The literature of the St. Paul and Pacific Railroad declared that "a man could buy land, break it and fence it, pay for the land, breaking and fencing, and all expenses *out of the first crop!"*

Well before the Civil War the tide of settlers was heavy. Whereas in 1857 Minnesota had 150,000 people, by 1870 there were almost half a million. Nebraska, the youngest state in the Union, starting as it were from scratch, already had 120,000. Dakota had a mere 14,000, clustered along the eastern fringe of the territory, but its hopes were high. "The mighty Missouri runs through the very heart of our territory," the legislature declared, "thus giving us the facility of cheap transportation by means of which we can bear away the surplus products of our rich, luxuriant lands to southern markets."

Everywhere small-town newspapers boasted of how many immigrants had passed through during the week. Some traveled as their parents had traveled West; by horse- or ox-drawn wagon, but before the war most of them came by steamboat up the Mississippi, packed on the lower decks of the excursion boats or freighters, half stifled by the heat and crowds. In one prewar year more than a thousand steamers docked at St. Paul. After the war, river traffic on the upper Mississippi declined as it did everywhere else, and settlers came by train—not much more comfortable, no better ventilated, dreaded by those who disliked foreigners with their strange habits and strange speech, but faster and cheaper, and reaching farther into the countryside. Special carriages were arranged for immigrants, with wooden benches and bunks and a stove where food could be heated.

Veterans of the recent war, small farmers, and city workers from the East, Germans and Norwegians and Swedes—where did they all hope to find land for farming? Not in the dense northern forests of pine, where the lakes were flush with the land, nor in the enormous treeless country along the Red River of the North. The preferred landscape was open and rolling, the parklike Big Woods, in the southern quarter of the state where there were streams and groves of hardwood trees, and the high grass reached as far as the eye could see. The country abounded with game, and wild fowl haunted the shallow valleys. It had a reassuring pastoral beauty, and the deep rich black soil stretched into Iowa and Nebraska. The farther west the settlers moved, the scarcer became the trees, though there were always stands of willow and cottonwood along the watercourses; and it was in the West that the game became even more plentiful—deer, wolves, antelope, prairie chickens, and at first even an occasional buffalo. Who would have wanted a better country to live and work in? The trouble was, not all of this land, despite its emptiness, was available. The railroads owned alternate sections (or square miles) sometimes five miles deep on each side of the right-of-way. Speculators had somehow managed to get ahead of the flood of bona fide settlers and take up quantities of the choicest land; and then the state government owned a great deal. There were Indian claims, and even within the townships open for settlement there were sometimes two whole square miles held out as school sections. Often the settler had to look in less accessible and less desirable areas away from the railroad lines, or buy land at a high price.

Nevertheless, tens of thousands of family-size farms were established in the Northwest in the years following the Civil War, and more than half of them were established under the Homestead Act. Minnesota indeed was more than two-thirds settled by homesteaders.

The passage of the Homestead bill in 1862 was the long postponed and bitterly contested triumph of a principle, more popular in the North than in the South, that held that every freeborn American had a right to a piece of land on which he could live. For more than three decades the question of how best to dispose of the public domain with the greatest benefit had been debated in Congress, in political campaigns, and in the press. Horace Greeley became an eloquent proponent of land reform and a supporter of the Free Soil Party of 1848; it was he who often best expressed the reasons for a more generous and more democratic distribution or sale of public lands. The rapid growth of industries in the East, especially after the influx of immigrants from Ireland, demanded new outlets for their products; more farms in the frontier regions would satisfy the need. There were many unemployed and underpaid workers in the

Eastern states; if they were provided with land and assured of
the prospect of a decent livelihood a difficult social problem
would be solved at least in part, and the United States would be
acting in keeping with a national ideal, first enunciated by Jeffer-
son, of a society of free and independent yeomen. Moreover, a
more democratic distribution of land would serve to check the
expansion of slavery into the West and do much to stop the
scandalous speculation in land, whereby large areas were held
out from settlement, only to be disposed of later at an enormous
profit. The moral side of the issue was not neglected: the Bible
clearly stated that land was not meant to be treated as a commodity, in Greeley's words as "mere merchandise, like molasses
and mackerel." Men had a natural or God-given right to it; it
was indispensable to the right of life, liberty, and the pursuit of
happiness.

The arguments against a more liberal distribution, usually
though not always advanced by Southerners, were on a different,
more pragmatic plane. The wholesale disposal of public lands
with no service in return would be not merely unconstitutional
but an invitation to idleness and small-scale speculation. It would
also undermine established land values in the older regions of
the country and bring about a wholesale migration of labor
from the North as well as the South; and what would then
happen to our developing industries? The deadlock lasted until
the outbreak of the Civil War; it was only the withdrawal of
the secessionist members of Congress that made it possible for
the House, and soon thereafter the Senate, to pass a Homestead
bill introduced by a Representative from Minnesota. In May
1862, Lincoln signed the bill into law, and on the first day of the
next year the distribution of homesteads was begun. The first to
take advantage of the Act was Daniel Freeman, a young soldier
from Ohio. His homestead, located near Beatrice in southeastern
Nebraska, is now the Homestead National Monument.

The Homestead Act gave a quarter section—a square of 160
acres—of the public domain to any citizen or prospective citizen
who applied. He obligated himself to build a house on the land,
farm at least a portion of it, and live on it for five years; then,
after paying a filing fee of $10, it became his to do with as he

pleased. There were, of course, other ways of acquiring land; it could be bought from private parties or land speculators or from the railroads or from the state or territory. It could be had by pre-emption, or by squatting on it before it had been surveyed, and then, after survey, paying a minimum of $1.25 an acre. Whole townships in Nebraska and South Dakota were settled in this manner. Each method had its advantages; but to the settler with little money and that little earmarked for farm equipment and the expenses of living, and especially to the foreign settler unacquainted with the pitfalls of land speculation, the government homestead seemed the safest and best. It is unfortunately true that the Homestead Act never lived up to its promise; it was far from a success in the frontier territories; but this became apparent only later. In Minnesota and Nebraska and Kansas, where the climate favored the small farmer, the Act left an indelible mark on the landscape. The two decades after the Civil War were in a sense the Golden Days of homesteading on public lands, when the tide of migration lapped against the line of continuous settlement and eventually pushed it west into the Great Plains. It was then that the Northwest received the imprint of the traditional American organization of space—the last region, perhaps, not only to receive but to retain it so that it is still discernible today: the square homestead farm in the square section which in turn was part of the square township of thirty-six sections. And in time fences, roads, fields, streets, and houselots all found their place in the overall grid. Nowhere in America is the rectilinear layout more impressive and more harmonious than in the old Northwest. The geometrical pattern is softened by the rolling terrain, the woods and valleys and streams; it is rarely distorted or hidden.

At the beginning of this postwar wave of settlement, there could not have been much that was idyllic about the homesteader's way of life. With little money and usually little experience, he and his family had first to build themselves a home of sorts—in Nebraska a dugout or a sod house, in Minnesota a house of log or slab—then a well had to be dug, the land had to be broken, and a vegetable plot and a small crop put in. All the while they had to survive the loneliness, the cruel winters, the hot summers, the violent storms. Gilbert Fite, in *The Farmers' Frontier*, describes their hardships: in 1873, a bad year for most Americans, the Northwest was struck by a murderous three-day blizzard that killed much livestock and inflicted widespread hardship. Two years before there had been hailstorms and prairie fires; grasshoppers in clouds that darkened the sun were a recurrent plague. "We have no money nor nothing to sell to get any more clothes with as the grasshoppers have destroyed our crops what few we had for we had not much broken yet as we have no team of our own," a young girl wrote the governor of Minnesota. "We almost perish here sometimes with the cold . . . Now if you would be so kind as to send us some bedding and clothes and yarn."

Fences were expensive and time-consuming to build; the farther west (where trees were fewer) the more of a problem they became. During the first years children herded the livestock out on the open meadows. Hamlin Garland, whose childhood was spent in Iowa in the seventies, herded his father's cows in this manner, and in *Boylife on the Prairie* gives a picture of the early homestead times and of riding across the still unbroken country, day after day, among the prairie birds and the wild prairie flowers and the tall grass. Despite all the striving for order and security, the increase in houses and farms, the landscape was still half wild. "Antelope and deer were occasionally seen, and to [the boy] it seemed that just over the next ridge toward the sunset the shaggy brown [buffalo] bulls still fed in thousands, and in his heart he vowed to ride away over there and see. All the boys he knew—all the young men—talked of 'the West,' never of the East; always of the plains, of the mountains, and cattle-raising and Indians."

Nevertheless the pioneer landscape of the Northwest, half homestead, half open range and woodland, started to change in the seventies. If at first the settlers had to think most of merely surviving and starting to farm, with little time for the outside world, sooner or later they undertook to raise a crop for money. It was not enough to earn a little cash, working to help build the new railroads or for the lumber companies in the nearby woods. Wheat was the crop that proved profitable; by 1872 almost two-thirds of the Northwestern farms were planted to wheat, and the area continued to grow.

The raising of wheat in the years after the war occupied the energies of most farmers. "Men work in wheat all day when it does not rain, lounge around talking about wheat when it is wet, dream about wheat at night," a Minnesota preacher complained, "and I fear go to meeting Sabbath Day to think about wheat." From this single-minded devotion several features of the Northwestern landscape ensued. Before the expansion of the railways, the favored areas for raising wheat had been the regions near the rivers; transportation of the grain was by boat, eventually down the Mississippi. But transportation by rail opened up a wider country, and instead of having to haul the crop to some riverside loading point, farmers went to the much nearer depot and grain elevators punctuated the prairie skyline. The village of Minneapolis, living for lumber and sawmills in the sixties, blossomed out, when rail connections with the wheat-raising regions became general, into a gristmill town. "Until I got there," Anthony Trollope wrote in 1862, "I could hardly believe that in these days there should be a living village called Minneapolis by living men"—a village of ox-drawn wagons and visiting Indians with painted faces, and one hotel, closed for lack of business. But it was soon on its way to becoming the flour-producing center of the nation.

More and more fields of wheat, and fewer fields of anything else, made the landscape increasingly uniform, a composition of immense honey-colored rectangles, impressive in its very monotony. But the fields of the Northwest were not only far larger than those in the East, they were planted and harvested in a new and different way.

Horse-drawn mechanized equipment was no longer a novelty to American farmers in the seventies. Hussey, and later McCormick, had each invented a horse-drawn machine—a combination mower and reaper—in the 1830s, and a machine for threshing the crop, separating the grain from the straw and chaff, had been invented and put on the market a few years later. No machine for harvesting corn had as yet been produced—one reason why the Western frontier farmer, always short of help, chose to raise wheat. It was this shortage of farm labor, particularly acute during the war years, that did much to speed the invention of new farm machinery and the improvement of the old; and as a result the yield of American farms actually increased after 1860. This was a source of pride. "Should a stranger to our nation's struggle visit our shores," an orator in Iowa declared in 1863, "he would observe no external sign to warn him that this land was engaged in a most titanic struggle for the perpetuation of its free institutions. New fields have daily been added to our breadth of cultivated land; houses and barns and orchards have sprung up as if by magic."

It was only in later years that the human consequences of this rapid, widespread mechanization became evident. Fewer farm workers were needed; an advantage in wartime, to be sure, but hardly a boon to veterans looking for jobs. Pioneering in the West ceased to be attractive to many; the *American Agriculturist* warned men with families to resist the temptation of a free homestead unless they could take with them at least $1000. Even the established, well-to-do farmer often found the increasingly complex machinery beyond his means, and well before the war the traveling operator of harvesting equipment, moving from farm to farm with his crew, was a familiar figure. As long as mechanization was confined to a few prosperous landowners the small farmer, the homesteader with a few bushels of wheat to sell, did not feel threatened. Using the traditional cradle scythe, the traditional flail, working with slow oxen and with his family doing much of the threshing in winter when time hung on his hands, he could still be oblivious of change. But when the large operations expanded and multiplied and when the price of wheat began to fall, he started to wonder how long it would be before he would have to become someone's tenant or even a hired worker.

Yet the size of the fields continued to grow, and the farms themselves grew larger. Oliver Dalrymple, a wheat farmer in eastern Minnesota, had 2600 acres in wheat, divided into three farms called "Grant," "Sheridan," and "Sherman." Later he was to achieve even greater renown by farming wheat fields of 14,000 acres. Enterprises of this sort gave a new luster to the

Northwest. The homesteaders had chosen the region because of its familiar qualities and because they had hoped to establish a familiar, small-farm way of life. But the frontier community was, after all, a twice-told tale; the tourist, and the journalist in search of a story, were far more attracted by the new, large-scale mechanized landscape.

Mary Dodge was a New England housewife who wrote volumes of essays as well as some verse under the name of Gail Hamilton. Given to frequent moralizing, she nevertheless turned out brisk and informative accounts of various aspects of postwar America. One hot summer in the late sixties she undertook to investigate the new Northwest; she traveled by boat up the Mississippi, explored the environs of St. Paul, then turned south. Her sketches of Tennessee and Washington are still easy to read. Everything she saw or heard or thought on the excursion seems to have been written down: her disapproval of the profane language of the deck hands on the river boat, the dusty, unimproved roads meandering across the still uninhabited stretches of Minnesota, the lonely, disreputable roadside taverns frequented by the teamsters hauling wheat to the docks, the naked little frame farmhouses with their makeshift comforts and the treasured pieces of china brought from back East. She saw and praised Minnehaha Falls. She went to a county fair; inquired as to why the flow of the Mississippi seemed so much reduced. The answer was, the increased area of plowed land now absorbed the rainfall which had once gone into the river. She pondered this information.

What amazed her most of all was the wheat country and the expansive way of thinking and acting that went with it. "The Minnesota farmers do not go on out there in the old ways in which their fathers trod," she explained to the readers of *Wool Gathering*, "for the very good reason they have neither ways nor fathers. . . . They make experiments. Indeed their farming itself is an experiment." She wondered at the amount of riding they did, either on horseback or in a buggy, and how little work was done on foot. She told about the men in the fields, about the harvesting crews with the steam-driven threshing machines in the middle, and the black smoke of other threshing machines in neighboring wheat farms rising along the hot horizon. The patterns of mechanized movement, so different from the traditional harvesting she knew in Massachusetts, delighted her and she described them in detail. She seemed to sense that she was glimpsing something out of the future.

2. BONANZA FARMING

Had she visited the region a few years later and traveled farther afield she would have seen her premonitions proven correct, for it was in the early 1870s in the northwesternmost corner of the Northwest—in the valley of the Red River of the North— that a new and spectacular farm landscape made its appearance, eventually to spread over much of the West as far as California.

The Red River of the North, so called to distinguish it from the Red River which borders Oklahoma, rises in the rolling country between North Dakota and Minnesota, and meandering erratically, flows northward to pass through Winnepeg; its waters ultimately reaching Hudson's Bay. For much of its length it is sluggish and opaque and given to overflowing its low banks, thereby creating areas of marshland throughout its broad valley, in places fifty miles wide.

Strictly speaking the Red River Valley is not a valley at all; it is part of a vanished lake, Lake Agassiz. Its soil is in consequence rich and deep and entirely without rocks. It is all but treeless and extraordinarily flat.

A hundred years ago when settlers were still few the valley must have presented an impressive spectacle. The traveler from the East came out of the gloomy evergreen forest of northern Minnesota and was all at once confronted by a vast, featureless boundless expanse of grassland stretching to the low flat horizon. Only along the river and its tributaries were there fringes of trees; everywhere else was grass and marshland grown to tall grass and reeds. It was without sound or movement, save for the call of meadowlarks and curlews, and the wavering lines of many birds in flight. It was not a view that caused elation, but its immense monotony was overpowering.

In some ways it was a land of abundance. The rivers teemed

with fish, sturgeon so numerous and large that early travelers had trouble navigating. The marshlands were the haunt of duck and geese, even of pelicans and eagles, and it would have been hard to find a region where beaver and mink and muskrat and marten were more plentiful. Trappers soon discovered the valley and by the early years of the nineteenth century had already exhausted its wealth. Indians hunted the herds of buffalo grazing year round in the valley. At one time the hunters had also practiced a kind of farming, but when they acquired horses they wearied of a sedentary life and most of them rode west in pursuit of still more buffalo. So the valley remained solitary. Beautiful in the spring and summer, golden under a transparent northern sky, in the winter it was indescribably cold and bleak, the grass beaten down and turned gray by the fierce winds straight out of the Arctic, when not buried under deep snow.

The northern third of the valley is in Manitoba, and farmers settled there in the first half of the nineteenth century. But in the portion within the United States only a few adventurous pioneers were to be found before the war. More came after; homesteaders who avoided the great empty spaces and preferred the more wooded eastern margin. For all its potential wealth it was a harsh environment; settlers complained of the wind, the mosquitoes, the recurrent plagues of grasshoppers. There was much superfluous water, not all of it of a wholesome quality. But when plans were made to build a railroad across the valley the region began to attract attention.

The Northern Pacific intended to build a line between Duluth and Puget Sound. As was the practice, the company received immense tracts of land from the government to help finance the undertaking. In the valley and its adjoining country it acquired strips of alternate sections along the projected line sixty and, in places, even a hundred miles wide; at one time two railroad lines in the Red River Valley controlled nearly one third of the entire area. A campaign to publicize the valley and promote colonization and the sale of the railroad holdings was soon underway. The usual inducements were offered; to Mennonites, Norwegians, Germans, Swedes, Englishmen, singly or in groups. Few responded; settlement proceeded at a cautious and sporadic pace;

villages remained rare and the scattering of homesteads, some of them ten miles from their neighbors, did little to enliven the landscape.

In 1870 construction of the line was commenced. Starting at St. Paul, it pushed rapidly westward, establishing towns as it went, and by 1873 had reached the valley. But in September of that year the banking house of Jay Cooke, financial agents for the Northern Pacific, went into bankruptcy. The ensuing panic plunged the entire nation into a three-year financial depression and brought work on the railroad to a halt. The bonds of the company dropped to one-tenth of their value, and the company finally announced that it would redeem them at par for some of its extensive holdings of land.

The offer proved to be an attractive one; in the two years following the panic the Northern Pacific managed to dispose of almost half a million acres in the valley, two-thirds of the amount being acquired by no more than twenty-three bondholders. They paid as little as fifty cents an acre for land which everyone agreed was worth at least $25; but as to what to do with it, they had no clear idea. With much of the public domain still awaiting homesteaders there could be little hope of selling the land to individual farmers: tenant farmers were not to be had. The solution finally arrived at was to hire a skilled and experienced wheat farmer to take over the exploitation and management of the various holdings.

The man chosen was Oliver Dalrymple, who, in 1875, had just sold his three much-publicized wheat farms in southern Minnesota. A native Philadelphian, a onetime lawyer, public official, successful farmer, and unsuccessful speculator in the grain market, he was the logical candidate. He took the job and at once set to work organizing the enterprise, plowing more than a thousand acres the first summer, planting them to wheat, and harvesting a gratifyingly large crop. He then expanded the operation, and in time was farming and managing some 34,000 acres, with at least one wheatfield larger in area than Manhattan Island.

The type of farming that Dalrymple helped devise was popularly known as "bonanza farming." It was characterized, to quote an agricultural historian, "by investments of large amounts of capital, a high degree of specialization in production, use of the latest agricultural machinery, and hired management." The manager, of course, was Dalrymple himself; the capital was provided by the absentee owners, most of them Easterners, who allowed management a free hand provided it show a substantial profit. Bonanza farming was thus not in the least concerned with the development of the rural community, with the family farm as a way of life, or with the long-range productivity of the soil; it was a process for producing wheat in commercial quantities.

Dalrymple was by no means the only manager of bonanza farms in the region; but he was the most important and the most successful, and the methods he evolved were imitated by others. He cut up the farms under his control into divisions or administrative units of 5000 acres, and on each division he installed a self-contained headquarters consisting of a dwelling for the superintendent, a boarding house for the hired hands, a stable, a granary, a blacksmith's shop, and a machine repair shop. In a countryside where cattle were scarce, fences were not necessary; neither were vegetable gardens or orchards, since all food was shipped in. The establishment was on a large scale; often as many as two hundred and fifty men were employed on a bonanza farm during the growing season, though during the winter ten men sufficed to take care of the four hundred or more horses and mules.

One consequence of the depression of the mid-seventies was the great number of jobless men who roamed the country. The public made no distinction between them and the tramps and bummers and hoboes who had been around for decades, and treated them with suspicion if not hostility; bonanza farmers welcomed them because they were cheap and temporary and unskilled, provided them with primitive housing, and subjected them to strict discipline in the field. And indeed the precision of the mechanized harvesting operation amazed all who beheld it; in describing work on a bonanza farm journalists invariably resorted to military similes. In the fall a row of twenty-five or more reapers in echelon drove across each field of wheat. "A superintendent on a superb horse," wrote one visitor to the valley, "like a brigadier directing his forces, rides along the line, accompanied by his staff of two on horseback. They are fully armed and equipped, not with swords but with . . . wrenches, hammers, chisels. They are surgeons in waiting, with nuts and screws, or whatever may be needed. . . . An army of 'shockers' follow the reapers, setting up the bundles to ripen before thresh-ing." Another observer described bonanza farming as "the army system applied to agriculture. This general marshals his men, arrays his instruments of war, and with mechanical precision the whole force moves forward to conquer and exact rich tribute from the land."

To a generation more familiar with army life than with indus-trial routine the military comparison was natural. But the bo-nanza farm had in fact more in common with the factory than with a wartime operation. The superintendents and foremen and repair crews did not correspond to officers in a military hier-archy; each was a specialist with his own particular job; his au-thority rested on his competence. And the precision and scale of the mechanized work in the fields was less a display of an irre-sistible force than of an obsession with the efficient use of time. It was consciousness of time, of the advantage of getting the product to the market as fast as possible, which prompted the bonanza farmer to thresh the wheat in the field instead of storing it and threshing it later. The raising of wheat was a complex and continuous process, not to be interrupted or delayed. It was doubtless his concern for industrial efficiency that inspired Dal-rymple to connect all his farms by telephone long before the telephone had become common in American cities.

It is easy, with the wisdom of a century's hindsight, to dismiss that misinterpretation of bonanza farming; it is less easy to dis-miss the poignancy many Americans saw in the disappearance of ancient ways of farming. There was inevitably much praise in the 1870s for what American brains and American skill and American capital had created; many grandiloquent prophecies of still greater yields, more land under cultivation, more Ameri-can prosperity to astonish the rest of the world. Yet even in the loudest paeans of the bonanza landscape there were hints of un-easiness, of a sense that the new agriculture spelled the end of many pleasant and valued traditions. With something like sorrow observers saw a landscape without fences or trees or gardens, without churches or schools or villages; periodically abandoned by its all-male inhabitants who left behind a collection of gaunt barracks and empty sheds. Perhaps there was wisdom in planting wheat year after year in the same fields, and no doubt it was ingenious to use the straw to fuel the threshing machines. But "Ruth never will glean in the fields of Boaz on American soil, or dip her bread in vinegar at the noon lunch on the plains of Dakota." Another writer found it impossible to forget "that plowing which we have seen in the fields of New England where Johnny steers the old horse carefully along the hillsides, and the old man guides the plow as best he can through the stony ground." The immense new farms excluded small farms; the tramp, the itinerant worker, excluded the hired man, almost part of the family. The flimsy villages were overshadowed by the immense new agricultural machines waiting at the depot for their owners. Even the promotional literature could not help dwelling (though in an exultant tone) on the rejection of the old ways. Years later the public relations releases of the railroads made much of the fact that "the typical farmer of the older regions, with his sunburnt face, his great horny hands, his coarse homespun breeches stuffed down the legs of his cowhide boots . . . is unknown here. The Dakota bonanza farmer dresses in the latest New York or Chicago style, and wears a diamond shirt stud. . . . His wife and daughter . . . have learned the last waltz or racquette step and are familiar with the latest opera airs."

By comparison with the intoxicating landscape of the Red River Valley the older parts of the Northwest seemed all but indistinguishable from the East. But here too, throughout the 1870s, changes, though of a less dramatic kind, were taking place, and the old pioneer landscape was fast disappearing. The frame houses, painted white, surrounded by saplings, multiplied. Fences went up, roads straightened out, hundreds of schools and churches and lodge halls and business blocks appeared. In the brand new villages and towns there were Grange picnics and Fourth of July speeches—all but identical, whether in Minnesota or Nebraska or the Dakota Territory. The railroads branched out everywhere; indistinguishable railroad towns, at regular intervals, dotted the pleasant countryside; and at almost every one of them a grain elevator rose higher than any courthouse dome or Methodist or Lutheran steeple.

When he was a grown man, in the 1880s, Hamlin Garland went back to the Iowa prairie where he had grown up. "Big hay barns and painted houses stood where the shacks of early settlers once cowered in the winds of winter. Pastures were where strawberries grew, and fields of barley rippled where the wild oats once waved. . . . All else of the prairie had vanished as if it had been dreamed. The pigeons, the plovers, the chickens, the vultures, the cranes, the wolves—all gone—all gone."

CHAPTER THREE

The Midwest

1. DEFINITIONS

What Americans have called the Northwest has changed location several times. The ordinance of 1787 defined the territory as all the land—it was then public domain—between the Appalachians, the Ohio to the south, and the Mississippi to the west; but in common parlance during the first decades of the Republic it seems to have meant Ohio; it was at Marietta that the first Northwestern civil government was established. By the 1840s the Northwest had shifted westward, being identified with the region north and west of the new states of Iowa and Wisconsin —Minnesota, in a word, but a Minnesota that reached all the way to the Missouri, more than halfway across what are now North and South Dakota. In the twentieth century, of course, the Northwest means Washington and Oregon and Idaho, and the day may not be far off when the term finds its ultimate home somewhere in Alaska. In the meantime, traces of the Northwest's peregrinations persist: Indianapolis once had a publication known as the *Northwest Farmer*, Chicago has its Northwestern University, and the Northwest Bell Telephone Company operates in Minnesota.

When the concept was monopolized by Minnesota and its

neighboring states in the middle of the last century, the remainder of the territory was left more or less without a name. How did Americans then refer to the newer states west of the Appalachians? In a variety of arbitrary ways: Ohio and Pennsylvania were each of them sometimes included in the East, at other times in the West—a term which usually covered all the country as far as the Mississippi. There were even those who called Missouri the Far West; that was at a time when the Southwest was Alabama and Mississippi; it was not until the 1850s that the latter description was applied to Arkansas instead.

Soon after the Civil War, perhaps in the late sixties, Americans finally hit upon a way of describing the region. It ceased to be the "West," and became the "Midwest," and although the word never received official sanction—"Middle West" being deemed more correct—it came into wide use. It had from the start far more than a geographical significance; it meant the heartland of the United States, the moral and social epicenter of the nation. With half the population, more than half of its agricultural activity, and a proud record of having given more than its share of wealth and men to the Union cause, the Midwest had entirely outgrown its frontier status and had acquired an exhilarating sense of its own identity.

It differed in many ways from the East and the South, and it believed that it possessed unusual virtues. The more worldly states along the Atlantic still retained remnants of an obsolete social order, and all too often fell victims to foreign fashions and ideas. But the Midwestern heartland, the product of brave and enterprising yeomen whose inspiration derived directly from the War of Independence and the new constitution, had always remained true to the basic traditions of the Republic. It was the American land of hope, the national conscience.

It was natural to want recognition of this new status; why not, for example, move the capital to the Midwest? Washington was not only inconveniently situated, it was too susceptible to Eastern financial influences, and since the war it had fallen into dissipated habits. St. Louis had many claims to being the largest truly American city, though fourth in rank in population after New York, Brooklyn, and Philadelphia. In many respects it was indeed the center of the nation; it stood in the midst of the very richest and most productive agricultural country; it was the terminus of routes from the West and Southwest, and the Mississippi linked it with the Northwest and the South. In 1867 construction of the great steel bridge across the river to Illinois had begun. It was the first structure in America to use steel instead of cast iron, and although all the leading civil engineers in the country had warned that it would be impossible to build a bridge with a 500-foot center span and a clearance of 50 feet—necessary for steamboat navigation—James Eads, the designer, built two piers in the swift and treacherous river, one of them beginning 136 feet below water level and 90 feet of shifting sand. It was during this construction that America first heard of the "bends"—the effect of increased air pressure on workers below the surface of the water. In 1874 the bridge was open to traffic. It is still in use by trains as well as vehicles, and the public was quick to admire it as a masterpiece of revolutionary engineering and architectural design. James Eads must have been an extraordinarily versatile engineer. As a young man he had worked on the Mississippi riverboats and had later invented a diving bell with which he salvaged many sunken river craft. He thus acquired a firsthand knowledge of the river, its treacherous bottom and swift currents, that stood him in good stead, not only when he designed the St. Louis bridge and supervised its construction, but when in 1875 he undertook to build for the government the jetties that were to wash away the accumulation of silt in the narrow mouth of the Mississippi below New Orleans.

Before the bridge was completed the St. Louis waterfront was one of the great spectacles of America. The river packets were constantly arriving from the South, and great barges loaded with coal and iron ore and lead left to proceed up the Ohio. Other barges with wheat came down from the Northwest, and from the Northwest forests there floated immense rafts of logs. Their crews of long-haired, wild-mannered woodsmen, rifles over their shoulders, swaggered through the downtown streets. Ferry boats crossed the river from East St. Louis in Illinois; in the crowds waiting for passage there could be seen families of German im-

migrants, Texas cattle drovers, "the poor white from some southern state, with his rifle grasped in his lean hand, and the tired
and ill-uniformed company of troops on transfer to some remote
frontier fortress." There was an incessant pandemonium of wagons
loaded with coal, panicky herds of long-horned Texas cattle;
troops of mud-bespattered hogs scampering among the roust-
abouts and longshoremen. But St. Louis was more than a prosperous commercial center; its cultural activity was distinguished.
Its fine botanical garden, the "wonder of the West," was widely
known; its parks—including the oldest public park west of the
Mississippi—were not surpassed by those of any other city. It
enjoyed an international reputation as a center of speculative
philosophical studies. Thanks largely to its many German citizens, it impressed visitors by its unpretentious, comfortable so-
lidity. Chicago was likened to New York, but St. Louis was paid
a higher compliment (in those days) by being compared with
Philadelphia. And, in fact, Philadelphia had served as a model
for the laying-out and naming of the streets in the newer part of
town. Even in architecture St. Louis had contributed to the development of an American idiom: the business section contained
numerous examples of buildings with a prefabricated iron skele-
ton and iron joists; an innovation derived from the iron store
fronts of pre-Civil War New York, and encouraged by the
abundance of iron ore in the nearby Missouri hills. Not the least
of its attractions was the famous mule market, the largest in
America; and the October fair drew visitors from all over the
Mississippi Valley.

Would it not have been appropriate to transfer the seat of the
national government here? Many Easterners endorsed the notion. "Our future capital may not be where the present one is,"
Walt Whitman wrote in 1868. "The main social, political, spine
character of the states will probably be along the Ohio, Missouri
and Mississippi rivers, and west and north of them, including
Canada." Horace Greeley, running for President in 1872, seriously considered a plank in his platform calling for the removal
of the capital to a more central site. And the fact that the center
of population in 1870 was not far from Columbus, Ohio, whereas
the westernmost town at that time was also Columbus—Colum-

bus, Nebraska—seemed to give an indefinable suitability to the choice of St. Louis, halfway between the two.

Accordingly, several conventions were held in 1867, in Cincinnati and Chicago and St. Louis, to promote the plan of moving the capital to the last-named city. For all its logic, the proposal failed to arouse much national interest. Veneration for the name Washington had at that period reached almost religious proportions: public outrage had greeted the publication in the country of *The Virginians;* Thackeray had had the temerity to introduce young Washington as a character in the novel. Moreover, the Capitol with its recently completed dome was already a powerful symbol of national unity. The only visible effect of the agitation—and it was temporary—was the calling of a halt to the erection of public buildings in Washington; Midwestern congressmen being reluctant to appropriate money for improving a city which might well be abandoned. The first sign that the crisis was over was the construction of the State-Army-Navy Building in 1872.

Still, even without the national capital, the Midwest was acknowledged not only by its inhabitants but by outsiders as well to be typically American; and the future promised an increase in its power and influence, for the subjugation of the regional landscape was by no means at an end. Except in the southern part of the state, much of Michigan was still forest; the exploitation of the Grand Prairie of East Central Illinois and adjacent Indiana was not yet complete; and throughout the Midwest sizable areas of vacant or abandoned farmland waited for a growing population. Even the areas first settled, the wooded valleys and draws along the Ohio, still contained untouched forests. The man-made landscape was, after all, barely fifty years old; but it was this landscape, the creation of the Land Ordinance of 1785 (which imposed on most of the United States the grid system of land survey), that endowed the Midwest with its most distinctively American traits.

We who fly over the grid landscape see it much more clearly than did those who passed through it by wagon or in a train. A century ago all that most travelers saw of it was a glimpse of a long, straight country road, slightly wavering between its fences;

a perspective of cornfields, wheatfields, and the checkerboard villages and towns. No less characteristic, however, were the widely, evenly spaced farmhouses. Many of these were new, brightly painted, encircled by a picket fence, though there were still many survivals of earlier days—houses built of logs with clay chimneys. The fields were large and often square, but there were remoter countrysides where the forest had only recently been removed and log cabins stood on the edge of fields where girdled trees rose above the corn. Groves of trees, remnants of the original forest, grew along the creeks and in the valleys: giant sycamores and oaks, often festooned with vines, and surrounded with expanses of grass. Each year saw fewer reminders of the wilderness; each year saw more farms laid out with new machinery stored in massive new barns. Dozens of villages sprang up along the railroads—some of them immediately shabby and swarming with flies, others neat and inviting. Widely scattered throughout the landscape—at crossroads, on the banks of streams, at railroad stops—were small churches, small school houses, a new Grange Hall, a mill, and sometimes a small factory where farm equipment was made. Whether the land was hilly or flat, the same dispersed pattern seemed to repeat itself—friendly, peaceful, vaguely untidy under its opulent trees. It was easy for the outsider to discover monotony in the Midwest and to think of monotony as its significant characteristic.

James Bryce, who traveled widely in the United States in the 1870s, came to that conclusion. "From the point where you leave the Alleghanies at Pittsburg, until after crossing the Missouri . . . a railway run of some thousand miles, there is a uniformity of landscape greater than could be found along any one hundred miles of railway in Western Europe. Everywhere the same nearly flat country, over which you cannot see far because you are little raised above it, the same thickets of the same bushes along the stream edges, the same solitary farmhouses and straggling wood-built villages. And when one has passed beyond the fields and farmhouses there is an even more unvaried stretch of slightly rolling prairie, smooth and bare, till after 500 miles the blue line of the Rocky Mountains rises upon the western horizon." Concerning the kind of life led in this landscape he added: "All over the

wide West . . . one travels past farms of two or three hundred
acres, in everyone of which there is a spacious farmhouse among
orchards and meadows, where the farmer's children grow up
strong and hearty on abundant food. . . . It is impossible not to
feel warmed, cheered, invigorated, by the sense of such material
well being all around one, impossible not to be infected by the
buoyancy and hopefulness of the people."

What the stranger might call monotony the native, more flat-
teringly, was inclined to see as a kind of wholesome simplicity
and lack of artifice. In a way both concentrated exclusively on
one aspect of the landscape: its reassuring sameness. But in
point of fact the Midwest, a century ago, was anything but
homogenized. A strong Southern tradition persisted in Indiana
and Ohio, and expressed itself not only in political activity but
in the quality of rural life and in the very composition of the
towns. However much they might have resembled one another in
outward appearance, the country villages of the Midwest were,
more often than not, defiantly unique in terms of population;
communities of Bohemians, Swedes, Hungarians, Vermonters,
Seventh-Day Adventists, Mennonites, Hutterites, Total Abstain-
ers, lived in all possible isolation in the midst of their orchards
and fields, from Ohio to the Mississippi. Nor was the fertility of
the countryside always a fair indication of contentment and com-
placency; the tidy Grange Halls resounded to denunciations of
the railroads and Eastern finance. In the late summer evenings
the forest groves thronged with country families eager for the
experience of a revival or a camp meeting, and there was scarcely
a farmer who did not find himself confronted by new and per-
plexing problems: should he give up the kind of farming he had
always known, and feed livestock as many of his neighbors were
doing? Should he borrow to buy some of the new, expensive
machinery and hope to repay with bigger yields? Should he
aspire to High Farming—a phrase much used a hundred years
ago to indicate scientific farming for immediate profits? There
was always the question of fencing—more and more costly; a
one-crop farm needed fewer interior fences; should it be wheat
or corn? Hedges perhaps were the answer: osage orange, locust,
barberry; wire was too brittle in cold weather, and lumber far

too expensive. At every county fair, at every Grange meeting, at the Agricultural Society, in every farm paper, there were alarming reports of the vanishing wood supply: if more railroads and houses and wagons were built, if more stoves and furnaces burned wood, soon there would be none left; streams would dry up, the climate would become harsher, the winds more destructive. As for the roads, they were no worse than they had been in the past, but now that he and his neighbors no longer rode horseback but traveled by wagon or buggy he noticed the steep grades, the rocks, and the mud.

2. FENCES

The fence, the boundary, was in a sense at the heart of many of the farmer's problems, and in more and more communities the first step toward a general solution was the passage of a herd or fence law—a law (that is to say) which compelled the owner to confine his livestock.

When the landscape of the Midwest was still new, when it was still in the process of settlement, the pioneering farmers allowed their cows and horses and pigs and sheep to forage for themselves in the nearby woodland or prairie. If any of his neighbors were raising crops it was their responsibility to build a fence to keep the wandering livestock out, and since they too had cows and horses and pigs on the loose they were not likely to complain. But in the course of time more and more land was devoted to farming, and less was available for stray animals; fenced out of the fields of wheat or corn, they grazed or rooted along the grassy margins of the roads, or looked for breaks in the surrounding fences.

The larger the area of land under cultivation the more time and money the farmers had to spend in building and repairing fences to protect their land from the depredations of the animals belonging to a steadily diminishing number of stockmen. Why should the majority be put to great expense by a minority— often a shiftless minority—too lazy to farm or to build fences of their own? It was when this state of affairs had been reached that farmers began to agitate for a law obliging the owners of livestock to confine them—either in the barnyard or behind a fence.

The residents of villages and towns supported the move; for the wandering livestock eventually invaded the villages as well, destroying lawns and gardens and forcing all landowners to fence their property. Even the village common and the cemetery were laid waste. A letter to a farm journal in 1869 complained bitterly about the cattle, geese, and hogs that got a starving living on the highways and streets. "They dodge into every open gateway, plunder the garden, tear down the roses on the trellis, break the shrubbery, eat the turnips, destroy the paling, and are the pest of the neighborhood." Nor did the damage from stray livestock cease with the destruction of greenery. The roads themselves suffered; profusely littered with manure, trodden into mires, they were so unsightly that farmers in the country used them as convenient dumps and garbage heaps. Here is the lament uttered by a farmer in upper New York State before a local fence law was passed in the 1860s. "It is an old-fashioned notion that highways were made to travel in, and belong to the traveling public. A few have discovered the error of this opinion and now employ them for barnyards by setting their buildings upon them. Others use them for coarse tool houses and pile old carts, wagons, sleds, rollers, plows, harrows, etc., along their sides; others use them for deposits of rubbish and throw piles of brush along the fences. . . . Others again make cattle yards and pastures of them, the cattle helping themselves to their neighbors' wheatfields, the hogs rooting up the grass walk—and all of them terrifying the little girls on their way to the district school and returning. We are old-fashioned people, however, and prefer clean neat roads, and quiet animals in good sheltered private barnyards or in rich pastures with good fences."

This in fact is what the fence laws eventually provided: roads which were safer and cleaner and more agreeable to travel. And once cleared of cattle, they were soon cleared of rubbish. Fences around lawns and gardens became unnecessary, and the village common, stripped of its picket fence, revealed itself to be a pleasant ornamental space. Thus there gradually evolved in villages and on farms throughout the Midwest the uninterrupted lawn stretching from the house to the edge of the street or road; and along the street or road trees were soon planted. It was thus that a familiar feature of the American rural landscape came into being, a feature so familiar indeed that few inquire as to its origin.

As they were enacted across the country, the herd laws not only freed farmers from an increasingly burdensome expense, they transformed the rural environment. Nowhere was the change more dramatic than in the Midwest. "One of the admirable features of the landscape in the new States and Territories," declared the *American Agriculturist* in 1872, "is the freedom from fences. In some of the prairie States they have begun right by compelling every man to take care of his cattle, and holding him responsible for all damage to his neighbor's crops. The fences mainly are on the boundary lines of farms, and these are often omitted. This gives full sweep to all the modern implements of husbandry . . . and prepares the way for the steam plow, which can not be far in the future." The editorial then added, "One great want of Eastern farms is to get rid of the heavy walls that our fathers have built at such expense. . . . If we compete with the West successfully, we must put our fences out of the way."

Memories of the older, simpler order died hard, yet much of it had already vanished; milk was shipped by daily train from Ohio to St. Louis, and Illinois, once proud of its fruit, now bought it in Missouri. There had always been men in the Midwest who owned no land of their own and worked for others. In the past they had been dismissed as indolent white trash, last vestiges of a generation of hunters and trappers; but now there were thousands of tenant farmers, men—some of them veterans of the war—who did not have the money to start farming on their own. Likewise there were landowners with thousands of acres and dozens of tenant farmers. What did these changes portend?

These were merely symptoms: the prairie vanishing, the corn belt taking over, the forests and woodlots dwindling in size; the cabins of the first settlers, their trees grown large, pulled down one by one. There were fewer boats on the rivers, fewer mill wheels on the streams, less life in the waterfront towns. Fences and hedges came down as fields expanded; new fences went up where a new kind of farming appeared. Towns reached out into the fields, rails crisscrossed the marvelous landscape of level green and gold. It was as if the whole man-made spatial order had begun to expand and flow; as if the rigid rectangles of the grid could not contain a new and mysterious force.

3. TOWNS

Farther west and later, the railroad dominated the landscape and at times determined its form. Illinois in the 1850s offered a preview of the linear organization of space that was to prevail in the decades after the Civil War.

In 1851 the Illinois Central Railroad came into being, handsomely endowed at birth with more than two and a half million acres of federal land (or Congress Land as they called it then) along both sides of its future right-of-way. By 1856 the road was completed, from Chicago and Galena in the north down to Cairo in the southern tip of the state: 700 miles of track, at the time the longest railroad in the world.

But by no means the most prosperous. Built as it had been across a relatively unsettled part of the state—the prairies were not much liked at first—it lacked passengers and freight traffic. The obvious solution was to sell as much of the granted land as possible, and to encourage rapid settlement.

A nationwide advertising campaign was launched to tell of the marvels of Central Illinois and of its economic promise. Like the later publicity drives in the Northwest, it addressed foreigners as well as Americans, but it seemed to have been particularly effective in New York and New England. Groups of families and whole Emigration Societies in Vermont and Massachusetts and upper New York State moved out to establish communities in Illinois, and in parts of New England real estate values fell alarmingly. It was not enough, however, simply to dispose of farmlands; towns centered upon a railroad station and a freight depot were essential, and the railroad company (or a subsidiary of it) undertook to lay out, at regular intervals along the line, thirty-three towns, identical as to plan—a grid bisected by the track and identical as to street nomenclature—essentially that of Philadelphia. Even the sequence of concocted names, most of them ending in "a"—Onarga, Loda, Pera, Urbana—had a certain similarity. The majority of the lots in these railroad towns were sold on the open market, but a few were donated as sites for churches, schools, and public buildings. The business streets were supposed to flank the railroad; parks were not thought of.

The plan was entirely without imagination, but no more so than that of most American towns of the period and region. It was within the national tradition of the grid, and since the landscape through which the Illinois Central ran was in general remarkably flat, the plans rarely did violence to the terrain. When the towns prospered, and many of them did, they soon obliterated their artificial origin. Nevertheless, the railroad-designed towns, eventually common throughout the West, represented an important development in our whole landscape. They and the new farms surrounding them were not, even in theory, part of a pattern of independent social spaces: they were integrated from the beginning into a well-designed economic process, into a linear system vividly symbolized by the lines of track and their accompanying telegraph wires.

The tracks were everywhere, and it was from the train that the traveler saw the Midwest. In summer when rows of trees shaded the streets and the houses and lawns, the towns seemed fresh and pretty. Sometimes a stream meandered through a valley, and children swam in it and waved at the train. Many steeples testified to the piety of the townspeople; there was a view of substantial brick houses with wide verandas on a height overlooking the town, and on the outskirts there could be glimpsed the large brick buildings and chapel of a sectarian college. Near the station was often a small factory which made cultivators or cast-iron stoves.

But when he found himself spending a night or two in Midwestern towns, especially in bad weather, the traveler saw them in a different light. In all of them, as Bryce remarked, was the same gridiron of broad, unpaved streets, most of them leading nowhere, with the same names or numbers; the same dirty, noisy horsecars with passengers clinging to the steps; the same enormous hotel with a desolate lobby occupied by men in rocking chairs; the same Chinese laundry, the same undrained swamps and stump-littered vacant lots on the edge of town; the same pretentious Second Empire architecture; the same flimsy frame dwellings crowded together near the tracks or the river, slum or soon to become slum, densely inhabited by recent immigrants or blacks; everywhere the same hasty construction, frantic speculation in real estate, the same atmosphere of impatient hope. Everywhere in every town the same food, immersed in flour gravy. Aside from the new church, the new school, the fine new residences, the traveler found less to admire than to wonder at, particularly if he came from the East or overseas. Drugstores (already serving ice-cream sodas) were to be found on almost every corner, but it was in the newer, more expansive towns of the Midwest that another feature of urban America best displayed itself: the Block; the large, four- or five-story building, in a central downtown location. New England had first devised the Block in the 1830s, but in the Midwest it came to full flower. Built as a speculation with no specific occupants in mind, it nevertheless suggested in the arrangement of its floors the various functions for which it was suited: stores on the ground floor, above that offices for lawyers and doctors, and on the third floor—a kind of *Piano nobile* with tall windows—there was often a large space for an opera house, lodge hall, assembly room, or library. Finally, in the uppermost stories, attic or mansard, were rooms for rent, without heat but with an extensive view of roof tops. This hierarchical arrangement represented less a traditional social order than degrees of accessibility: two flights of stairs were enough for the average citizen to climb; three flights were for the poor.

As for the hotel, large and elaborate, it had already begun to play a role unique to America: as social center, place for public gatherings, and permanent home not only for single men but for single women and for whole families. The day of the squalid backwoods inn with its total lack of comfort and privacy was long past in the Midwest, and since the Civil War the shortage of moderately priced houses forced many families to stay in hotels; and career women, more and more numerous in offices

and factories and stores, found hotel living satisfactory enough
when they could afford it. Public opinion disapproved of boarding houses and hotels on moral, social, and dietary grounds, and
an Englishman writing in 1869 believed that the custom indicated that "Americans do not attach the same value to homes as
we do."

Three cities in the Midwest rose above the regional level, not
only in size but in wealth and worldliness: St. Louis, Chicago,
and Cincinnati. In 1870 the last-named city, with a population
of more than 200,000, was undergoing a short-lived return of
prosperity with the opening of the Ohio and the Mississippi to
shipping and the renewal of commercial ties with its southern
neighbors. In 1869 it had organized the first professional baseball
team, the Red Stockings—an innovation which in the eyes of the
amateur gentlemen players spelled the doom of the game. It was
in Cincinnati, moreover, that the traditional baseball uniform
originated, designed by a local dressmaker. It had art galleries,
an unusually active musical season, and (like every other American city of the period) it prided itself on its beautiful residential
district where expensive houses, surrounded by gardens and
lawns, gazed over the valley of the Ohio. Its most celebrated
park was Spring Grove, a cemetery of some 600 acres, widely
acclaimed as the most beautiful cemetery in America. It had
been designed shortly before the war by Adolph Strauch, a
German horticulturist who had come to live in Cincinnati.
Though his name is now largely forgotten, he was long held
to be the foremost designer of cemeteries in America, and Olmsted declared that when he sought inspiration it was to Spring
Grove that he went. It was Strauch who in effect first created
what is known as the lawn cemetery; one in which the size and
design and placement of the monuments are subject to esthetic
control, and where all extraneous ornaments—railings, plantings,
cemetery furniture—are forbidden in order to preserve an open
and harmonious environment. With Strauch the cemetery became a landscape more spacious and parklike. It ceased to be a
motley collection of monuments of every style, each enclosed in
its own well-defined space, and became instead an integrated

composition of lawns and clusters of trees. As a reorganization of a highly traditional kind of space, Spring Grove was a small but significant instance of the rejection of obsolete boundaries and the perception of a larger, more "natural" unity. It remains to this day an extremely beautiful place.

Despite these assets, Cincinnati had begun to fall in national esteem. Its age—it was by far the oldest city north of the Ohio—was forgotten, its honorable role in abolitionist activity, as influential as that of Boston, and the fact that *Uncle Tom's Cabin* had been written there, were both overlooked and the Southern sympathies of many of its citizens during the war constantly recalled. Its location on the Ohio was splendid, but never was there a city, said its detractors, so dirty, so grimy, thanks to the bituminous coal burned in its furnaces and stoves, in the factories and steamboats. It was true that its wealthy sections were imposing, but the crowded, dilapidated frame houses down by the river harbored a sensational slum. "Within a stone's throw of the most aristocratic portions of this city," a citizen of Cincinnati wrote in 1870, "there is another civilization, or rather absence of it, where thousands of human beings are crowded like cattle in pens, and lose all the sympathies of humanity in a greedy struggle for their common pittance of air, and light and water." Anthony Trollope, whose mother had passed three unhappy years there, and who perhaps wished to vindicate her unfavorable verdict on the city, called it "slow, dingy and uninteresting." Like St. Louis it had its large and well-behaved German population and again like St. Louis it had copied Philadelphia in the layout and naming of its streets; but whereas in St. Louis this imitation had seemed highly appropriate, in the case of Cincinnati it was held to be evidence of the provinciality of its citizens. "They patterned their city after Philadelphia," one commentator scornfully remarked, "the most magnificent city their eyes had ever beheld, and anything more splendid than which their imaginations were powerless to depict." The Queen City, as it called itself, its river traffic failing, the railroads taking its trade away, seemed sadly aware that it had somehow failed to fulfill its earlier promise.

4. CHICAGO

Even in those years just after the war and before the Great Fire there was no city to be compared with Chicago. St. Louis was larger (though it was fast losing its lead) and Cincinnati had a far more beautiful site; but the "Lightning City," the "Electric City" on the flats by the shores of Lake Michigan surpassed all other cities (except New York) in vitality and brilliance and in its capacity to astound. Its streets were broader, longer, incessantly alive; its buildings, whether the homes of the rich or the immense hotels in the central district or the rows of grain elevators near the Lake, were invariably sensational. Chicago was already the most active railroad center in the nation, the meat-packing center, the milling and lumber center, the center for the manufacture of farm machinery; it was here that the westward-moving settler met the land speculator and the supplier, and the regions where he went to live and farm became (in the eyes of Chicago at least) part of the city's empire—potentially the greatest and richest and most populous the world had ever seen.

It was also the "Windy City"—not because of its weather but because of the tendency of its inhabitants to brag of its accomplishments. These were certainly impressive: situated on what had originally been a hopelessly flat extent of land, barely higher than the nearby Lake, for weeks on end a vast sea of black mud where wagons sank three or four feet deep, it had been destined by nature to be a prairie Venice, a maze of drainage canals. But it had rejected the role, refusing any compromise with the environment, and instead had undertaken to raise itself by as much as twelve feet—a long and strenuous process of building-up streets, jacking-up and moving houses, and filling-in the low-lying sections of the city. Furthermore, it had reversed the flow of the sluggish Chicago river so that instead of dumping the city refuse and sewage into the Lake it carried it away in the opposite direction—to fertilize (in the words of a historian) the shores of the Illinois and Mississippi rivers. This done, Chicago constructed an elaborate system whereby drinking water was taken from two miles out in the Lake—a pure and inexhaustible supply.

Still another attempt to remedy the native shortcomings of the landscape was the creation in 1869 of a system of public parks. Before the war all that the city had possessed by way of pleasure grounds was a scattering of small and unimpressive green spaces and a few residential streets planted with trees and shrubbery; also, an area north of town of some 120 acres, originally a cemetery, but taken over by the city in the fifties as a park. This piece of ground was to become the nucleus of a local park system which in time included the Lake Shore Drive and Lincoln Park.

Its benefits, however, were confined to the Northside of the city; the Southside felt neglected and demanded parks of its own. Accordingly, in 1869 a commission was established to meet the need. The landscape architecture firm of Olmsted and Vaux, already celebrated for the designs for Central Park in New York and Prospect Park in Brooklyn, was hired. A comprehensive plan, sufficiently magnificent for the fifth largest city of the nation, was drawn up, submitted, and eventually adopted. Despite the fact that Chicago in this case was merely belatedly copying New York and Brooklyn and Philadelphia and even Baltimore, it discovered still a further ground for self-congratulation: it adopted as the city motto *"Urbs in Horto"* and thereafter referred to itself as the "Garden City."

Unfortunately before the plan of Olmsted and Vaux could be executed, the Great Fire of 1871 destroyed the preliminary paperwork, and the commission had to start much of the undertaking anew. To reorganize and carry out the designs for what were to be known as South Park and Jackson Park, the services of a relatively obscure landscape architect were engaged: Horace William Shaler Cleveland.

In his late fifties, Cleveland had recently moved to Chicago from Boston, where he had practiced with Morris Copeland. He was a native of Massachusetts and shared the background of Olmsted and Eliot and Copeland—rural New England and the New England tradition. Cleveland in fact belonged to a literary club in Boston whose members included Longfellow and Sumner, and toward the end of his life he undertook to defend the New England he had known against the criticisms of Henry James. Also, like his contemporaries in the field, Cleveland had had no formal training in landscape architecture, though he had managed to acquire experience in farming and horticulture and engineering; for a while he owned an orchard and vineyard in New Jersey. It was only after his removal to the Midwest that he developed his talents as a designer of parks and parkways. For almost three decades he was undoubtedly the leading landscape architect of the region.

It is rare to find mention of him in the histories of the art. The great parks and avenues which he created still adorn many cities, but Cleveland himself remains a relatively unknown figure; it is only with the recent republishing of one of his essays, with an appreciative introduction by Roy Lubove, that the current generation has been reminded of his existence. One reason, perhaps, for his tacit exclusion from the ranks of the Olympians is his identification with the Midwest. It is true that Cleveland had designed Sleepy Hollow Cemetery in Concord and Roger Williams Park in Providence, but his greatest works were the park systems of Minneapolis and St. Paul, Indianapolis and Omaha, as well as Southside Chicago; and his most important publication was entitled *Landscape Architecture as Applied to the Wants of the West.*

There is another and more likely explanation for his neglect by the Establishment: he was a different kind of landscape architect, with a different concept of the purpose of the art—a concept which the second half of the nineteenth century found uncongenial but which the present generation automatically accepts. He disliked the very term landscape architecture as pretentious; to him the art was "the subdivision and arrangement of land for the occupation of civilized men"—a definition which suggests urban and suburban and even regional planning. Most writers on landscape architecture, and by implication most landscape architects in his time, were chiefly concerned, Cleveland believed, with serving a class of well-to-do patrons "inhabiting districts already brought to a condition of elaborate culture and who would therefore be mainly interested in details of decoration." But in the West and Midwest the problems were of a less sophisticated sort. New towns and cities were being built almost overnight, and existing cities—Chicago among them—were expanding along every country road, every horsecar line, into the fields and pastures. Coming from New England where woods were omnipresent and where a second growth of forest had already transformed much of the rural environment, Cleveland was struck by the absence of trees in vast areas of the plains. What the landscape architect could contribute was therefore the systematic and wholesale introduction of tree plantings—to beautify the country, to alter the climate, to insure future supplies of wood for construction and fuel, and to soften the harsh outlines of the new towns. In 1873 he wrote his essay on "Forest Planting on the Great Plains," and for many years thereafter remained actively interested in the question.

His enthusiasm for tree planting, and his conviction that trees were an essential element in all kinds of environmental design, were matched by his detestation of the grid system and his efforts to modify it where he could. These two sentiments formed much of the basis of his philosophy as a landscape architect: the transformation and improvement of the environment for human occupancy by means of a more varied vegetation, and the dividing and arranging of spaces in an efficient and harmonious manner. The grid system not only ignored topography and imposed a hideous sameness on every town and city, it prevented the development of functional divisions and handicapped cross-town movement. "The government surveys of public lands [have] formed the only basis of division, the only guide in laying out country roads, or the streets of proposed towns. . . . Every western traveler is familiar with the monotonous character of the towns resulting from the endless repetition of the dreary uniformity of rectangles which they present." The blind allegiance to the grid had produced steep streets and all but inaccessible building sites, expensive grading and cutting; and at the same time an almost total neglect if not destruction of natural beauty as part of the urban scene. "All of these evil results might be obviated by due forethought and the exercise of taste and judgment . . . and now that we have reached the point where vast regions may be controlled by companies or individuals, and the sites and plans of towns can be selected and preordained, it is unworthy of the progress of the age . . . that no advance should be made in a matter of such importance."

Thus it was the mission of the landscape architect to help the new and expanding towns free themselves from the tyranny of the grid, and to achieve beauty by planting and adorning the streets and roads and pleasure grounds. At a period when it was still almost mandatory for the landscape architect to take his inspiration from classical or romantic landscape painting and to use the vocabulary of the painter, Cleveland insisted on the collaboration of landscape architect and engineer; and it was his Chicago partner, French, who wrote *The Relation of Engineering to Landscape Gardening.*

Given Cleveland's preference for creating environments, urban and rural, and his disdain for providing what he called "details of decoration," Chicago was a good place for him to be. In 1872 he was appointed landscape architect of the South Park and the network of connecting boulevards which Chicago was already planning. It was the boulevards that most excited his imagination; the parks, although incomplete in terms of landscaping, presented less of a challenge. Even before taking the job, he expressed some doubts as to the transcendent importance of parks as the chief place of public recreation. Central Park in New York was, to be sure, a brilliant success, but that was chiefly because New York, being situated upon a long, narrow island, with no access to the country on either side, was obliged to create a park near the center of population. Other cities, notably Chicago and Boston, were more favored by geography; open country was within easy reach in almost every direction. All that was needed was a series of broad, handsomely landscaped boulevards which would not only lead to the open country but provide pleasant avenues of greenery and fresh air for those who lived nearby. Furthermore, these boulevards could be cut diagonally through the city, thereby improving crosstown communication and remedying one of the defects of the grid. He envisaged a park system composed of a series of "grand avenues or boulevards . . . having roadways on each side of a central mall, lined with trees and adorned with fountains and other objects of attractive interest." It was all very well, he observed, to refer to parks as the "lungs of the city," and no doubt they could be made into beautiful and useful places for enjoyment and relaxation; but Chicago had no badly congested areas in need of this therapy, and what pleasure did parks afford to people who lived five miles away? He cited the late afternoon traffic jams which developed when people sought to travel by streetcar to Central Park after work. Diagonal boulevards more than two-hundred feet wide would be less costly to build in a busy city than more extensive parks; and they would have a virtue which no park could claim—they would make movement through the city faster and more agreeable.

The parkway, broad and well landscaped, linking a series of smaller parks throughout the city, was not an idea original with Cleveland. Like so many mid-nineteenth-century innovations in American urban design, it derived from the example of Haussmann's work in Paris, and the Ring in Vienna. And indeed Olmsted had proposed a similar parkway for Brooklyn, and Philadelphia was planning its own version. Cleveland, however, was inspired not only by esthetic considerations but by concern for traffic flow and the promotion of better health among those who might live near to one of the broad avenues of light and fresh air. Nor did he overlook the opportunity offered by these boulevards to promote his other ambition: the planting of trees. Years before he was placed in charge of the parks, he described in minute detail how the Lake Shore Drive could be made into a ten-mile-long arboretum—a systematic display of all the trees indigenous to the region. How else was the featureless Chicago terrain to be enlivened? For the existing attempts to landscape the parks of Chicago, he had nothing but scorn: "Mountain ranges are introduced which are overlooked from the chamber windows of the surrounding houses; lakes of corresponding size are created apparently to afford an excuse for the construction of rustic bridges. . . . A lighthouse three feet high serves to warn the ducks and geese of hidden dangers of navigation." Whereas, if the Lake Shore Drive were landscaped according to his suggestions, "Chicago would be in possession of a public promenade, perfectly unique in its character, and of an arboretum."

Like many others, Cleveland had hoped that the reconstruction of Chicago after the fire would result in an improved layout, but he was soon disillusioned. "Chicago now adds her experience," he wrote in 1873, "in proof of the fact that except under a despotic government, any essential alteration of the original plan of a city must be regarded as hopeless." Beginning in 1872, some twenty-six miles of boulevards, linking the various parks with one another and with the center of the city, were laid out, graded, and planted, and though few of them came up to Cleveland's lavish specifications, and none of them was diagonal, they were noteworthy additions to the city environment. Their breadth as well as their treatment indicated the increasingly important status which streets were acquiring in the American city, for they had been taken from under the control of the city administration and placed under that of the Park Board. It was the Park Board that regulated their use, and excluded all commercial traffic—to the indignation of the residents of parallel streets who found themselves submerged in more than their share of dust and noise; it was the Park Board and not the city which assessed adjacent property owners for boulevard improvements; and it was the Board, undoubtedly inspired by Cleveland, which prescribed uniform planting, not only on the boulevards themselves but along the property frontage. For many years the boulevards in the outskirts of the city were lonely and unused—"as inappropriate to their respective neighborhoods," in the words of a Chicago historian, "as would be a cathedral in a country village." But by the end of the century the foresight of the seventies had been amply vindicated. Chicago was not unique in its system of boulevards; had the authorities followed Cleveland's advice the system would have been larger and far more splendid; but the city provided a good example, especially during the seventies, of the growing tendency in America to interpret every civic improvement in terms of linear design, in terms of more and better streets. Already in the fifties Chicago had begun its self-raising project by elevating the streets—a move which entailed much litigation and a court decision, important in its day, that the city had exclusive control over street grades. Twenty years later, when Chicago began to aspire to a system of parks, it was the street (or the boulevard) which received a goodly share of the attention. And it was Cleveland, perhaps more than any other designer, who recognized the new role of the street and sought to give it artistic form.

The street or road as a kind of megastructure of the landscape was likewise exemplified in the residential suburbs of Riverside, which Olmsted and Vaux designed in 1868. This was not the first Chicago suburb laid out in a "picturesque" manner. Twelve years earlier in 1856, a St. Louis landscape architect by the name of Jed Hotchkiss laid out the suburb of Lake Forest, socially far more successful than Riverside, and containing in the midst of its maze of curving roads and avenues a "University Park," destined to be the campus of Lake Forest College. The suburb created by Olmsted and Vaux never achieved the distinction of Lake Forest, and was characterized in its early days by "a plentiful lack of improvements and an overwhelming generosity of prairie wind and waste prairie land which were anything but inviting." A group of Chicago businessmen, calling themselves the Riverside Improvement Company, had bought some 1600 acres of land on the banks of the small Des Plaines River near the line of the Burlington Railroad. The site was only six miles from the city, and well suited for country living. Olmsted and his partner produced a picturesque plan, with winding roads and open park landscapes along the river. Nothing like a commercial center was provided for, and the houses, many of them designed by Vaux, were to be pleasantly isolated, each in its own sylvan environment. An atmosphere of prosperous domesticity was sought for and attained; Riverside became a desirable if expensive place to live, and there was even a project for a carriage road leading from the suburb into Chicago. Olmsted paid special attention to the layout of the roads in Riverside; they were deliberately curved, despite the generally level topography, to "suggest and imply leisure, contemplativeness and happy tranquility." This was to be in welcome contrast to "the ordinary directness of line in town streets, with its resultant regularity [suggesting] eagerness to press forward, without looking to the right hand or left." The roads were slightly depressed between grass-grown banks, and afforded frequent glimpses of open public areas near the river—spaces which Olmsted recommended be used as ball grounds or for croquet. In keeping with the advanced taste of the time for open, undefined spaces, he urged the proprietors of Riverside to discourage the use of fences and walls.

So, for all its flatness, Chicago got the varied landscapes that it wanted. The city, the totally man-made environment, proved harder to control. It was wonderful to have it grow so fast, and to see it spread all over the prairie; it was gratifying to note the amazement of strangers when they were shown the elegance of Prairie Avenue, the new parks with their floral designs depicting the profiles of famous men or a camel or an immense globe, the continents indicated by succulents. But to many Chicagoans the expansion had its disquieting aspects: block after block of jerry-built frame houses, fronted on unpaved streets; even in the center of town there were wooden sidewalks with rickety flights of steps where the street elevation changed. The influx of a black population had begun to produce a recognizable "back alley" culture and environment in the older sections, and a series of "patches"—collections of dirty and disreputable shanties—not only harbored numerous brothels but a large and troublesome floating population of sailors; as many as thirteen thousand vessels a year docked at the waterfront, with cargoes of wheat and lumber. The banks of the river constituted a particularly sordid neighborhood. The original plan had been to slope the banks and pave them, but the deep-hulled lake craft, unlike the light-draft Mississippi boats, would have been unable to reach the shore to unload, so the adjacent landowners proceeded to build unsightly wharves and storehouses into the water; and nearby there evolved a squatter village, largely inhabited by poor Irish, that became known as "Kilgubbin"—a region of incessant fighting and scandal, and (because of its flimsy wooden dwellings and the proximity of the great lumber storage yards) a potential fire trap.

But then the whole city was by way of being tinder for a fire: of its sixty thousand buildings, forty thousand were of wood;

most roofs were shingled, and there had been several disastrous fires in the past. The summer of 1871 was exceptionally dry and the *Tribune* warned its readers that the marble and iron fronts of the newer buildings concealed a wooden structure underneath. On Sunday night, October 8, Mr. and Mrs. O'Leary, who lived in a wooden house on de Koven Street, gave a party. Around nine o'clock the O'Leary barn caught fire. A wind spread the flames, and by the time the fire had been brought under control —thirty hours later—2200 acres, containing the homes of 98,000 persons as well as much of the business section of the city, had been devastated, and 275 lives had been lost. Fortunately the O'Leary house was undamaged.

The lesson which America drew from this calamity was the obvious one: cities of frame buildings were entirely too dangerous to be allowed; the sidewalks in parts of Chicago had contributed to the spread of the flames, and it was rumored (but later denied) that the wooden paving blocks had also caught on fire. "It is earnestly to be hoped," wrote the editor of *Appleton's Journal*, "that the new Chicago which shall arise on the ruins of the old will establish the beginning of a new order of ideas in American architecture. Let it be such a city that fire cannot destroy, with far less of ornamental trickery, and very much more of substantial strength in its buildings, than now mark any of our frail and dangerous centers." And Joseph Medill, elected mayor a month after the fire, declared that "a blind, unreasoning infatuation in favor of pine for outside walls, and pine, covered with paper and tar, for roofs, has possessed many of our people." He proposed that "the outside walls of every building hereafter erected within the limits of Chicago should be composed of materials as incombustible as brick, stone, iron, concrete or slate."

And in fact the reconstructed Chicago proved to be a city of brick and stone, and the title of "Capital of the Gingerbread Style" was ceded to San Francisco. But the rebuilding of the burned-out area produced in terms of urban morphology an unforeseen result: it brought into being all at once the first of those typically American central business districts where thousands worked during the day, and no one lived by night.

There was some question, after the fire, as to whether the homeless merchants and bankers and other businessmen would try to return to the center of town. Most of them had moved to temporary quarters to the south and west—where whole rows of residences were converted into hotels and offices—and many were half inclined to stay. But the City Council offered to lease small plots of ground on the open lakeside to persons needing temporary accommodations while reconstruction was underway, and in no time a long row of shacks and booths appeared. "Derrick time" was what Chicago called the months after the fire, when every hour of every day throughout the year a new masonry building was completed. There had been some thirty-nine churches in the stricken district, and all of them had been destroyed. None was rebuilt; not only was the land too valuable, but the congregation had dispersed, for no landowner could afford to rebuild a dwelling in the center of the city. In consequence, downtown Chicago ceased to be part of the lives of many of the oldest and most substantial families; in a matter of months what had been a diversified but close-knit area with strong local loyalties became a densely packed district of stores and offices and lofts, destined to exchange its tenants every few months, uniform in its daily rhythm, entirely without the incidental spaces, without the greenery and solitude of gardens and backyards; compact, convenient, and more specialized, perhaps, in its functions than any comparable urban fragment in America. In place of the former centralized society, held together by propinquity and church and family ties, there began to evolve in Chicago three distinct suburban groups, none of them much concerned with the cultural life of the city.

Furthermore, the city ordinance forbidding the erection of frame buildings within a prescribed area had the effect of inducing residential development immediately *outside* the limits, since frame houses were cheaper to build, and if isolated on large suburban lots presented no fire hazard.

What speeded the physical recovery was the help, financial and material, contributed by thousands of well-wishers all over the world, but as a lumber center Chicago was fortunate in being able to help itself. The local Relief and Aid Society put up more than five thousand houses—many of which (as is the peculiarity of this kind of structure) survived the emergency by thirty years. Originally produced in New England and New York, the first portable or ready-cut houses of America were severely utilitarian in nature, and enjoyed a temporary popularity at the time of the California gold rush when they were shipped around Cape Horn, and later as field hospitals during the Civil War; but it was in Chicago that they were first produced in variety and number. The opening of the western plains to settlement with the completion of the Union Pacific created a demand for instant housing and provided the means for satisfying it; and the forests of Michigan and northern Wisconsin lay within easy distance of the Chicago mills. Samuel Sloan, an architect of some distinction and the editor of the *Architectural Review and Builders Journal* of Philadelphia, was greatly impressed by this industrialization of building. "A large contractor in Chicago keeps [portable houses] ready to be put up to order," he wrote in 1870. "Colonel Bridges has an order for a house where it is a necessity to put it up at once in order to save the title [on homesteads] and he has had the house completed, ready for use inside twelve working hours. He has had orders from Connecticut for seaside buildings, and had the buildings on the ground and ready for use in ten days. Just now," Sloan continued, "he is sending out seven meeting houses for Presbyterians to be put up at new towns on the line of the Pacific Railroad."

"There is a firm in Chicago," the historian James Parton wrote in 1867, "which is happy to furnish cottages and villas, schoolhouses, stores, taverns, churches, court-houses or towns—wholesale or retail—and to forward them, securely packed, to any part of the country. No doubt we shall soon have the exhilaration of reading advertizements of these town-makers, to the effect, that orders for the smallest villages will be thankfully received; county towns made to order; a metropolis furnished with punctuality and despatch; any town on our list sent, carriage paid, on receipt of price; rows of cottages always on hand; churches in every style."

Even before the completion of the Union Pacific, much of its westbound freight consisted of portable houses. Travelers reported seeing trains loaded with doors, sashes, door and sash frames, all in bundles of twelve. In the course of his travels in the same region, Cleveland reported in 1871, "Last summer on the plains between Lincoln, Nebraska and Fort Kearney I asked a new settler at whose home I stopped to dine, where he got the lumber for his house, not a tree being in sight. The answer was 'I ordered it from Chicago to Lincoln by rail, and hauled it out from there (thirty miles) with my team.'" Sloan saw the portable house as a solution of the problem of how to provide working-men with homes of their own, and investigated the matter in Chicago. "No one who has not visited these huge manufacturies of portable houses can have any correct idea of the magnitude of their operations. They are in keeping with the gigantic scale on which businesses of all kinds are carried on in the West. On their premises one may see millions of feet of lumber piled up for use. In the factory is machinery of the completest description for the purpose. Labor is thus wonderfully economized, and lumber is worked up with the least possible waste. Every class of customers are accommodated, exactly as is done by the great manufacturers of packing boxes. Houses are annually turned out by the thousand." He not only saw this process as the introduc-tion of "exact science" into the art of house building, but as an incomparable aid to the development of the West. "By im-mediately relieving the settler from the care and delay of build-ing in a new region where roads are few and supplies a great way off, with wages at a maximum, they have served as stimu-lants to the purchase of tens of thousands of acres, and to this day constitute an important element in Western prosperity." And he then wondered why similar portable houses could not be erected in such Eastern cities as Philadelphia, where the urgency was no less great.

In his *American Building Art,* Carl Condit calls the portable or ready-cut house "probably the greatest social consequence of the balloon frame; yet" (he adds) "in the twentieth century this valuable technique was nearly lost by the resistance of pseudo-cultivated taste and by the opposition of architects, building trades unions, and the entrepreneurs themselves." The portable house industry continued to flourish until the Depression, and its history, particularly in the latter decades of the nineteenth century, is very much part of American settlement history. The plausible assumption that all the portable houses, whatever their size and pretentions, were temporary and therefore eventually demolished, has induced many architectural historians to believe that most specimens, especially the earlier ones, have long since disappeared. Quite the contrary: even now they form a substantial part of many small railroad towns throughout the High Plains, and a little investigation would undoubtedly not only identify them as to age but even as to origin in one factory or another. To try to understand the distribution of house types throughout the United States without recognizing the role played by the factories in Chicago and other Midwestern cities would be a hopeless undertaking.

One further contribution made by Chicago and the Midwest to the new organization of space that began to evolve after the Civil War calls for mention, even though it has been investigated in detail by Siegfried Giedeon in *Mechanization Takes Command.* The Union Stockyards were open for business in the summer of 1865. They were essentially the creation of two meat packers, G. F. Swift and P. D. Armour, who together undertook to systematize the handling and processing of the cattle brought by train to Chicago to be slaughtered. Giedeon rightly emphasizes the "mechanization of death," the assembly line aspect of the butchering and rendering, the triumph of the impersonal and mechanical over organic life; but scarcely less significant is the spatial organization which made the process possible, and from this point of view the stockyards were prophetic.

Previous to the appearance of these two men, the handling of the livestock had been wasteful and confused: the animal freight of a half-dozen different railroad lines, arriving at widely separated stations, had to be switched from one line to another or herded through the streets. Buyers and sellers and processors had no common meeting place or common source of information; the animals suffered from harassment and lack of water and shelter; and for the processor the most serious shortcoming was the uneven flow of the work. What Swift and Armour provided was an area of some 345 acres, divided into 500 pens, capable of holding a total of 118,000 animals. The stockyards were laid out in a grid, with a main street, named Broadway, a mile long. But unlike the urban grid, the stockyard grid was designed to expedite movement: an intricate system of gates and light fences allowed herds of cattle to pass from the train to holding-pens to their ultimate destination without disorder or delay. It was the first large space in America designed for processing, and it was quickly imitated not only in other cities but in countless small cattle towns and on farms and ranches where livestock had to be sorted out and dispatched to market. While it is impossible to disassociate this ingenious planning, this complex linear design, from the bloody process it served, it nevertheless represented a new departure in spatial organization. Space is not only a container, a cage; it now becomes part of a movement, an orderly system of events leading up to a product. Strauch and the Midwestern farmer abolished the container; Cleveland and the railroads laid out space in terms of the line or the street; but it took the manufacturer, the packer, to organize space for the expediting of a process.

CHAPTER FOUR

New England

1. THE WOODS

Youth accounted for the hope and energy of the Midwest, youth accounted for its shortcomings. It was long to remain a region where, in the words of one of its sons, there could be "no question of origins, only of derivations." If its social forms (and many of its older landscape features) derived from the South, intellectually the Midwest looked to New England as home. No doubt the future of America lay in the prairie states, but the past had to be sought for elsewhere; even Chicago accorded priority to Boston in matters of intellect and scholarship. Michigan and Ohio, nearest to the East and largely settled by New Englanders, outdid all the other states in their loyalty to what they still thought of as an ancestral land.

In the sixties, when he was the twenty-three-year-old author of a small volume of verse, William Dean Howells journeyed from Columbus to Boston on a literary pilgrimage, made financially possible by an assignment from a Cincinnati paper. At first New England disconcerted him. Contrary to his expectations he was not overwhelmed by the antiquity of the scene. "With its wood built farms and villages, it looked newer than the coal smoked brick of southern Ohio. I had prefigured," he wrote much later, "the

New England landscape bare of forests, relieved here and there with the trees of orchards or plantations; but I found apparently as much woods as at home." But Boston and Cambridge were everything he had hoped for, and he was enchanted by a stage-coach ride between Lowell and Concord one fresh summer morning; he passed through newly mown meadows where the hay lay in long windrows among the boulders. "The land was lovelier than I have ever seen, with its old farmhouses, and brambled grey stone walls, its stoney hillsides, its staggering orchards, its wooded tops and its thick brackened valleys." The road went through cool forests and emerged into the glisten of the open fields.

More than once in his account of that early visit to New England—he was to return seven years later to live in Cambridge —Howells remarked on the many woodlands, the profusion of trees. He was in fact noting a characteristic of the New England landscape that was still relatively new and that would become more pronounced in subsequent decades: the gradual return of the forest. A generation earlier New England could have been described as an open countryside of farms and villages and towns. The original forest had been pushed back and frag-mented by two centuries of stubborn pioneering, and in the 1830s it is probable that at least two-thirds of the region (minus Maine) had been cleared of sizable stands of trees. The high tide of fields and meadows was perhaps the end of the first third of the nineteenth century; then ensued the long slow ebb tide, still not at an end, when the forest re-emerged, first on the hills, then in the valleys.

It was in the sixties that the decline of rural New England first became striking. In 1869, Nathaniel Shaler commented on the deterioration of the New England scene. "There is something sad about the look of the land. One never sees an acre gained from the forest; around the pasturelands there is often a belt where the wood marks its gain upon the cultivated tract. It is question-able," he added, "whether more than one-third of Massachusetts was ever at one time cleared from its forests. If things go as they are now going, there will be much less than that within the century."

But the signs of decay were not new; the process had started after the Revolution. No sooner had the war ended and the lands west of the Appalachians been opened for settlement than the population had begun to move. Young men, young families, whole congregations and villages left for New York State or Ohio or Illinois. The small farms with their difficult terrain and poor soil could no longer contain them. Seventy years later, after the Civil War, the exodus was still underway, only now it was to the Northwest or to Colorado or Kansas or California. Maine, and large parts of Vermont and New Hampshire saw the eclipse of innumerable hamlets; in Massachusetts and Rhode Island more than ten-thousand farms were abandoned during the sixties. Cedars and wild vines grew in the empty fields, and little by little the birches and alders and sumac and brush took over. Any farmer who stayed behind saw the fields of his onetime neighbor turn to wasteland, and before long a young forest had engulfed them, hiding a labyrinth of tumbled stone walls. William Brewer, Professor of Agriculture at Yale, described the condition of the New England woodlands in the *Atlas* of 1870: "The large timber used in house and shipbuilding is unquestionably rapidly diminishing, but the area of woodlands is not decreasing in the same ratio. In many places the large trees suitable for sawing are cut, without clearing the land of the smaller growth, leaving it still *woodland*. . . . As a whole, the *area* of woodlands in this region is but slowly, if at all, diminishing, and in large districts it increases from year to year. . . . This extension," Brewer explained, "is by natural process. Few if any forests have been planted, except on the sandy regions along the southern part and on the islands. . . . The extensive planting of trees for shade and ornament, however, increases the actual amount of wood in this region. To appreciate how much it is only necessary to see many of the new England villages and cities from some height in summer, where the abundance of trees gives the appearance of a forest to the scene. Some of the cities have more actual wood growing in their streets and parks than is sufficient to be termed a heavy 'forest' or 'timber' in the sparsely wooded regions of the West."

The resurgent woods were not the equivalent of their predecessors; they were younger, for one thing, and composed of a great mixture of species; but for those country people still around to use them they served several purposes. They were by way of being welcome extensions to the traditional family woodlot which provided material for a score of local crafts and winter occupations. The great variety of woods in the second-growth woodlands produced tool handles, shoe pegs, shingles, spools, baskets, furniture, barrel staves. Some served as fence posts or as board lumber. Much of it, perhaps most of it, was consumed as fuel, either in the nearby towns or in the home. It has been estimated that the average New England farm household in the days before the domestic use of coal needed between fifteen and twenty cords of wood a year, a cord representing roughly a half acre of woodland. Even the sugaring-off of a hundred pounds of maple sugar took the wood of a half acre. In this exploitation of the local woods there was little system and much waste; Americans in those days interpreted any natural resource in what might be called domestic or private terms. The small landowner rarely thought to exploit it in a businesslike manner or to improve it as an investment. To him the woodlot was much like an attic: a storage space where the family went to supply some unforeseen need; the space itself bore small relation to the contents; finding what was wanted was a matter of hit or miss. "Instead of using first the dead and dying . . . for firewood," an authority on forests later remarked, "body wood of the best trees was considered none too good for the stove, and the best trees of the best kind were chosen for posts, rail fences and other inferior uses."

The decline of commercial lumbering in New England that set in during the sixties did much to increase the areas of second growth. In the steep mountains of New Hampshire and Vermont where farming had never gained a foothold, and in the immense back country of Maine, the vast stands of spruce and pine had been vigorously exploited since the turn of the century. An insatiable demand for lumber for houses, ships, telegraph poles, railroad ties, and the extravagant means by which it was satisfied, eventually stripped much of northern New England of its virgin forest. While the boom lasted it was exciting and profitable. It was then that modern techniques of logging got their start on the large individual or family forest holdings. The owners sold the cuting rights to the lumberers and paid little or no attention to the methods used. In the valleys of the Machias, the Penobscot, the Kennebec, the Androscoggin a new breed of logger or lumberjack made its appearance, better equipped, more skilful in the felling of trees, the cutting of logs, and in the dangerous process of driving them down the lateral streams to a tidewater mill. The Maine lumberjacks, often of Canadian birth, considered themselves in a class apart, heroic figures of the sort Whitman praised in his "Song of the Broadaxe," and they enjoyed a special kind of prestige in camps elsewhere in the United States.

Lumbering in those days was blind in its widespread destructiveness. Clean cutting—the removal of all trees, not simply the usable ones—continued to be the practice, and wild fires, sweeping through the litter of chips and dead branches over a whole mountainside, were frequent. "Tonight the forest is on fire upon a mountain just above this house," an English tourist wrote from a hotel in the White Mountains in 1854. "The sight is grand, but rather terrific. . . . For some days past we have observed these forest fires in many directions. Sometimes they are intentional, to make clearings, but in general they are regretted." William Murray, the celebrated Boston clergyman, was less tolerant. "Go where you will in Maine," he wrote in 1867, "the *lumbermen* have been there before you; and lumbermen are the curse and scourge of the wilderness. . . . A lumbered district is the most dreary and dismal region the eye of man ever beheld. The mountains are not merely shorn of trees, but from base to summit fires, kindled by accident or malicious purpose, have swept their sides, leaving the blackened rocks exposed to the eye, and here and there a few unsightly trunks leaning in all directions, from which all the branches and foliage have been burnt away. The streams and trout pools are choked with sawdust, and filled with slabs and logs. . . . Every eligible site for a camp has been appropriated; and bones, offal, horse-manure, all the *débris* of a deserted lumberman's village is strewn around, offensive to the eye and nose. The hills and shores are littered with rotten wood."

Still, there were many rural New Englanders who welcomed the logging industry into their midst. It built roads and railroads, it built dams and mills, it provided work (of a very rugged sort) in places where farming was another word for poverty. Not a few towns in Vermont and New Hampshire and Maine, now venerable in appearance, came into being as centers of logging or milling or the processing of wood; and when commercial logging left New England to move west to New York and Pennsylvania and the Great Lakes states many towns languished. Even today hunters and explorers in the remoter New England woodlands tell of finding the remains of small logging communities, undisturbed for more than a century.

Trees everywhere—trees along the streets and roads and in the parks, trees growing into small forests in the abandoned fields, trees covering the hills and mountains once again—and yet this was the time, immediately after the war when America began to cry out in alarm that we would soon run out of wood, that the day was not far off when there would be no forest left east of the Rockies. This was the time, in other words, when the cult of the forest succeeded the cult of the tree.

There were in fact local (and often temporary) justifications for anxiety. During the war the supply of wood for fuel in the larger Eastern cities had run short, and branch line railroads had been obliged at times to burn hay. Out West the settler was beginning to discover that wood for fencing, for fuel, for construction took a great deal of money, and in the Midwest, where much of the original stand of forest had been destroyed, farmers complained that "the face of the whole country is becoming denuded, and wintry winds and summer storms sweep our farms with more fury than formerly."

Most of the blame for the impending scarcity was laid on the railroads. It was obvious that much lumber went west for the building of the new lines across the treeless Great Plains, and wherever railroads appeared the local wood supply was soon exhausted. "Ohio today has one mile of railroad for every ten sections of land," a farm editor wrote in 1869, "with thousands of locomotives and tens of thousands of cars, and shops, depots, docks, bridges, tanks, ties, sheds, and shanties without number.

The shrill scream of the locomotive whistle reverberating through every forest proclaims its doom."

But where was the remedy? To most country people it did not lie in preserving the existing forests. "We do not regret as some do," wrote an anonymous contributor to the *Country Gentleman*, "to see the old forests melting before the hand of civilization— though the want of economy in the waste of wood is much to be regretted. We do not ask landowners to keep their old woods untouched. It does not pay." What would presumably pay was "a general and extensive planting of new timber" in the form of windbreaks and plantations on hillsides and rough terrain— sources of profit when the trees had matured.

So it was not the threatened destruction of forests which worried most Americans but the threatened scarcity of a cheap and essential commodity. The well-being of several million domestic establishments was at stake, and the measures taken to remedy the situation were consistent with that point of view. This is not the place to mention the various federal and state actions designed to encourage tree planting by the individual landowner, nor the steps taken by the railroads to provide themselves with plantations of trees in the otherwise treeless expanses of Kansas. Arbor Day, instituted in Nebraska in 1874, was a small but typical manifestation of the approach, and so for that matter were the tree-planting activities of the Rural Improvement Societies. Whether or not all these efforts had any effect on the supply of wood is immaterial; Sherry Olson, in *The Depletion Myth,* effectively disposes of the notion that America in the seventies and later was menaced by a "timber famine." Their real significance is the attitude toward the natural environment which they implied.

Rural America in the postwar decades was still loyal to the cult of the tree, to the piecemeal domestication of nature; it was the scientists, the members of the learned professions, the writers and artists who had been converted to the cult of the forest and who eventually converted the government. "Many people," E. C. Fermow, onetime Chief Forester of the United States, observed, "have the tree sense well developed, but do not have the forest sense developed. Ever so many trees do not make a forest. . . .

The forest must be treated as a unit, not merely as a collection of trees, any more than a city is treated as a mere collection of houses." He could hardly have made a more apt comparison, for what he was saying (and what many others were thinking) was that the forest is an environment with specific characteristics of its own.

So the solution to the problem of the scarcity of wood was environmental and not merely social or legislative.

It is scarcely necessary to point out that America at that time already had a well-established cult of the wilderness dating back to the early years of the century, and that the celebration of the forest and the forest experience had long been a favorite theme of many writers and artists. It is logical to assume that the enthusiasm for forest preservation that possessed so many persons after the war derived in large part from the American version of the Romantic tradition. Moreover it is clear that the emphasis was almost always on the *preservation* of the forest, rarely on its elimination or reduction. But at the same time we cannot afford to overlook the radical change that had already begun in the attitude of Americans toward their natural environment, causing them to see the world around them less with the eye of the poet and more with the eye of the engineer. The worship of the forest as a kind of sacred grove was fast disappearing. Fermow warned that if one was to understand forests and forestry "he must get it out of his head that natural forests are necessarily perfect forests. From the standpoint of products, man can grow a much better forest than the major part of the natural forests. Natural forests are likely to be as weedy as neglected cornfields." Horace Greeley expressed the same notion with deliberate crudeness: "I am not at all sentimental— much less mawkish—regarding the destruction of trees. I realize that trees exist for use rather than ornament. . . . Understand then that I urge the planting of trees mainly because I believe it will *pay*, and the preservation and improvement and extension of forests, for precisely that reason." Forests were essential not only because they produced a valuable crop but because they retained moisture and discharged it throughout the year; even more important, they affected the climate. The belief was strong among Americans that the planting of trees in the West would produce more rainfall. The journalists who went to cover the building of the railroad across treeless Nebraska and Wyoming wrote back that the few tree plantings already in existence were modifying the climate. A report in 1868 on Nebraska by the geologist Hayden stated, "It is believed that the planting of ten to fifteen acres of forest trees on each quarter section will have a most important effect on the climate, equalizing and increasing the moisture and adding greatly to the fertility of the soil." The Mormon practice of planting trees had resulted in more summer rain in Utah, it was said, and a rise in the level of the Salt Lake. And if the planting of a few thousand young trees could thus influence the climate of the Great Plains and cause a marked increase in rainfall, what must the role of the great forests of the East be in influencing climate and rainfall in that part of the country?

The year 1873, so disastrous in the economic life of the United States, was a fateful one in the rise of the new forest awareness. It was then that New York State set up a commission to study the causes for the diminished flow into the Hudson and the Erie Canal. Both bodies of water were greatly reduced in depth, and it was feared that it might soon be impossible to ship produce to New York from the West by the canal and river. After some deliberation the commission reported that the flow had been reduced by increased lumbering in the Adirondacks, and it recommended that the forests of the region, covering about 715,000 areas, be declared a forest preserve. To be sure, no action was taken for another twelve years, and then only because the volume of water in the river and canal was once more below normal; but the recommendation marked the first official recognition of the preservationists' point of view, and of the forest as a definite environment. A topographical survey, to establish the boundaries of the proposed forest preserve, was immediately authorized.

In that same year Nathaniel Shaler published an article in which he speculated on the relationship between types of forest and types of climate. The preceding year had been an extremely dry one [which might have accounted for the drop in the water levels in New York] with an unusually cold winter in which many pine trees had been killed. Would another such drought and cold spell, Shaler wondered, end by producing a forest cover predominantly deciduous? If so, New England was in for a change of climate, for a deciduous forest did not moderate the extremes of weather so effectively as did a forest of conifers. Brewer of Yale also concluded his studies of the American woodlands by stating that there was a relationship—how close he could not tell—between rainfall and forests, and implied that unless some government control was exerted over forest exploitation, droughts could be expected in the future.

Then in September 1873, the American Association for the Advancement of Science met in Portland, Maine. It was addressed by Franklin B. Hough on "The Duty of Governments in the Preservation of Forests." Hough, later to be the first United States Forestry Commissioner, was by profession a doctor and the author of several learned local histories. By avocation, however, he was the first of those tireless and eloquent spokesmen for conservation who have since played so important a role in arousing public interest in the landscape. In his Portland speech he dwelt on the continuing destruction of the woodlands of the United States and demanded their preservation, not only to insure supplies of wood but to protect sources of water. The assembled scientists listened to him attentively, and before adjourning, petitioned Congress to make a study of the influence of forests on climate. Hough then went on to further triumphs, expounding his favorite topic in other cities; in 1874 he gave a series of lectures at the Lowell Institute in Boston.

Subsequent developments in the forest preservation movement saw a decided split between the advocates of a more scientific and professional management point of view, and the defenders of the forest as a wilderness; but in the years immediately after the war both were merely aspects of the new attitude toward the forest that had started first in New England and then spread throughout the country. The forest, and by extension the woodlot, ceased to be defined as a convenient warehouse to be raided with impunity and occasionally restocked by the random plant-

ing of trees. It became, in theory at least, a special environment
with its own "natural" boundaries.

In retrospect, so many forces, intellectual, social, and economic, are seen to have been at work producing the reappraisal of
the forest, that the influence of any one man is not easily dis-
tinguishable; but the writings of George Perkins Marsh constituted the most eloquent as well as the most scholarly expression of the new philosophy of the relation between man and
nature. *Man and Nature* was the title of his book when it was
published in 1864; ten years later the second edition was retitled
The Earth as Modified by Human Action. Marsh was a native of
Vermont, and as a young man engaged in a variety of rural
occupations—sheepbreeder, operator of a woolen mill, dealer
in lumber—he had had the opportunity of observing the impact
of lumbering on the economy and landscape of New England.
Later, as Minister to Turkey, he traveled throughout the Near
East and saw how the hand of man had altered and often laid
waste the face of the earth. Finally, as Minister to Italy, he
began to accumulate materials on the subject, and after seventeen years of study and reflection produced a book whose thesis
was that man was destroying the balance of nature, but that
with foresight, knowledge, and technical skill he could still
reverse the destructive process.

The book was enthusiastically received, and later acknowledged as the source of inspiration of the new forestry; Lewis
Mumford has called it "the fountainhead of the conservation
movement." Marsh, however, wrote not merely to alert men to
their destructive actions but to urge them to study and know
their environment, especially the forest environment, in order
to manage it more efficiently. "We have felled forests everywhere, in many districts, far too much. Let us restore this one
element of material life to its normal proportions," he wrote,
"and devise means for maintaining the permanence of its relation to the fields, the meadows and the pastures, and to the
rain and dews of heaven, to the springs and rivulets with which
it waters the earth." The years spent in what was then still the
pioneer landscape of Vermont had served to discourage any

romanticism in his view of the relationship between man and nature; man was a predator, entirely concerned with his survival in an alien setting. "Nothing is further from my belief than that man is part of nature," he declared, "or that his action is controlled by the laws of nature; in fact a leading spirit in my book is to enforce the opposite opinion and to illustrate the fact that man . . . is a free moral agent working independent of nature"; working, that is to say, with his own material well-being exclusively in view. Consistent with this philosophy was Marsh's belief that when the needs of man necessitated it, the natural environment could and should be radically transformed, provided it were done with intelligence and awareness of the consequences. Though expressing some scepticism of the more extensive effect of forests on climate, he was in general agreement with the notion that the natural forest—and therefore much of the natural environment—was capable of great improvement by human intervention, and repeatedly proclaimed "the great general superiority of cultivated timber to that of strictly spontaneous growth." The ideal forest was an "artifically regulated" forest, which had the additional virtue of having an artificially graded terrain for the greater control of the discharge or retention of the moisture.

If we look for Marsh's intellectual progeny we are more likely to find them among the proponents of scientific forest management than in the membership of contemporary wilderness or nature conservation groups; he had little time for any theory of a mystic link between man and the organic world. Although almost every page of his book speaks of his feeling for nature, of his loving scrutiny of all aspects of the natural environment, nowhere is there an acknowledgment of men's response to the beauty of the world around them nor of men's unceasing efforts to modify the environment in order to glorify it. A book which (we are told) was the product of a lifetime of study and reflection devotes not a single passage to speculation, however tentative, on the mystery of the complex relationship which is its chief topic: the relationship between man and nature. Marsh was apparently content to define man entirely in terms of his opposition to a natural order; as a "hostile influence," "a destructive power," an intruder; and it was only when man was taught to perceive that his physical survival was at stake that he would learn to control his violence and abide by the mechanical rules governing the balance of nature. Had *Man and Nature* been written a generation earlier it would have uttered the conventional pieties of an unquestioning age; were it to be written now it would contain much more of doubt and less of optimistic assurance, more awareness perhaps of the complexities of both man and nature. But it was written at a time when men were impatiently rejecting the traditional organization of the world, and were sure that the discovery of environments and of how to create and alter them was the key to material progress. The priest, the artist, the individual citizen had none of them succeeded in organizing space on an efficient basis; that task was one which only the engineer or the expert in nature technology could accomplish.

2. THE COUNTRYSIDE

If the forest had imperceptibly re-emerged onto the New England landscape, it had done so chiefly as scenery. Now that the lumberers had departed, it could safely be left alone. In New York there still survived an aristocratic tradition of the forest as a hunting ground for big game, and much of the pressure for the preservation of the Adirondacks came from well-to-do New Yorkers who owned hunting lodges in the region or belonged to one of the hunting clubs. New England, however, approached the forest in a different, more detached frame of mind: either in search of spiritual uplift or (as was more common) in search of a cool and restful vacation spot.

In 1869, The Reverend William H. H. Murray, recently called to the pulpit of the Park Street Church in Boston, wrote a book about the Adirondacks: *Adventures in the Wilderness.* Deplored by literary critics—"'Loud' is the word we might best apply to it"—it was nevertheless an instant success, and the following summer witnessed what was called "Murray's Rush" to the Adirondacks. "Mr. Murray's pen," a contemporary commentator wrote, "has brought a host of visitors into the Wilderness such as it has never seen before—consumptives craving pure air, dyspeptics wandering after appetites, sportsmen hitherto content with small game and few fish, veteran tourists, weary workers hungering for perfect rest . . . come in parties of two and dozens, and make up a multitude which crowds the hotels and clamors for guides."

Inevitably there were disappointed and frustrated visitors, and angry letters appeared in the press denouncing Murray as a liar for his accounts of the fishing available, or for attracting such a motley public to the Adirondacks and thereby threatening its widerness character. Yet his intentions had been honest enough; he had written a flamboyant and enthusiastic book about his excursions into the Adirondacks because he himself was flamboyant and enthusiastic. In a church noted for sensational preachers he had attracted unusually large audiences. "Mr. Murray," said a reporter for a New York weekly, "lectures, edits a paper, drives a fast horse—several of them—keeps himself in front, and draws a large crowd. He has an immense choir, supported at great cost. The musical feature of the worship is very prominent." In 1874, Murray withdrew from the Park Street Church and embarked on a colorful career of horsebreeding, ranching, and lecturing. Undeterred by the consequences of his first literary venture, he soon wrote another, a volume of stories about the Adirondacks. One of them, "A Ride with a Mad Horse in a Freight Car," was published in the *Atlantic Monthly*.

His original intention had simply been to tell his readers of the joys of hunting and camping in the woods, and he conscientiously listed all the necessary equipment: tin cups, rifles, an assortment of fishing rods, and a pair of "stout pantaloons." No doubt many took his advice and went to the Adirondacks to relish primitive living. But most did not; they went to stay in hotels, to take boat rides and picnic excursions into the mountains. "The woods are thronged," the superintendent of the Adirondack Survey sadly observed, "bark and log huts prove insufficient; hotels spring up as if by magic, and the air resounds with laughter, song and jollity. The wild trails . . . are cut clear by the axes of the guides, and ladies clamber to the summits of

these once untrodden peaks." The defiant pronouncement of
G. P. Marsh that man was no part of nature was never more
clearly vindicated than in the behavior of Murray's Adirondack
public. Camping out, a new and delightful way to spend a vacation according to contemporary guidebooks, was still not
popular with the majority; few Americans saw its attractions,
and even Professor Shaler, traveling on foot with a group of
geology students from Cambridge to Tennessee, was followed
by a wagonload of equipment and a competent cook. To the
city-bred Easterner the forest was merely a picturesque setting
for a holiday; an element—and not the most essential—in mountain scenery. In modern parlance it had not yet become a
significant feature in the popular perception of the environment.

So, despite the omnipresent second growth, visible to everyone, New England was still envisaged as an open landscape of
farms and meadows and tree-embowered villages, fresh and
green and beautiful. It was accorded a quality—acquired or
retained, it would have been hard to say—that distinguished it
from other regions: a smallness of scale, a neatness and simplicity, a rich diversity of scenery that elsewhere in the United
States were lacking. Never reluctant to tell its own virtues, New
England ascribed them to its being the most truly American
part of the country, but the rest of the states ascribed its unique-
ness to its age.

And indeed much of the rural New England landscape, a century ago, recalled a pre-industrial society. There were valleys
which the railroad had still not found it profitable to invade, the
coast of Maine and Massachusetts and Connecticut had seaports which were half asleep, and in the mountains of Vermont
and New Hampshire it was possible to discover dying villages,
unchanged for fifty years. The remoter parts of the region invited
exploration, and after the war summer vacationists from Boston
and New York and Philadelphia began to rediscover the landscape which lay so close. Increasingly resentful of city dirt and
city crowds and city corruption, resentful of the rising tide of
foreign immigrants, they set out to find evidences of the "real"
America in New England.

The hills of western Connecticut reverting to forests, and the more open valley of the Housatonic, contained many villages where an older America survived. There was Newtown, where Americans met their first elephant, imported after the War of 1812 by Hackaliah Bailey; there was Litchfield, the site of the first law school in the United States and of the first female seminary. How agreeable it must have been to ride or drive through the woods and rolling green country from one white village to another! There was not only the scenery to relish and the old pre-Revolutionary houses and churches, there were the old American "types." In an account of a leisurely trip taken in 1874 through "cozy little villages that nestle so lovingly among the hills of northern Connecticut" a journalist remarked that this was a region "where the traveler can fill his notebook with quaint folk phrases . . . elsewhere obsolete, but here like fossils in a social formation eocene to observers whose studies have been limited to densely settled tracts." He speculated on the Yankee idiom as he heard it, noting that the peculiarities of the language seemed related to the physiological structure and inner life of the speaker. "The New Englander, with his preference for closed sounds, presents a curious example of the closed nature. He declines to open his mouth."

Farther north in Massachusetts was Stockbridge, with its memories of Jonathan Edwards and William Cullen Bryant and Hawthorne and Melville, and the Sedgwicks and the Fields. The mountain setting was no less an attraction, and it was in Stockbridge that the first Village Improvement Society, the "Laurel Hill Association," was founded in 1853. It took its name from a wooded knoll in the center of the village, and the first object of the new Association had been to convert the hill to a public park; next followed the planting of trees along the streets and roads. Gradually it extended its efforts into the outlying country and into the improvement of the cultural facilities of the village itself, until Stockbridge, twenty years later, was looked upon as a model community. George Waring was one of the admirers of the Village Improvement Associations as propagators of new ideas of community organization; rural beauty was by no means all that they could contribute. "It is beyond dispute," he wrote in *Scribner's*, "that the United States is *par excellence* a land of beautiful villages. North, south, east and west, there are plenty of hideous conglomerations of poor-looking houses with an absence of every element of beauty, but there are thousands of other villages scattered all over the land which are full of the evidences of good taste. . . . The real elements of beauty in a village are not fine houses, costly fences, paved roadways, geometrical lines, nor any obviously costly improvements. They are rather coziness, neatness, simplicity." Justifiably opposed to the elaborate fountains and statues and public buildings which New England villages were already receiving as memorials to prosperous or famous sons, Waring drew up a model set of regulations for a Village Improvement Association. The introductory article stated that "the object of this association shall be to improve and ornament the streets and public grounds of the village by planting and cultivating trees, establishing and maintaining walks . . . securing a proper public supply of water . . . lighting the streets, encouraging the formation of a library and reading room, and generally doing whatever may tend to the improvement of the village as a place of residence."

The Laurel Hill Association, prototype of hundreds such groups throughout the United States, was by way of being a successor, in terms of public responsibility, of the traditional New England town meeting, whose environmental authority was increasingly limited. In the 1870s there were no less than two hundred Village Improvement Societies in New England alone; Horace Bushnell and B. G. Northrop, both of Connecticut, brought the institution to California, and Waring's model bylaws were widely adopted in other parts of the nation.

After the explorers came the summer residents. Beginning soon after the war the demand for old houses in "unspoiled" townships became so insistent that few villages, however remote, went uncanvassed by scouts and agents, and articles appeared in magazines advising readers where to look and what to pay. Those who had money built houses of their own, attempting, not always successfully, to harmonize the design with the colonial village environment. Vincent Scully, in *The Shingle Style*, has described the efforts of American architects of the seventies to devise an idiom suitable both for country living and for the renewed awareness of the American past.

The vacation region extended up the Maine coast to Mt. Desert, a century ago still very much a recreation frontier. Bar Harbor was described as "an ill-kept village of perhaps one hundred dwellings situated partly on a hot, treeless plain, and partly upon a very boggy bog," and the promoters of the new resort were sternly warned to do better if they wanted visitors to return. "It will never do to trust to scenery as a magnet if the walks are dusty, the lawns broken and clayey, the streets un-shaded. . . . A little Haussmannizing will place Bar Harbor in a far better condition."

No such crudeness obtained in the White Mountains. The Boston, Concord and Montreal Railroad carried its passengers into the heart of the vacation region. In the many summer hotels "the halls dazzle with beauty," according to the guidebook, "their parlors rustle with fashion; their corridors resound with mirth; and their drives are a whirl of excitement." From the broad verandas the guests watched the shadows of the clouds pass over the forested flanks of the mountains. Paths led to a nearby waterfall or an unusual rock formation; opportunities for sketching or painting in watercolors abounded. Here was a rich source of inspiration for the writer of romantic short stories, as was the vacation spent more modestly in the New England country boardinghouse or as a paying guest in a farmer's family. Howells and Stockton exploited the theme, as did Lucretia Mott Hale in the *Peterkin Papers*. The eternal Peterkin search for the edifying experience ended as usual in farce, but always the quest was for a bucolic simplicity, for a return to an earlier American innocence; and it was the brief glimpse of an elusive past which introduced into many of the novels with a summertime New England setting a note of regret. The same sentiment pervaded the sculpture groups of the New Englander John Rogers, as well as innumerable landscape paintings. William Morris Hunt, the fashionable portrait painter brother of the architect, startled and delighted Boston in 1874 by displaying a number of New England landscapes—among them an old frame mill on the bank of a stream, with a tall brick chimney rising prophetically in the background. "Such places," wrote a critic, "as these are chiefly made interesting through the pen of writiers like Thoreau or Emerson. . . . Till lately it has not been the fashion to crystallize them into works of art worthy to hold side by side with 'vineclad cots,' 'wild ruins,' or 'old cathedrals high and hoary.'" Hunt (he said) was to be congratulated for "delineating our unique, unfinished, but most interesting and individual American life."

From the perspective of the artist and writer, from the vantage point of the hotel veranda, the charm of New England lay in the reminders of an established American landscape tradition, and the landscape itself seemed to encourage the genre painter, the antiquarian, the collector of historical lore. The gray-roofed farmhouses with their brood of sheds and barns stood among tall elms and maples, and elms and maples flanked the narrow winding roads leading from village to village. Stone walls divided the holdings into small fields, which in much of New England averaged no more than four acres apiece. Each contained a patch of corn or wheat or potatoes; there was a rock-strewn meadow, and a decrepit orchard, survivor of a time when the making of cider had been an art. Oxen plowed the fields, oxen hauled the loads of firewood and hay into town. At the county fair oxen always attracted the largest crowd; there were plowing contests in the afternoon with sometimes as many as ten teams of two yokes of oxen apiece taking part. These were enormous animals, often weighing three thousand pounds. In the evening everyone listened to the Annual Address. The topic was "Neatness in Farming" or "The Blessings that Surround the Farmer and his Calling" or perhaps a poem on country life. Professor Agassiz spoke, denouncing the erroneous theories propounded by Charles Darwin; Charles Sumner spoke, and even Emerson spoke at the county fairs. The farmers and their families went home persuaded that their lot was an enviable one. The soil might be poor, the yields smaller and smaller, and each year there were fewer neighbors and less help to be had. The letters from sons telling of the wonders of farming in the new lands in the West were briefly disturbing, but there was comfort in the remembered words of the orator, comparing the mountain landscape of New England with the plains of the Mississippi Valley. "No man can pretend that agriculture in the West is the intellectual exercise that it is with us. It may indeed be true that there is as much mind employed upon the land there as in New England; but let no one assume from existing facts that the equality will be maintained through generations and centuries. The West has no character of its own," he said. And what food for thought there was in his assertion that "the inhabitants of Caledonia County, Vermont, produced more than any equal population on the Globe!"

It was picturesque; it was ideal as a vacation background; but another way of thinking and working had begun to manifest itself. Francis Amasa Walker at just such a county fair bade the farmers of Massachusetts educate themselves in new agricultural techniques before it was too late. George Waring, celebrated in those years as the author of the "Letters from Ogden Farm," told them that they did not know how or where to plow, that they knew nothing about soils or about chemistry and that they would do well to learn. Bolder spirits borrowed money and bought farm machinery, harnessed their oxen to mowers while sceptical neighbors looked on. It took little time to discover that the five-acre meadows were ridiculously small for this kind of operation, and that hillside pastures strewn with rocks and scrawny brush were ruination on the blades. They demolished some of the walls and made pastures of twenty-five acres or more; concentrated on plowing the flat valley lands and seeding them to new kinds of grass; as for the hillsides, they were left to whatever wild growth chose to take over. A cycle of sorts was thereby completed: the man-made landscape of New England had got its start back in the seventeenth century on the hilltops cleared by Indian fires; it had slowly expanded, generation after generation, into the wooded valleys. And now, in the second half of the nineteenth century, the fields were retreating from the hills and leaving them to the forest.

New crops were called for: it was no longer a question of simply providing for the family—pumpkins, beans, wool, wheat, corn—it was a question of raising crops to sell. For all its reluctance to experiment, New England had had its share of fashionable novelties. "Merino sheep, China tree corn, Rohan potatoes, grama grass, *Morus Multicaulis*," a farm writer wearily complained, "were each in their turn loudly extolled as speedy stepping stones to agricultural wealth. The 'hen fever' followed them. What is to follow it?" But the poultry craze proved lasting: after the respective merits of White Shanghai, Black Spanish, Bolton Grays, Plymouth Rock, and Rhode Island Red had been weighed, New England took to poultry farming in earnest. Towns were growing. The urban population demanded not only poultry and eggs, but milk and butter and cheese and vegetables and fruit.

The valley lands were reorganized to satisfy the new market; neglected pastures were plowed and drained and seeded; hay— to feed the dairy stock or to be sold in town to feed the draft horses there—became in many parts of New England the most important crop, and when in the sixties the hay bailer was invented it became possible to ship hay by rail long distances; even remote farms started to raise it in large quantities. The landscape of grass expanded. During the war New England, bereft of cotton and in need of cloth for uniforms, had reverted to the raising of sheep. Outside of certain areas of intensive farming—the tobacco and onion-raising districts of the Connecticut Valley, the truckgardening districts around Boston and along the Sound—New England turned green. An Englishman traveling in America in the 1860s thought New England "resembled a vast sheep farm."

The emphasis on dairying and on raising feed for cattle produced a new kind of barn: larger, better built, and more elaborate in plan. Previously any makeshift shelter for the animals had sufficed, and indeed cows and horses had spent most of the year foraging along the roads and in the woods. The improved barns were handsome structures, the pride of their owners, conspicuous features of the landscape; and the adoption in the seventies of the tall round silo for the preservation of forage in a green state contributed much to the imposing character of the new barn complex. Usually the work of local carpenters and cabinetmakers, the new barns were sometimes designed by experts like Waring; plans and specifications could be bought from builders' firms and from the agricultural magazines. In New England most if not all of them, even until a half century ago, were built in the traditional manner: with a stout and heavy frame of rough hewn timbers mortised and tenoned together, covering with sheathing. The merits of this massive construction (so the New England farmers believed) lay in its ability to withstand any horizontal thrust and to support the heavy loads of hay. But in fact the balloon frame barn, almost universal in the West, was equally sturdy and far easier to build, and the reluctance of the Eastern farmer to adopt it provides an interesting insight into regional differences in technology. New England and most of the East persisted in building barns so massive and so intricately subdivided that in time they proved all but impossible to remodel or adapt to changes in farming practices. The heavy central king posts supporting the gable prohibited the use of the convenient and laborsaving horse fork—a horse-powered contrivance for lifting hay into the loft of the barn. As a consequence the New England farmer, unlike his Midwestern colleague, was obliged to unload and store his hay on the ground floor. The cattle were housed in the basement underneath, and the hay was pitched to them through chutes or trapdoors. This in turn necessitated building the barn on a slope, so that the cattle could have access to the basement on the down side.

The bank barn (so-called because of its siting) originated in Pennsylvania and among the Pennsylvania Dutch it achieved an almost architectural quality. In New England it was likewise very often a beautiful structure, well proportioned, precise in workmanship, with an ornamental cupola or turret for ventilation, and a massive silo rising next to it. It was in its day an excellent solution to the new problems of dairying: it permitted work to be done indoors, and it permitted the accumulation of manure to spread on the fields and meadows. But stubborn loyalty to the traditional heavy, rigid frame, strong enough to last forever, eventually hindered any change or growth in the layout.

New barns, in any case, were a necessity, once new kinds of

farming were introduced, and New England made a virtue of that necessity. New dwellings were another matter. The most the average farmer was willing to do to improve the homestead was to paint it another color when a new coat of paint was called for. White, whether paint or whitewash, had long been the accepted treatment, but ever since Downing had denounced the practice—"chalky white in their clapboards," he had said of the early nineteenth-century farmhouses, "and *spinachy* green in their blinds"—there had been timid experiments with color. The fashionable popularity of brownstone in the cities in the 1850s and 60s had naturally encouraged many farmers to paint their houses brown, and even when possible to paint the shutters verdigris bronze. The taste had not lasted; and after the war a new standard—not without its spatial significance—had been adopted. No longer was it a question of imitating some other building material, marble or brownstone, with its social connotations; now it became a question of choosing a color which blended with the rural environment. Calvert Vaux, the onetime partner of Andrew Jackson Downing and later of Olmsted, and an architect in his own right, spoke out eloquently for the new approach to color. He condemned white as too glaring, brown as too somber, and red as too bold. Shades of buff or yellow were what he recommended; a neutral tint for the body of the house, and the trim around the doors and windows and cornice several shades darker. Furthermore, the barns and stables and other farm structures should all harmonize and blend into the surrounding landscape.

How much the boxlike Colonial dwelling could ever be made to "blend" with an environment it had been originally designed to defy was questionable; but newly built farm dwellings showed a greater adaptability. The studied picturesqueness of the "irregular" style promoted by Downing and Vaux had its influence on the architects who compiled books of plans and specifications for rural dwellings of every price; but farm life, and farm incomes, imposed restrictions which the suburban resident did not have to take into account, and at the same time inspired significant changes in the plan. The old Colonial layout with its large rooms and inflexible symmetry was no longer desired;

a more complex family life required individual rooms for each member of the family when possible: spaces with specialized functions were introduced. "I am aware," wrote a designer of moderate-cost farm houses in 1873, "of the partiality for large kitchens, or rather combinations of kitchen and dining room, and the many arguments brought in their favor. But cannot all that is claimed for them, ease of work included, be found in the . . . arrangement of dividing this great room into a moderate-sized dining room and small cook room? . . . After meals the table can be cleared in a moment, and all removed out of sight. Then how delightful the thought that when weary of washing, ironing or baking, by a step or so you can retreat to this bright and pleasant room, with its cool refreshing atmosphere!" So the new farmhouse had a dining room, and it even had a study or library; a room where the children could do their homework and the man of the family keep his books. The establishment of cheese factories and butter processing plants throughout the dairy country of New England and New York relieved the housewife of one of her most onerous and time-consuming duties, and the farmhouse of the seventies was rid of one of its spaces for work. In return it acquired the wide veranda or porch; not the traditional narrow porch which was simply a shelter and a shade from the sun, but an outdoor living space, a transitional zone between the dwelling and the immediate environment of garden and lawn.

This flexibility of design was largely achieved by the introduction of a modified balloon frame construction. Though the Eastern farmer resisted the balloon frame in barn building—for reasons which are still unclear—he welcomed it at an early date in the building of his new house. As might be expected the shift from the traditional methods to the new methods imported from the Midwest did not take place without modifications and adaptations; mortise and tenon persisted for some years, while elements of the balloon frame were used in the less critical parts of the structure. By 1860 the modified balloon frame seems to have been generally accepted for dwellings in the East—encouraged no doubt by the use of speculative housing construction in the cities and factory towns, and made cheap and convenient by the multiplication of lumber and planing mills throughout New England. As with the new barns, plans and specifications for the new-style frame dwellings were widely circulated in books and magazines, and in the catalogs of architectural publishers.

It was in these various ways that rural New England changed in the mid-nineteenth century: the fields moved down into the valleys and (in accordance with the nationwide tendency) became larger. More and more, topography was recognized as a factor in location and boundary. Grass took over, denser and brighter green than the old wild grasses, and imposing barns now stood on the slopes above the fields. Where the expanded pastures merged into the hillside woods the cattle grazed under the trees, eating the undergrowth, eating the lower foliage of the trees themselves and thereby creating an open, parklike margin to the forest. Whatever the delighted vacationist supposed, this was no longer the traditional New England landscape, it was a pastoral landscape of smooth expanses of short grass, bordered by translucent groves of trees. It was amid that calm and spacious beauty that Olmsted and Cleveland and Copeland and (later) Eliot had passed their childhood, and it was this that they unconsciously sought to reinterpret in their urban parks when they were middle-aged men; pastoral New England—rocks, browseline, short grass, and shallow streams— was transplanted to Central Park, to Brooklyn, to Omaha, to Chicago.

Henry James, who had briefly experienced this aspect of New England in the rolling hills and sheep farms of Stockbridge, came back to it late in life; in 1906 he could still discern the pastoral quality of backcountry New England. "Why was the whole connotation so *delicately* Arcadian, like that of an Arcadia of an old tapestry, an old legend, an old love story in fifteen volumes, one of those of Mademoiselle de Scudéri? Why, in default of other elements of the higher finish, did all the woodwalks and nestled nooks and shallow, carpeted dells, why did most of the larger views themselves, the outlooks to purple crag and blue horizon, insist on referring themselves to the idyllic *type* in its purity?—as if the higher finish, even at the hand of nature, were in some sort a perversion, and hillsides and rocky eminences and wild orchards, in short any common sequestered spot, could strike one as the more exquisitely and ideally Sicilian, Theocritan, poetic, romantic, academic, from their not bearing the burden of too much history." He spoke of the apple tree in New England, which "plays the part of the olive in Italy . . . and becomes infinitely decorative and delicate." But the future of this lonely landscape, as James saw, lay not in the hands of farmers but in those of the Summer People.

3. TOWNS

By the seventies the Summer People, reinforced by tourists, seekers after health or solitude, amateurs of country ways, had taken over much of the abandoned or underpopulated sections of the backcountry of New England; and they and their descendants were to maintain and consolidate this control during the hundred years to come.

Much the same urban element began to covet the New England seacoast as well. Seaside resorts had already been popular with an earlier generation of well-to-do city dwellers. Newport dated its discovery by the world of fashion from the 1850s, and all along the beaches and rocky inlets of Cape Cod and the North Shore as far as Old Orchard in Maine there were well-established summer communities, each with its own characteristic public. The years after the war saw the advent of something new in vacation facilities: the planned, privately financed and controlled resort village. If Mt. Desert was the most elaborate of these, Oak Bluffs on Martha's Vineyard, a Methodist summer community of some seven hundred cottages, had the distinction of being designed by the Boston landscape architect Morris Copeland in 1871. Falmouth Heights on Buzzard's Bay, likewise designed by Copeland, was another such planned resort, complete with "serpentine walks and drives," and a grand waterfront avenue.

In addition to these seasonal attractions the New England coast possessed a number of picturesque seaports and fishing villages extending from Bath, Maine, down to Greenwich, Connecticut. They dated from Colonial times, and at one time or another had been prosperous and important, involved in fishing or shipbuilding or the export of lumber, or in overseas trade. They had come to full flower in the early years of the Republic, but by the time of the Civil War they had lost much vitality. New sources of oil had gradually eliminated the whaling fleets of New Bedford and Edgartown; New Bedford in one arctic disaster lost twenty-one of its whaling ships in 1876. In Maine the hinterland of forest had been harvested of its best timber. Boston and New York had monopolized the foreign trade of such ports as Salem and New Haven, and ships from the Maritime Provinces competed successfully with those from the old fishing ports around Massachusetts Bay. The once active waterfronts had become deserted, and their warehouses stood empty. Marblehead, for long an important fishing town and at one time second only to Boston in population, in the 1870s sent out no more than a dozen vessels a year, and its narrow harbor briefly came to life when the New York Yacht Club paid its annual visit. In the somnolent seacoast towns great foursquare mansions, painted buff and white, stood back among old-fashioned gardens on streets bordered by tall elms and maples and chestnut trees. Down by the harbor, shops stood empty or decaying. In old-fashioned parlors, around stoves in grocery stores, along the idle waterfront, talk was of the more glorious past—when ships had gone to Africa or China, when Lafayette had stopped overnight, when a disastrous storm at sea had taken the lives of fifty young fishermen. In their all-but-empty churches clergymen still prayed for those "who go down to the sea in ships, and who have business on great waters." The cult of the past assumed a variety of forms: historical societies and family museums flourished, privately printed memoirs and biographies recalled the happier years at the turn of the century. Portsmouth had its society for the preservation of the old trees, and loyal townsmen bequeathed money for the planting of more trees or for the maintenance of some monument or ancient graveyard. Thomas Bailey Aldrich wrote of an old lady in her nineties "who had known Washington very well . . . The President was the staple of her conversation during the last ten years of her life." A visitor to Marblehead had the impression that all the inhabitants were related and shared a common past. Howells, first exposed to the New England genealogical enthusiasm in Salem, saw in the universal veneration of family and family tradition evidence that he was in the midst of a civilization far more complex than the one he had known in Ohio. And somehow the veneration for the past was identified with the "real" America, as the old towns fell under the protective custody of the nearby Summer People. On the example of Stockbridge their citizens established Improvement Societies, and tentatively opened their houses to visitors. The sterling tea service, the Revolutionary sword, the embroidered ancestral waistcoat were displayed, though not offered for sale.

What threatened the survival of the seacoast towns was not poverty or inner decay but a new and discordant form of prosperity and a new kind of inhabitant. Industry on a small scale had already invaded the outskirts of Portsmouth and New Bedford and Portland and other quiet cities; few places, after the war, remained totally untouched by the new steam factories and the influx of foreign-born operatives. The assignment which Howells had had from the Ohio editor had been to collect information on the mills and factories of New England, preparatory to editing a book "on the operation of the more distinctive inventions of our country." Coming down from Canada he had dutifully visited a foundry in Portland "where they were casting some sort of ironmongery." In a Haverhill shoe factory he looked at a machine "which chewed a shoe sole full of pegs, and dropped it out of its iron jaws with an indifference as great as my own." Lynn was the center of the new shoe manufacturing industry. Howells, in Salem to pay his respects to the memory of Hawthorne, vowed that he would visit Lynn and its factories. Some thirty years later he did so.

The instinct which kept him in Salem admiring the House of the Seven Gables was undoubtedly a sound one. What Howells himself called his "pitiful literary antipathy" to the technological environment was by way of being the obverse of his love for the older humane New England tradition. Lynn, already creeping up on Salem and invading it with its shoe factories, symbolized the new order in a harshly unmistakable manner. The older textile mills had been located on tumbling streams in the foothills; but the shoe factories were on the waterfronts or railroad tracks of crowded cities, near where coal could be delivered by rail or by barge. The textile mills in their architecture had paid respect to an attenuated classical tradition. The shoe factories were far larger, and designed (if that is the word) by engineers. Because they had been remote from sources of labor, the textile mills had recruited help from elsewhere, had provided houses, and shown a degree of concern for the welfare of their operatives, but the shoe factories in Lynn got all the help they needed from among the recently arrived immigrants, and housing of a sort was either already there or would be provided by speculative builders. In brief, the textile mill had been a kind of social institution, paternalistic and homogeneous, whereas the shoe factory was a structure where a certain process took place, where (to quote the official census definition of a factory) "raw material can be converted into finished goods by consecutive, harmonious processes carried along by a central power." The new type of factory as an organization of space had more in common with the contemporaneous stockyards of Chicago than with the neighboring textile mills in the Merrimac Valley.

This is not the place to discuss the wider impact of the factory system on the American landscape. A hundred years ago it was still too new to be recogized for what it was. If to our generation the most familiar symbol of the coal-powered factory—the tall chimney emitting a cloud of black smoke—has come to stand for industry's irresponsiblity toward the environment, for almost a century it stood for prosperity and progress. A group of some seventeen Boston fire insurance companies in the sixties assumed the responsibility for passing on the design of new factories, prescribing safety and fire prevention regulations and even furnishing on request ready-made designs for buildings. Though their basic interest was financial they inevitably introduced new concepts of industrial engineering. Powerful machinery (it was noted) produced such extreme vibration in the upper stories that the only solution seemed to be the building of one-story or at most two-story factories. Yet the cost of land dictated a greater height and it was the engineers on the payroll of the insurance companies who devised more effective structural systems, as well as better fireproofing and better insulation. The textile mills required their own microclimate—a degree of humidity all but unbearable to the operatives—and this the engineers also produced. Gas lighting was considered a serious fire hazard; unhampered by traditional ideas of harmonious fenestration, the engineers made larger and more numerous windows. Exterior ornaments disappeared, concern for proportion disappeared, the cheap and useful mansard roof replaced the classic gable, the freight elevator replaced the imposing tower and belfry. A new kind of structure, uncompromising, frequently unsightly, was the outcome of all these innovations. The factory emerged as an autonomous form—noisy, dirty, hot, immense in scale; an environment defined not by its human but by its mechanical contents.

Whenever this new factory appeared in the late nineteenth-century New England, it produced dramatic changes. The industrial communities which evolved in small villages or on the outskirts of the larger towns and cities bore little resemblance to the neat and compact textile towns with the company-built dwellings and boarding houses of an earlier period of industrialization. In empty fields and lots there arose long lines of frame dwellings—two-family cottages to begin with, then larger three-story houses, often occupied by three families. Contractors, usually operating on a small scale, built most of them, borrowing the designs from one another or taking them out of builders' books. Artistically and structurally they were far from impressive; whatever the size of the lot at the builder's disposal, they were placed as near the street as possible, since it was in the street that the gas and water lines were eventually to be laid. Built in great numbers during the decades after the war, they were criticized by architects and social reformers, despised by the more affluent, and none too enthusiastically accepted by those compelled to inhabit them. Just the same, they represented a radically new concept of the dwelling as an industrial product, and contributed greatly to the restructuring of the American city. Discussing this period when housing took its place "as an economic activity within the city, calling upon investors independently of any connection with manufacturing," the urban geographer James Vance remarks, "Not only the physical form of the building in which housing was provided but also the general urban plan was transformed. The cellular nature of the urban structure [the clustering around the factory] was replaced by *urban stratification* wherein the 'means test' came to substitute for place of employment in determination where within the city a man and his family would live." The worker, in short, began to choose (insofar as his means allowed of it) his domestic environment: how convenient was the neighborhood? What was the rent? Was it near to his church and lodge and school? Again, the Chicago pattern was repeated: downtown, where the factories were located, was abandoned in favor of outlying residential developments each with a distinct characteristic—ethnic, religious, or economic.

Public reaction to these developments was immediate but variable. The defenders of the ancient and picturesque objected to the pretentiousness of the new row houses, comparing them unfavorably with the older, smaller, quainter cottages in farm villages. Henry Ward Beecher probably voiced a widespread criticism when he spoke out against "this method of building houses by the architect's plans and not by the owner's disposition." They were houses, not true homes. E. C. Gardner, an architect as well as perceptive commentator on current domestic architecture, likewise lamented the impersonality of the new workers' houses. In an essay entitled "One of King Kole's Cottages," written in 1875, he remarked of the villages produced by the coal-powered factories, "A row of twenty-nine white houses, exactly alike, just two rods apart and one rod from the street, makes a pleasant gleam in the landscape when seen from a point ten miles away, over hill and valley . . . Seen from a back alley within a range of ten rods, the artistic effect is different . . . King Kole is a landholder and a practical philanthropist; it isn't necessary that he should be hopelessly sentimental in order to object to these bare, heartless-looking buildings in which hardworking mechanics are vainly trying to cultivate a love of home."

Nor was the new factory social system easy for New Englanders to understand. Even before the war Edward Everett had sought to explain and justify the changes in the shoe industry— a subject of wide concern in the rural villages. Mechanization and centralization were beginning to do away with the small scale domestic aspects of shoemaking, the sewing and pegging by hand which had occupied many winter evenings on the farm and brought a small income to the women of the family. The new pegging machine (which Howells had so coolly gazed upon), the new shoe-sewing machine concentrated production in the city factories, and with the introduction of steam-powered machinery after the war there came minute subdivisions of the job of making a shoe, so that, in place of three, and possibly four, persons who would have once performed the labor, the work was now shared by as many as thirty-four.

It was work which could be performed by any able-bodied person, regardless of education or skill, willing to submit to the monotony, the confinement, the long hours, and the prospect of layoffs between seasons. "The work people of both sexes," Everett noted, "as might be expected from the sedentary nature of the occupation are, generally speaking, of a reflecting and meditative character, somewhat impressionable, and subject to emotional influences"—foreigners in short, men and women with frequent economic grievances.

The social transformation did not spare the older textile centers. Visitors noted with regret the change of tone in the working force. New England was still proud of Lowell and the Lowell girls who worked in the mills and yet found time to attend lectures and edit a literary magazine, but there was no disguising the fact that the golden years of "Mind among the Spindles" had passed. "Time and progress have wrought many changes in Lowell," a reporter for *Harper's Magazine* noted; "Factories have sprung up all over the land, and as the demand for labor has increased, it is supplied by immigrants from the Old World, bringing with them the ideas and habits peculiar to their condition at home. Experience has shown that cotton cloth can be manufactured at a cheaper rate by operatives who prefer beer to literature, and the Utopian dream of combining money-making with the moral virtues has faded somewhat."

The tourist, it is true, saw little of this unromantic aspect of New England, but to the native there was much that was disquieting in the changes underway. A writer remarked in 1872 that the "traveler by railroad sees here and there a specimen of the old spacious farmhouse, surrounded by its colony of barns . . . but these are now rare, and his attention is chiefly attracted by the villas of the successful manufacturers, with their pretentious variety of Americo-Italian, transatlantic Tudor, and nineteenth-century Gothic styles of building. If, however," the writer added, "our supposed traveler . . . is in the habit of observing closely . . . his experience will at first glance lead him to question whether this era of industrial activity is an unmixed blessing. Clustered about the mills, with their ugly uniformity of brick and their tall chimneys, he will see collections of squalid cottages, or rows of tenement houses redolent of poverty, and disfiguring the landscape like blots upon an otherwise fair page. These are the homes of the operatives. These are the structures, crowded, unventilated, undrained, infectious, which have replaced the cottages in which the labor of seventy years ago found its home."

This indictment of the New England milltown of the seventies was corroborated by the Report (the first of its kind) of the Massachusetts Bureau of Statistics of Labor for 1871. It noted that the old Lowell system of mill operation had long since become extinct, and that a secondary period had succeeded it, in which the labor was supplied by "low-grade European operatives," who would possibly be succeeded by an even cheaper element—Chinese, for instance—since factory work repelled anyone of education. In 1870 a group of some seventy-five Chinese strikebreakers were in fact imported by a shoe factory in North Adams, Massachusetts. When the strike was settled many of them remained in the town. "The *tenant houses*: who has not seen their fine array on sloping hillside, in seeming order, with fair show of external comeliness of form, suitably adorned by paint? But he who stops to observe . . . may clearly and easily perceive that this glitter of external show but imperfectly covers the misery and want, degradation and wrong, within that calls loudly for redress."

If the factory town had degenerated, how was it to be redeemed? Chiefly, so it appeared to the postwar generation, by improving the physical environment. In South Manchester, Connecticut, the Cheney brothers sought with some success to create a model industrial community around their silk-weaving factory. "The grounds around the mill," wrote a commentator, "are laid out like a park . . . Fences, which are always so ugly in a landscape, unless by their decay they please a sentimental love of the picturesque, and which are normally so objectionable for the isolation and selfish distrust of our neighbors which they suggest, are abolished all over the domain." The workers' cottages were all designed "with an artistic taste," and their rent was modest. Management provided a library and a hall for social entertainment as well as for Sunday services. Liquor was forbidden and so were chickens (because of the absence of fences around the garden plots). The new factory was remarkable for providing adequate light and ventilation, and there was a wooded park with picturesque walks. "It has been found advisable," the account continues, "to locate the homes of the different nationalities at points remote from each other, thus avoiding any possible turmoil which might grow out of petty discords."

Edward Everett Hale, indefatigable idealist and advocate of social reform, wrote voluminously in the seventies on homes for workmen; in his novel telling of the rise of the model workers' town of Montgomery, he proposed a suburb, thirty miles from the city, where blue-collar workers could own their own homes and commute to work by railroad, and in his Utopian novel *How They Lived at Hampton* (written much later) Hale was to reiterate his proposals for solving social as well as housing problems in terms of a small, self-sufficient community.

It was almost as if the vision of Lowell haunted all attempts to improve the industrial town: the vision of a small semi-rural center, its inhabitants united in their loyalty to a traditional code of hard work, self-improvement, and church-directed action. But though Lowell and its sister cities had long since lost their Utopian quality to become shabby and uninspired, it was still hard for New England to look for other models. Trollope, who visited Lowell during the war, sensed the beginning of its decline. Its strength lay in its smallness, its compactness as an environment as well as a society. "Steam, it may be presumed, will become the motive power of cotton mills in New England as it is with us; and when it is so, the amount of work to be done at any one place will not be checked by any such limits as that which now prevails at Lowell. Waterpower is very cheap, but it cannot be extended; and it would seem that no place can become large as a manufacturing town which has to depend chiefly on water. It is not improbable that steam may be brought into general use at Lowell, and that Lowell may spread itself. If it should spread itself widely, it will lose its Utopian characteristics."

Had Trollope included Lynn on his itinerary, he could have seen the vindication of his prophecy; but Trollope, like Howells, like many other well-intentioned observers of the New England landscape, avoided Lynn and all that it stood for until it was too late and Lynn had spread itself everywhere.

4 · BOSTON

On the evening of Saturday, November 9, 1872, a fire broke out in a building on Summer Street, in downtown Boston. The building, which was of granite, housed a wholesale dealer in drygoods, a wholesale dealer in hosiery, gloves, and lace, and in the mansard roof a manufacturer of hoopskirts. It was empty at that time of day; a passerby noticing the blaze rang the fire alarm and a hand-drawn fire engine shortly appeared. It played its hoses on the lower floor of the building where the fire had started, but when the flames reached the frame mansard roof with its tarpaper surface they leaped high into the air and showered the neighboring roofs with innumerable fire brands. In no time the fire had crossed the narrow street and had started to race from one mansard roof to another, out of control.

Though it was now midnight, word spread that downtown Boston was in flames. The streets were soon crowded with the tenants and employees of the threatened buildings, trying— usually in vain—to save some of their stock. Cases and heaps of merchandise covered the sidewalks. Spectators came, as did the usual contingent of drunks and looters.

The fire raged throughout the night and the following day,

fanned by the violent winds which it had created. There were occasional bursts of brilliant flame and these could be seen as far as fifty miles away. Smoke enveloped much of the city and the gold dome of the State House was wreathed in black rolling clouds. By the time the fire had been brought under control, some sixty acres of downtown Boston had been reduced to ashes and rubble.

This included most of the wholesale and warehouse district, the oldest part of the city where the houses were wedged together and where the streets were so crooked and narrow that a balky horse or an overturned cart sufficed to bring all traffic to a standstill. A generation earlier the section had contained many substantial houses with gardens, and the streets had been quiet most of the day; but commerce began to move south along the waterfront, and the owners of the houses sold out, one by one, to move south themselves—to Beacon Hill or the South End. The residences were transformed either into offices and workshops or into lodgings for the immigrants who in the fifties were beginning to arrive in great numbers. At the time of the fire the last of these remnants were being replaced by massive five- or six-story buildings, combination offices, warehouses, stores. Austerely correct as to facade and built entirely of granite and brick and iron, they were designed to last forever and to resist all the elements, including fire. Their one concession to fashion was a mansard roof. These imitated the current Second Empire idiom in France, and it was generally agreed that they gave Boston a metropolitan aspect. Moreover they were convenient; the frame superstructure provided an extra story without overburdening the walls and foundations. In addition to these handsome buildings the downtown district was being improved by a local slum clearance project (not completed at the time of the fire) and by the cutting-through of a new street or two. Finally there were grounds for hoping that the Old State House, still encumbering State Street and universally condemned as unsightly and absurd, would soon be done away with.

It was natural for the public to compare the Boston fire with the Chicago fire of the previous year; but the differences were far greater than the similarities. In Boston the area devastated was much smaller, and comparatively few persons were rendered homeless. Nor was there ever any question of Boston's survival and recovery. Indeed even during the fire the neighboring sections of the city continued to function normally. Intellectually and emotionally the catastrophe had manageable dimensions, and the reactions of the public as well as of the press remained surprisingly matter of fact.

For one thing it was painfully obvious the the fire could have been prompty controlled but for two circumstances: first, there was an inadequate supply of water. Boston had been warned several years before to modernize its water system, especially for fire fighting. It had not done so; "Consequently," said a historian of the fire, "there were more engines than water. . . . The water pipes were too small to supply the draught of more than two engines." A second and no less fatal handicap was the total absence of fire horses. The East that year was suffering from what was called the epizootic, or "horse disease"—an ailment which incapacitated the animals and sometimes killed them. Shortly before the fire the horsecars in Boston had ceased to circulate. Oxen were used to haul the heavier loads through the downtown streets, while carts and wagons were dragged by men. The public seemed to take the inconvenience in its stride, and a brass band playing "Oh dear! What can the matter be?" preceded some of the improvised teams. But when Boston caught fire the absence of horses was no longer amusing, particularly when suburban brigades, coming to the rescue, were obliged to drag their engines twelve miles. The large crowds of spectators, not personally involved in the catastrophe, felt free to criticize the techniques of the firefighters and the inadequacy of their equipment. A newspaper commented on the behavior of this public: "Their conduct gave Boston a strange, unnatural look; made it present spectacles more like what one might look for in a French city than a puritanical American place . . . Strangers thronged unceasingly from morning till night, looking contented, interested, and happy . . . carrying themselves for all the world as if it were a festival they had journeyed hither to see, rather than the destruction of a great section of a great city by fire."

The same detachment fostered an almost scientific scrutiny

of the strange and erratic progress of the fire itself. Air currents set in motion by the heat whirled around the upper stories and vaporized the jets of water before they could reach the flames. Though elsewhere in the city the air was perfectly calm, the wind near the fire blew so fiercely that it was hard to stand erect, and how to account for the inclination of the fire to burn *against* the wind instead of with it? The same phenomenon had been noted at the time of the Great Fire of London and then forgotten; was there perhaps some undiscovered natural law at work? If so, should it not be investigated? What then corresponded to the Weather Bureau wrote a report to Washington on the winds generated by the fire. To many residents of Boston it became clear that there was much to learn about how to design and build fireproof structures. Thick walls of granite were not enough; there was no boxing-in of a raging fire. What was called for was a study of the patterns of air circulation within and surrounding a building; a proper design involved the creation of an artificial internal climate.

But most clearly of all, fire prevention and fire control meant doing away with mansards. As soon as reconstruction was undertaken various public groups petitioned for two reforms: the widening of the streets and action on the part of the City Council to "prohibit any further construction of mansard roofs." No such ordinance was ever passed, however, and in the new Back Bay section the mansard roof continued to flourish.

The burnt-out area was soon reconstructed, most of its streets no wider than before, its buildings taller and plainer, the last vestiges of open space obliterated. Though much construction was the work of "building brokers," indifferent to architectural niceties, the public in general approved the uniformity and absence of ornamental details; severity was appropriate to a part of town now largely occupied by warehouses and impersonal business establishments. The fate which had overtaken Chicago now overtook Boston, though on a smaller scale: the downtown district became the almost exclusive preserve of one kind of activity. But Boston had previously contained a diversity not only of architecture but of occupations and people, unparalleled in any other American city, and this was destroyed. When relief was first organized immediately after the fire it was discovered that the most numerous victims were the thirty thousand "sewing girls" abruptly thrown out of work. The list of their jobs revealed a Dickensian motley of doll dressers, bugle trimmers, tassel-makers, as well as a group mysteriously engaged in "cloud and nubia making." Small establishments devoted to crepe folding, and ruffling and fluting, and the making of burial clothing and of feather dusters, briefly appeared before the public gaze as they scurried out of the flaming buildings into suburban obscurity and eventual extinction. Downtown Boston lost something with their departure.

In terms of money the greatest losses were those suffered by the shoe and leather trades, both of which were concentrated in the area of the fire. The great warehouses and wholesale establishments were partly looted and entirely destroyed; they were rebuilt, larger and more impressive than before. What was likewise destroyed, and destroyed forever, were those ancient places of business identified with the small shoemakers who operated in country towns. Before the fire it had been the practice of these men to come into Boston on Wednesdays and Saturdays with a wagonload of boots and shoes to sell. They had their favorite taverns and dining places, their favorite leather merchants from whom they bought a load of leather to take home at the end of the day. Their horses and wagons immobilized all traffic on certain streets, and their countrified behavior was noticeable; nevertheless they were links of a sort between the village and the city, between the craft and the factory. The fire put an end to their visits, eliminating them and their gathering places altogether. The effect of the fire was thus to speed up the transformation of downtown Boston from being a place of complex relationships into a place with much less variety but much more efficiency; into a typical American business section with offices and banks, and a retail shopping fringe.

But as a matter of fact Boston in the seventies was well on its way to becoming a collection of distinct sections, each with its own social and economic characteristics—a development facilitated by the variations in topography. What now seemed to matter most in the choice of a location for work or living was not established relationships with people and institutions, but the possibility of controlling or taking advantage of some fragment of the environment. Manufacturing had found a congenial setting in the flat lands of Roxbury along the railroad tracks; there the steam-powered factories had easy access to coal, and room for indefinite expansion. Shipping activity likewise preferred the proximity of the railroads, and expanded beyond the old center, to the south. The pursuit of environment—the word was little used in those days—was especially striking in the growth of new residential quarters. Prior to the Civil War Boston had been a compact, tightly built-up city where most people could walk to work; beginning in the sixties a number of streetcar lines were built leading from the center of town out into the nearby villages, and there ensued a rapid and extensive development of residential areas within a five-mile radius of City Hall. In his book *Streetcar Suburbs* Warner has given a vivid and detailed account of how Boston grew along the streetcar lines serving Roxbury, West Roxbury, and Dorchester—a growth in many ways duplicated in the outlying sections north and west of the city. Rejecting the traditional brick row houses and the growing congestion of the older quarters, a population of small-business men, store proprietors, contractors, teachers, lawyers, moved out into a semi-rural landscape of old farms and pleasant views. Rows of frame houses, each with its own garden and trees, lined the curving streets. A streetcar took the men into the city to work. It was an environment no one could fail to relish: green, remote, and well isolated from the city. Furthermore many of the new streetcar suburbs possessed a reassuring homogeneity; houses resembled one another in design and cost, incomes and way of life were similar for street after street. There were other districts (usually nearer the city and with less attractive approaches) where the houses were closer together and accommodated two or even three families; districts (easily identified by the experienced suburban dweller) with a pronounced ethnic quality. On the other hand the farther one traveled by streetcar the more affluent, the more spacious the suburbs became.

If the pursuit of environment led the middle-class Bostonian to invade the leafy confines of Roxbury and Cambridge, the old established and well-to-do families often preferred city life. In the 1850s public authority had undertaken to convert the mudflats of the lower Charles River into made land—an engineering enterprise calling for much skill and imagination. In the late sixties the Back Bay district had been created, and laid out by the architect Gilman with the possible assistance of Horace Cleveland and his partner Copeland; an avenue 200 feet wide extended its length, crossed at right angles by a succession of broad streets named alphabetically after English towns. The general effect was of Second Empire elegance, and Back Bay rapidly became the most fashionable section of Boston.

Grandeur of this sort was new to the public. "Here the art of street planning is refined upon to the most luxurious extent," wrote a visitor to Boston in 1872. "Parks are devised, and the new avenues are so wide as to admit of a strip of grass-plot the entire length. The surveyor's maps picture a city Arcadia, with all the toys of statues, fountains and memorials." He mentioned with awe the "red brick and white marble *chateaux* with gorgeous stables, painted roofs, gilded ornaments of iron, encaustic tiles and massive oaken doors."

The attractions of Back Bay were never hard to define: it was detached but not remote from the business quarter, its neighbors were Beacon Hill and the Public Garden; it was new and expensive; in short, a class environment of an unusually homogeneous kind, and like most of the other new planned environments it had no nucleus, it was simply an orderly collection of totally autonomous structures. But there was a further reason for the popularity of the Back Bay that ought to be remembered: it was one of the few desirable parts of Boston where it was possible for an architect to design a house to the tenant's taste; where, in other words, it was possible within reasonable limits to create (or have created) one's own environment.

This was indeed one of the important distinctions between the Back Bay and its predecessor, the South End. The South End came into existence as a prosperous residential district in the sixties, perhaps the first of the developments created by the streetcar. No effort was spared to make it desirable. Whitehill describes it in its heyday as "a region of symmetrical blocks of high-shouldered, comfortable red brick or brownstone houses, bow fronted and high stooped . . . ranged along spacious avenues, intersected by cross streets that occasionally widened into tree-shaded squares and parks, whose central gardens were enclosed by neat cast iron fences." The street layout was the work of a reputable engineer, and a well-known Boston architect designed most of the rows of substantial houses. And possibly that was the trouble, for the floor plan of the average South End dwelling, however elegant it may have been, was inflexible and inconvenient; and it so happened that most of these houses went on the market—either for rent or for sale—at a time when the more worldly citizen was beginning to tire of the traditional arrangement of rooms—a series of formal containers, separated rather than joined by large heavy doors. Houses were already being built—only for the very rich, to be sure—which had spacious halls and rooms flowing into one another. The South End was respectable and suggestive of refined taste—"which," a commentator on the district noted in the seventies, "makes its appearance on every hand. It is not at all uncommon to catch the shadowy outline of a fine statue or a bust of marble facing inward upon the room from the street window; or an elegant bronze, or a rare and invaluable antique vase . . . or a model of a work famous for its artistic merit—it may be a Rogers group." He might have been peering into the house of Silas Lapham, who moved into the South End just as it was beginning to deteriorate.

It deteriorated for a variety of good reasons, not the least important of which was the opportunity afforded in the new Back Bay section for people to build their own house according to their own taste. To us the Back Bay is impressive chiefly because of the pleasing uniformity of its architecture; but compared with earlier parts of the city it contains a fantastic variety of styles, of facades flirting with Gothic and Second Empire and Classical. Bunting's *The Houses of Boston's Back Bay* is a remarkably complete study of the history and architecture of the district and of its artistic experimentations. The South End had allowed for none of this; it had been an environment imposed

The distribution of the population of the United States in 1870; from Walker's *Atlas*

A Missouri Barn; from *The American Agriculturist*, 1875

Haying on the Dalrymple farms in the Red River Valley, 1876

he prairie near Lincoln, Nebraska; from an advertisement of the Burlington and Missouri Railroad, 1875

The improvement of roads after the passage of the Fence Laws

St. Louis and the Eads Bridge, 1876

Cincinnati in the 1870s as seen from Covington, Kentucky

A business "block" designed for Olmsted's Riverside, 1873

"Chicago in flames"; from *Harper's Weekly*

Moving and storing hay on the small American farm in the 1870s

Shipping cattle from Halleck, Nebraska, in the 1870s; from *Leslie's Weekly*

A herd of Texas cattle crossing a river

Buffalo bones at a western Kansas railroad station, 1875

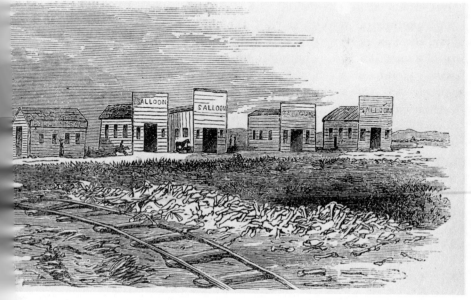

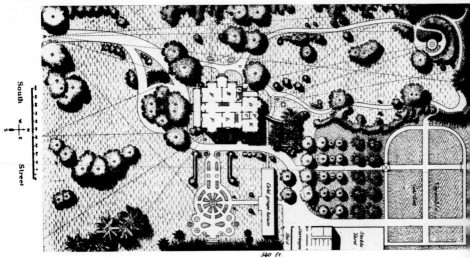

Plan for "a first-class Suburban Residence and Plantation on a Corner Lot"; fr[om]
F. J. Scott's *Suburban Home Grounds*, 1870

The eastern side of Commonwealth Avenue, Boston, in the 1870s

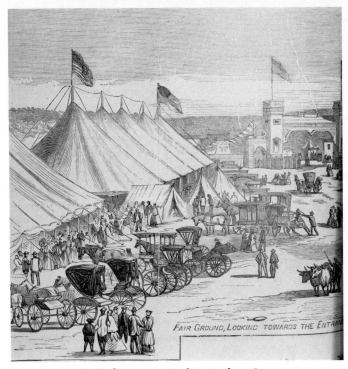

An Indiana county fair in the 1870s

The epizootic, or horse plague, in New York City, 1872

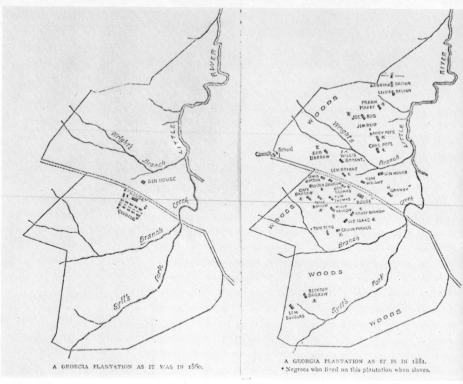

A GEORGIA PLANTATION AS IT WAS IN 1860.

A GEORGIA PLANTATION AS IT IS IN 1881.
* Negroes who lived on this plantation when slaves.

A Georgia plantation as it was in 1860, and as it was in 1881; from *Schribner's Magazine,* April 1881

Market scene in Macon, Georgia, 1873

The Great Smoky Mountains; from *Picturesque America*, 1874

Shooting buffalo from the trains of the Kansas and Pacific Railroad, 1867

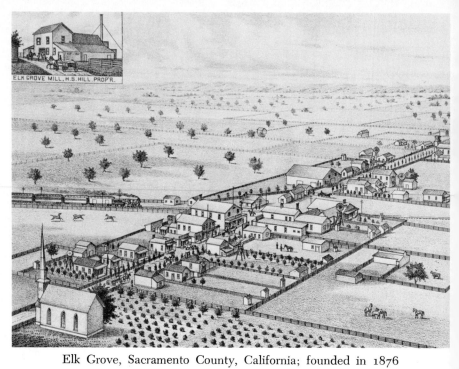

Elk Grove, Sacramento County, California; founded in 1876

Market Street, San Francisco, looking toward the Palace Hotel in the 1870s

Willard's Gardens on Mission Street, San Francisco, 1875

San Francisco in 1870

Broadway, looking up from Exchange Place, 1872

A New York tenement house in the 1870s

The Leow footbridge across Broadway at Fulton Street

A street of small homes in Philadelphia; from McCabe's *Our Country and Its Resources,* 1876

President Grant and the Emperor of Brazil start the Corliss Engine at the Centennial Exhibition

on its inhabitants. But more and more people wanted to make an environment of their own—whether in Somerville or on the waterside of Beacon Street.

But if you could not afford it? If, for example, you were a factory worker or a hodcarrier or a onetime maker of tassels or trimmer of bugles? Then you were likely to live in a rigidly structured environment designed for another age or class; in a wooden tenement in South Boston, in a row of "cottages" down a narrow alley, in a brick row house near the Roxbury factories, in a dilapidated eighteenth-century dwelling in the North End or the South End. There were many such neighborhoods to choose from, and with each of them there was a time when they promised to be secure and respectable communities, urban villages. But eventually they became slums as more people, many of them very poor, moved in, as streetcar lines invaded them and as factories and warehouses overshadowed and crowded out the dwellings. A community had to be rich and influential to survive the omniverous city; it was not every citizen who could achieve and preserve his own environment.

5. COPELAND

The Boston of legend was going strong in the seventies and pretty completely overshadowed the Boston of fact; what every visitor and tourist most wanted was to see for himself some of the legendary features: bespectacled females who (in the words of an English writer) were "so intellectual that they needed to use double eyeglasses when they looked at the gross objects of sense around them;" or a small child (also bespectacled) lugging home from the public library the two volumes of George Eliot's latest novel; or the elderly absentminded Emerson scattering pages of notes as he lectured in Tremont Temple. There was even a delight of sorts in hearing the Boston accent, observing that special Boston gravity of manner and dress, "that strictness and hard temper, and that coldness and formality which was so happy after all." To the average tourist, even then, Boston meant cobbled streets and colored doors; old signs, and the sight of a church where a famous man had preached. The city, at least the historic part, seemed old-fashioned and almost provincial; but it forestalled laughter by reminding the world that it was the birthplace of our national liberties, the most "truly American" city in the United States.

This despite its population being more than a third foreign-born. But that element lived in the other Boston which the patriotic antiquarian rarely bothered to explore: a Boston which counted among the fastest-growing cities in the East. By 1874 it had annexed Roxbury, Dorchester, Charlestown, and Brighton and had thus accumulated more than a third of a million inhabitants. No longer clearly delimited by its harbor and rivers, merging into the low wooded hills to the south and west, it had lost forever its old neatness, its almost geometrical form; it was now a loose collection of distant suburbs, residual farmlands, marshes, strings of factories, close-packed rows of workers' houses, islands and red brick towns. What held it all together? The many railroad lines and streetcar lines, and country roads doing duty as avenues leading to the center; ferry boats and bridges; all of them served downtown Boston. Tens of thousands of citizens, traveling each day the same route to work, saw the city and came to know it well from the window of a train or the platform of a streetcar. They watched it grow over the months and years and learned to interpret its existence as a process of ceaseless change. Howells, who went by horsecar from Cambridge to his office at the *Atlantic Monthly*, gave an attractive literary form to the almost universal commuting experience. Most of the lines terminated at Scollay Square, the traditional place of arrival for all strangers—farmers, sailors, travelers, just as it had been the terminal point for stagecoaches and wagons; it was one of the last remnants of the old heterogeneous Boston. Trains, even commuter trains, to the outrage of all, arrived at a variety of inconvenient stations, remote from one another. But the train journey, speedier and more detached than the journey by streetcar, revealed the city and its structure with unequalled clarity. "Hundreds of work-people with their dinner pails halt in their walk to gaze at the flying train," a contributor to *Appleton's* wrote in the seventies, "and the kitchenmaids pull aside the curtains to see us pass. Gigantic mills upon the edges of narrow streamlets are ready to burst into the roar of manufacturing at seven o'clock, and the endless columns of bluish smoke arise from the early morning fires. As we near Boston, we see the city clerks gathering at the stations for the accommodation trains, and gentlemen prowling about their flowerbeds, with their gardeners at their heels, trowels in hand. Villages become towns, and towns become continuous and merged into each other; and everything is clean, cheerful and prosperous."

Whether or not this way of viewing the city affected the way men perceived their whole environment, it impressed the commuter mind with the vital importance of railroads and of rail traffic of every sort. It was no secret that the business of the Port of Boston had declined since the war and that the prosperity of the city was therefore likely to depend more on railroads, particularly on good rail connections with the West. For almost twenty years work had been underway on the Hoosac tunnel which was to pierce the mountains between western Massachusetts and New York State and bring directly to Boston the wheat and other products of the West to be then shipped overseas; it promised to make Boston once more the commercial and maritime rival of New York. In 1875 the tunnel was finally opened to traffic; but well before that date there had been much speculation about how the forthcoming influx of rail traffic would affect the economy of the city: factories would want new locations, there would be grain elevators and freight depots to build. Was this to be left to the discretion of the railroads themselves? Boston apparently thought so, for no concerted effort was made to accommodate the great increase of business. On one occasion fifteen miles of freightcars stood waiting to be unloaded. If Boston expected to grow, why did it not prepare for growth?

This was the question asked by the landscape architect, Robert Morris Copeland, in his pamphlet "Essay and Plan for the Improvement of the City of Boston," published in 1872 in anticipation of the completion of the Hoosac tunnel. He maintained that a plan for the city was essential. "If a group can be planned for," he argued, referring to the already general practice of planning factory and railroad complexes, "why not the town or city? . . . We have supposed that, for some unnamed reason, planning for a city's growth and progress can only be done as it grows; that no one can foresee sufficiently the future requirements of business to wisely provide for them. This is a fallacious belief," he declared; "The city whose area is carefully studied, which shows by plan where wharves are to be laid out, and where factories may congregate . . . will grow in a sure, orderly and progressive way, and as it grows will have all the central vigor of the great railroad or manufactury, merchandise can be easily transported, business done, water and gas supplied, amusements furnished, fires limited, and sewage provided for." And he added, "When a man or company wish to begin a new or a valuable business they can adapt their wants to the city plan. If they own land in the domestic part of the city they will exchange it for a site in the business or manufacturing part."

When Copeland likened the well-ordered city to a factory or a railroad system—two conspicuous examples of space devoted to processes—he undoubtedly used a familiar simile; he belonged to a generation which had ceased to think of the city in social or political terms. And indeed, later in the essay he defined the city as "a warehouse for the collection and distribution of the products which contribute to the luxuries or necessities of life . . . The town or city grows in numbers because many persons must be employed to buy and sell, collect and distribute the merchandise which rolls in over the railroads, comes down the river, or is landed on its wharves."

As a result of this conviction, Copeland proposed to make Boston an efficient and expanding center of collection and distribution. The basis of his proposal was "a broad and well-made avenue open to teams and [street]cars," all along the entire waterfront. Even the new Back Bay mansions were included; "It would be agreeable," he conceded, "to their owners to devote this waterfront to some ornamental use. But the city cannot afford to give up any of her internal deep water to ornament." The waterfront or marginal avenue was to be connected by radial avenues following the easiest grades with the freight yards, the grain elevators, and the factories in other parts of the city. This would have the effect of reducing downtown congestion and would eventually allow the center to revert to residence and public buildings. Near the new warehouses and factories workers' communities would rise. Copeland was emphatic in declaring that all level land in the city appropriately belonged to industry or commerce: the hills and valleys were suitable for residence or recreation. All in all, his scheme was calculated to "develop [Boston's] natural resources and make its disadvantages of surface useful and ornamental, and leave the city as convenient as if it were a level piece of land, and infinitely more beautiful." For the beauty of Boston was as important as its economy.

The second half of the essay is devoted to a discussion of how to preserve and enhance the natural beauties of the extended Boston area. Copeland writes feelingly of the tree-grown, semi-rural scenery of the hills of Roxbury, where he had evidently spent happy childhood days. "The stranger drives from the city through our suburban towns, winding through lanes whose ferny and rocky sides are full of shrubs . . . or ascends hills that give the most varied and extended views over the bay, or far inland to the mountains." But how long would this beauty survive the growth of the city? Each year saw the straightening of more country roads, the filling up of ponds and streams, the cutting down of trees; even the Boston Common was not immune to this sort of vandalism. Soon there would be nothing left of natural beauty within easy reach of the city. Here Copeland writes not so much in the role of the landscape architect as that of a eulogist of times past, and his proposals for a system of small parks located on rocky hillsides, in stream valleys, beaches and marshlands—lands unsuitable for industry—are essentially attempts to preserve the topography he had enjoyed as a child, regardless of whether it was suited to the needs of a crowded urban population.

In any case, neither of his proposals was adopted or for that matter given much attention. They were put forward at a time when not only the commercial future of Boston was under discussion but when there was much public agitation for a city

park system. Outside of the Common and the newly completed
Public Garden, Boston had little in the way of public space for
recreation, and a great many suggestions were advanced in the
press and in public meetings; Copeland's was merely one of
them. The Park Commission, created in 1876, decided on a
system of moderately sized parks located not on a basis of
topographical features but on that of population; and these
parks (in keeping with the nationwide fashion) were to be
linked by parklike boulevards.

So Copeland's essay with its map of how Boston was to be
improved failed to make much of an impression, and it is doubt-
ful that many students refer to it now. Yet in more ways than
one it is an interesting piece of writing. It has been said that
Copeland in this essay was the first to use the phrase "city plan"
and that consequently we indirectly owe to him the phrases
"city planner" and "city planning." Even if so, we need not
presume that the expression came to him as a sudden inspiration; as a landscape architect he must have been familiar with
the parallel phrase "garden planner," and for all we know "city
plan" may have been in current usage in the seventies. Still,
like the egg of Columbus, someone had to think of it, and Copeland apparently was the man. Much more significant was the
new meaning he attached to the word "plan": the *continuing*
spatial organization or reorganization of a whole community
for its better functioning in the future. Planned cities, in the
sense of their being designed on paper, numbered in the hundreds in the United States of a century ago. But a city whose
future was not so much predicted as provided for—this had not
been heard of. Copeland used the word in a novel sense: to
him (and no doubt to many of his contemporaries) a plan
meant not an artistic design but a program, a blueprint for a
process.

When men start redefining the city, no matter how casually,
they are redefining and questioning a great deal more than they
realize. Copeland's parents and grandparents undoubtedly saw
the city as an institution not unlike the family or the church,
divinely ordained and subject to divine law. Without bother-
ing to repudiate that definition, Copeland and his generation

thought of the city as a kind of environment where certain transactions took place, and since it *was* an environment they believed that it could be modified to facilitate the transactions, whatever they might be. A city had no ideal permanent form; it could and should be changed as circumstances demanded.

He was thus giving expression to what was still an unorthodox point of view: that the city was an environment subject to human modification. But there were plenty of earnest and intelligent men who believed that the city on the contrary was an institution governed by immutable laws, and who further believed that when these laws were violated the city was sure to be punished; and the Boston fire provided an occasion for a confrontation between the two philosophies.

On the Sunday after the fire almost all the Protestant clergymen in Boston preached a sermon on the catastrophe and the lessons to be drawn from it; and as was their custom the newspapers reported the sermons, either in full or in a condensed form. With few exceptions the preachers declared that the fire was the work of Providence, a direct visitation from on high to remind the people of Boston of their spiritual shortcomings; they had been guilty of greed and undue haste in building "mushroom blocks" with inflammable mansard roofs; they had taken too much pride in their magnificent warehouses and public buildings. The fire was to teach men obedience, and should be received as a lesson. According to the newspaper accounts the sermons were listened to with the greatest attention, and the congregations seemed to agree that Providence had admonished Boston not to set its eyes upon things so vain, vexatious, and uncertain as earthly possessions.

The fire was the topic of sermons in other cities as well; Henry Ward Beecher preached about it to his large Brooklyn congregation. "Let us not," he said, "in looking upon so great a calamity as this, be led into speculation as to its significance, and try to find interpretation of the meaning of Divine Providence . . . There is a moral use of this calamity; but it is one that looks toward the future. It asks not why this was done; but, this being done, how are we to make benefit out of that which is disaster? We are to interpret in the future, not in the past

. . . Instead of asking if God meant to humble Boston, let us look into the future, and see what are the lessons to be learned from such a conflagration as this."

Beecher noted that while cities were the grandest product of civilization, much in their growth was left to "bungling chance or individual caprice and whim." Here was one place where Boston could improve on the past; why should there be narrow streets, dark, crowded, and unhealthy? Was it necessary to build tall buildings that were not fireproof? What was called for was a new city of broad avenues with "here and there an open square or some small park." And it was no longer enough to put up buildings that were efficient. Architects now knew enough to design heating and ventilation systems; the next step was to design buildings that controlled the spread of fire. Cities, like men, were capable of learning through adversity, but what they learned was not so much the inscrutability of Providence and the folly of earthly possessions as it was how to build better and more wisely. "Let us hope," he concluded, "that, in ten years hence, Boston, that tonight mourns the calamity, will give thanks to God for the benefaction."

CHAPTER FIVE

The South

1. RECONSTRUCTION

When F. A. Walker in the introduction to the *Atlas* of 1873 referred to the "imperial sweep" of American growth in the decades to come, he was using language that most Americans had no trouble understanding. The future of the country as they saw it was to be the continuation of the past, the vindication of a hundred years of piety and hard work.

But how did Southerners respond? They were once more part of the Union, of course, but much that they had contributed had been rejected. Moreover, they had their future to think of, their own problems to solve. These were far from being all of philosophical or political nature: towns and cities had to be rebuilt, farmlands redivided, natural resources exploited intelligently and profitably. What was called for was the almost total reorganization of the Southern landscape—an undertaking scarcely less arduous than the creating of a brand-new landscape in the West.

Four years of war and neglect had inflicted much damage on the whole environment. Northerners who came down, beginning in the spring of 1865, to explore the South were prompt to tell of the sad conditions they saw, though often they could not distinguish between the impact of the war and the results of an economy which for decades had been inefficient. Their accounts described the widespread destruction of the centers of population, uprooted railroad lines, factories and mills and plantations gutted and abandoned, whole countrysides lapsing into wilderness, their inhabitants, black as well as white, moving away and drifting into the already congested towns.

These things were easy to perceive; even the least experienced travellers, looking out of the train window, could appreciate some of the damage done. Invariably they were struck by the absence of fences. The most usual type in the South had been the snake fence or worm fence: a construction of poles or rails, laid zigzag along the edge of roads and fields, it is still common in regions where lumber is plentiful. The worm fence consumed a great deal of time in its preparation and construction, a great deal of space, and needed often to be repaired. There were persons who found it unsightly. Nevertheless it was all that most of the South had by way of protection against wandering livestock or as indication of property lines. The war destroyed hundreds of miles of it. Northern raiding parties, troops of cavalry suddenly descending on a remote rural community, went for the fences, finding them a convenient source of firewood. More important, their destruction meant that cattle were free to invade the fields and trample or devour the crops. The burning of a few lengths of fence was thus an easy way to destroy a farm. Fences of this sort were not to be speedily replaced, especially with the men off in the army; yet without fences there could be no crops. Undoubtedly their destruction by the Northern troops was often a calculated move, but Southern soldiers did their share. Toward the end of the war when the rations became more and more scanty and irregular, "Lee's Miserables" (as the Southern troops sometimes called themselves) butchered the homeless livestock and helped themselves to the vegetable patches. Generally speaking, whenever groups of soldiers, Northern or Southern, had passed through a country neighborhood it was in poor shape from then on. Stands of trees suffered in particular. Many were cut down, either for fuel or for shelter, and many were damaged by shell fire. Years after the war it was still very evident by the condition of the woods where there had been military action. Although much of the rural South survived the war without destruction, there were wide strips of country, notably in Virginia, North Carolina, Tennessee, and Georgia, of great desolation, where all buildings had been destroyed, all livestock seized, where abandoned fields had been cut by erosion and overgrown with sedgegrass and red cedar. Young Whitelaw Reid, touring the South with an official party in the summer of 1865, wrote of traveling "through a boundless common, waving with goldenrod and covered with luxuriant grass. Every fence, for miles, was gone. Here and there, solitary chimneys marked the site of an old 'Virginia mansion,' and sometimes a little of the shrubbery had been spared about the ruins, but there were no other signs of human habitation . . . Few trees were standing to show the scars of shells; the country seemed an absolute solitude."

The emptiness and solitude of much of the Southern landscape impressed every Northern traveler. "The visitor is constantly astonished at the apparent absence of human life along the vast stretches of good land," a journalist wrote in 1873; "he may ride twenty, thirty, and sometimes forty miles without seeing a habitation or encountering a human being, and then may suddenly come upon a log meeting house or a little village, in which five hundred negroes will be assembled for a 'meeting' or festival . . . It is only on Sundays or on some special occasion that one sees them flocking together along the roads and through the forests which cover so many thousands of acres. Now and then one encounters a party of white men, hunting, fishing, or 'riding to court'; but the loneliness and silence in many of the counties is almost oppressive, despite the beauty of the scenery."

The same destruction, systematic or otherwise, had done away with timber bridges on country roads, and the roads themselves, never good in the best of times, had become rutted trails and paths, cutting across fields. The desertion of a countryside sometimes had the effect of producing woodlands where there had been none before. Natural prairie land in North Carolina, used for grazing livestock, grew up into a forest when the cattle were taken away. In the back country quail and partridge and red fox multiplied; Northerners saw themselves coming back to hunt.

Over and above such evidences of violence, there was much in the Southern landscape to suggest slovenly workmanship. This many Northern observers ascribed to the Southern temperament, but it was also the outcome of four years of poor maintenance and neglect. Tools were lacking, materials were lacking, manpower was lacking; it was impossible to find even the simplest parts for repairing equipment. Levees along the Mississippi and other rivers were not properly kept up, and some were deliberately destroyed by the military. This was bad enough, but two years of unusually high water came to flood thousands of acres of the most productive land in Louisiana and Mississippi. The Mississippi itself grew so choked by silt that New Orleans wondered how it could survive as a seaport. Other rivers in the South suffered from enforced neglect; sandbars accumulated and fallen trees made navigation hazardous. Travel became slow and uncertain.

Without question the most serious obstacle to movement, and the greatest handicap to reconstruction after the war was the almost total disruption to rail traffic. Two-thirds of the railroads in the Confederate South had been put out of use, and many towns and factories were completely isolated. Engineers in the Union forces had devised effective means of heating the iron rails and twisting them around trees, and in addition to the roadbed, bridges, depots, shops, and rolling stock had also been destroyed. Southerners suspected the Northern Army of having a deliberate policy of destroying every Southern factory or mill, especially every cotton mill, this being its way of protecting Northern industries from competition. It was certainly in those days not a competition to be much afraid of: a single New England milltown possessed more spindles than there were in all the cotton mills in the Confederacy. Yet there were a number of flourishing milltowns in Georgia and North and South Carolina, including one or two, like Graniteville, South Carolina, built and organized on the "philanthropic" plan of

Lowell, with model dwellings and a paternalistic social order. Altogether they employed some ten thousand people, most of them poor whites from the hill country. These were thrown out of work, and further swelled the number of homeless refugees.

Whoever traveled by train in those first months after the war had plenty of time to observe the destruction and disorganization of the rural South. Long and unexplained delays ensued when work on the roadbed held up the train, or when passengers had to transfer from one rail gauge to another, or when the overtaxed equipment collapsed. Made up of dilapidated coaches, baggage cars, and freight cars, the train proceeded at twelve miles an hour, stopping every thirty miles or so to take on a load of firewood for the locomotive. In the country silence the traveler could overhear loud political discussions and tales of the war in the other coaches and the voices of the black passengers, relegated to the freight cars. Nearby stood a chimney in the midst of rubble—the remains of the depot. Frowzy women and children peered out of freight cars on a siding or from hastily built huts. Throughout the South this railside community was much the same. In Tennessee and Alabama in 1867, Gail Hamilton saw station villages composed of "a huddle of dirty white frame houses, small, disorderly, mean . . . Groups of unkempt, unshorn, unwashed men lounge at the stoops, men and villages are dirty white together . . . By far the larger number [of houses] on the road . . . are huts, cabins, built perhaps of logs, sometimes of the roughest boards . . . Black and white live side by side, as is easy to see, for the doorways are generally filled with gazers, looking even more wretched and squalid than their houses. One door is adusk with swart faces at various distances from the ground, and ten feet away another hovel overflows with towheads." Not far distant there were usually untidy patches of corn, or cotton, or greens; and a red road snaked wildly into the woods. What lay a mile or so beyond, what thoughts lay behind the dirty faces, black or white, the traveler from the North had no way (and perhaps no curiosity) to find out.

Those traveling South by ship saw the cities first. Because of its conspicuous role in the war and the events leading up to it,

and also because of its past reputation for an exotic and aristocratic way of life, Charleston was the place most Northerners
wanted to visit. The dramatic change in its fortunes was immediately evident; the wreckage of ships obstructed the harbor;
fortifications, from which cannon still protruded, hid the bright-
colored houses along the Battery. Though the city had suffered
comparatively little serious damage from bombardments there
were many signs of shell fire, and the spirit of the place seemed
subdued. "Alas! dear old CHARLESTON!" exclaimed a native
on his return in 1867, "The blight is still upon her. At every
step the marks of a cruel war. The streets are still unpaved.
The wharves comparatively deserted. There is no life or activity visible." It is true the restaurants and many of the stores
had closed and that the houses of the well-to-do remained
silent within their splendid gardens. But elsewhere the animated street life, always characteristic of the South, had resumed, though with new ingredients: Union soldiers, Confederate soldiers returning from captivity, up-country refugees
and blacks from the plantations kept the town crowded and
noisy day and night. The reappearance of organ-grinders was
a happy event recorded by the press. And it was not long before federal authorities, civil as well as military, discovered how
pleasant it was to live in a requisitioned house on the Battery.
Already in 1866 Charleston began to recover; the first streetcar
line was built, and money from the neighboring phosphate beds
compensated in time for the loss of income from the large
plantations. By 1870 its population had increased by a fourth.

Nevertheless the city did not appear to accept prosperity with
much grace. It became the prototype of those Southern cities—
Natchez, Beaufort, Augusta, Savannah—which chose to identify
themselves with the past. There existed, on the other hand,
towns which soon rivaled in energy and brashness the newer
cities of the West. It was in 1871, in a north Alabama cotton
farm where two railroad lines crossed, that a land company,
interested in exploiting the nearby deposits of coal and iron
ore, laid out a town with broad streets and parks and named it
Birmingham. In less than two years it had a population of four
thousand and was already known for its wickedness, its law-

lessness and violence. Nearby the town of Anniston was built
in 1875 by an iron company; celebrated architects including
(many years later) Stanford White were brought in to design
what was to be a model town. Farther north and west, Memphis
on the Mississippi knew a remarkable prosperity as the greatest
inland cotton market in the United States in the years immediately after the war. Its gayety was periodically dimmed
by recurrent outbreaks of yellow fever, and during that of 1873
the principal streets were deserted except for the unending
funeral processions. Each night most of the population fled to
the surrounding countryside, not daring to sleep in the unhealthy city. Once the epidemic was over the municipal authorities engaged the talents of George Waring to completely
modernize the water and sewerage system—an accomplishment
which established him as the national expert on sanitary engineering. Even the yellow fever did not prevent the townspeople from celebrating their annual carnival; the pageant of
the mysterious Memphi filled the downstreets in a different manner, and fancy dress balls were nightly events in the theaters.

The third of the Southern cities to be revitalized was Chat-
tanooga. Before the war it had been little more than a village in
an extraordinarily beautiful natural setting. A Northern general
with an eye for geology who had campaigned around Lookout
Mountain and Missionary Ridge returned shortly after the war,
organized a mining company, and soon started to produce iron,
and he was followed by other veterans from the North. Chat-
tanooga, they all decided, was to be the Pittsburgh of the South;
the town grew so rapidly that a visitor in the early seventies
found it hard to repress a fear "that someday all these natural
beauties will be hidden by the smoke from the five hundred
chimneys which will be erected in honor of the god Iron."
There was renewed talk of reconditioning the Muscle Shoals
Canal, begun forty years before, to make the Tennessee one of
the great navigable rivers of America.

But of all the newer cities Atlanta was the most spectacular
in its recovery and subsequent growth. A comparatively young
community, arbitrarily located in 1839 where two railroad lines
were to cross, Atlanta had first been known as Terminus. It

had been one of those small Georgia villages whose boundary was a circle. There still are in fact more than two hundred places in the South—most of them in Georgia and Alabama—which are round in shape. With villages little more than a crossroads cluster of houses having neither the means nor the ambition to survey their territory with any precision, the device seemed sensible enough: it was when the villages started to grow and to raise taxes that the shortcomings of perfect round-ness became apparent. Atlanta chose as its center the depot, and it had a radius of a mile and a half. No attempt was made to lay out the town; for many years it was merely a disorderly collection of farmhouses, residences, stores, and churches, each of which made its own road or path to the railroad station or to its neighbors.

Nevertheless it started to grow, and was an active town, important as a rail center, when the war broke out. Sherman, as we all know, very nearly obliterated Atlanta when he set fire to it in the spring of 1864, and its few remaining residents were evacuated. Aside from one brick building and a number of out-lying farms, little was left of it when the Union Army resumed its march to the sea. Yet a year later the town was in a fever of reconstruction, building stores and warehouses and blocks as fast as material and workmen became available. Southern capital was exclusively responsible for the reconstruction, and Atlanta acquired the nickname of the Chicago of the South—appropriate not only because of its vitality and devotion to money-making, but also because it, too, almost overnight, had replaced the countrified diversity of its downtown section with the uniformity of buildings entirely devoted to commerce. And also like Chicago, Atlanta had made no attempt to alter and improve its pattern of streets.

Richmond was another instance of the same transformation. Far older than Atlanta, acutely aware of its political and cultural eminence and still the unofficial capital of the South, the city after the war rebuilt its entire downtown area. Just before surrendering to the Union forces in April 1865, the public authorities of Richmond decided to burn the warehouses of tobacco and cotton, lest their contents fall into enemy hands. But the fire got out of control, supplies of food and liquor as well as quantities of dwellings went up in flames, and the downtown section was still smoking when the first Union soldiers entered the city; nine hundred buildings had been destroyed. Southern capital again came to the rescue, and the emergence of a new-style downtown district, exclusively devoted to offices and warehouses and wholesale concerns, took place with extraordinary speed; the old dwellings and riverside tenements vanished for good.

Whether or not towns in the postwar South had suffered destruction, whether they welcomed material progress with open arms or withdrew into aristocratic isolation, they all eventually underwent their own version of the nationwide process of disintegration; all broke up into distinct sections, each with its own character. If the homogeneous downtown business section was largely a postwar phenomenon, so was the racially (or economically) segregated residential district. Before the Civil War racial segregation in terms of residence was not conspicuous in the South. The white population had always feared the formation of any predominantly black district, lest the free blacks (of which in the South there were almost half a million) have a disturbing influence on the slaves. "In every city in Dixie," Richard Wade remarks in *Slavery in the Cities*, "Blacks and Whites lived side by side, sharing the same premises if not equal facilities, and being constantly in each other's presence." Skilled labor and the crafts were almost entirely in the hands of the blacks; in the more prosperous residential quarters, slaves usually lived near the house of their master, and black artisans, free or slave, lived near their place of work. This arrangement was not of the blacks' choosing; they would have preferred to live among others of their race, and even before the war there were small areas where blacks predominated. To many white city dwellers the only solution to the danger of a large black population was to send as many slaves as possible back to the plantation, and to discourage the free blacks by bringing in white craftsmen and skilled labor.

Even so, the two elements, however distrustful of each other, were interdependent. The end of the war changed the situation. Town slaves found themselves liberated from their one-time masters who in any case rarely had money to employ them. The traditional slave quarters in alleys and back streets and compounds near the houses of the masters were abandoned. Far from diminishing, the black population of the towns grew; blacks from the country, from farms and plantations, came to the centers to enjoy their new freedom of movement and to look for work. Where were they to live? The towns were already crowded. At first many congregated in makeshift groups on the edge of town, along the tracks, down by the river, or on unlikely hillsides.

It was only later that these settlements were clearly defined as black; they were in the beginning settlements inhabited by transients and the very poor, defined more in terms of class than of race. It is possible that the building of black churches and the formation of black congregations contributed to the development of the all-black ghetto. In any event the segregation took place, and a part of town once lived in by blacks and familiar to them soon became identified only with the place of work: the household, the store, the warehouse to which they went early in the morning, returning in the evening to their own distinct part of town.

In Chicago, in Boston, in Atlanta and Richmond, in other stricken cities the old order yielded to the new, and C. B. D. fulfilled itself in many ways. But the factor of race, rarely thought of as contributing much in the way of beauty or happiness to the American city, served in the South to modify the abruptness of change.

Until comparatively recently Southern cities retained a produce market in the downtown section. Unlike the produce markets of Boston or New York, where the truck gardener or farmer sold directly to the wholesaler, the markets of the South were conducted on an informal, inefficient, person-to-person basis. Moreover, buyers and sellers were all likely to be black. A Northern farm journal described in 1869 the whole procedure for the benefit of its readers. It was the custom in the South to have two market days a week, and early in the afternoon of the day before, large, slow, cumbrous wagons moved into town

from the farms. The drivers backed up to the sidewalk, un-
hitched the mules or horses, and prepared to enjoy themselves
until the start of business the following morning. "By nightfall,"
according to the farm journal, "the streets present a grotesque
and lively appearance to a stranger, with the many odd-looking
wagons, and numerous animals bivouacked in two long rows."

Twice a week, therefore, the downtown section was invaded
by farmers and teamsters and their customers; the Second Empire pomp of brick blocks with cast iron cornices and gold-
lettered windows served as the setting for street corner auc-
tioneers, sellers of firewood, of food and refreshment. "A vendor
of patent medicine," wrote a visitor to Atlanta, after an excursion to the downtown market after dark, "has set up a rough
platform and hung about it some flaring parafin lamps. . . .
Two negroes . . . dressed in the regulation burlesque style
familiar to us in the minstrel shows at the North, are dancing
jigs, reciting conundrums, and banging banjo, bones and tam-
bourine to the amusement of two or three hundred delighted
darkies." Down every alley there was music, he said.

2. THE COUNTRYSIDE

What the cities and towns of the South underwent in the first
years after the war was in most ways peculiar to them and their
predicament; but the result was that they began to be like the
cities of the North in makeup. Local problems of rebuilding and
social reorganization may have been unique, but everywhere
the solution arrived at produced much the same kind of American city: one with sections and districts quite distinct from
one another, each lived in or occupied during daylight hours by
a relatively homogeneous group.

What the rural South underwent during the same period was
something else again: a much more drastic and painful transformation, and a less successful one. Out in the coastal plains
and in the hills and woods and mountains the way of life and
the status of almost half the population had suddenly changed,
and to leave the place where they had lived and worked none too
happily was what they wanted. Alone, or in groups, the blacks

set out to discover what freedom meant. It meant in most cases leaving the farm or plantation of their former owner, especially in the rice-growing regions of South Carolina and Georgia, where climate and routine of work were especially hard to take. In one postwar year, so we are told, Georgia lost twenty thousand blacks. Many of them migrated westward: to Mississippi and Louisiana and even to Texas, where wages were supposed to be higher and opportunities for real independence greater than in the old South. But the majority of the footloose population made for the nearest large town or city, vaguely hoping for work, or federal relief, or at least some excitement. The poorer whites likewise migrated in sizable numbers to Texas, and files of covered wagons were a common sight in postwar Alabama and Mississippi. "In the long main street of [Jackson, Miss.] at the proper seasons," wrote a postwar traveler, "one sees long lines of immigrant wagons, filled with hard featured men and women bound for Texas or 'Arkinsaw.' These Ishmaels are not looked upon with any especial love by the inhabitants who intend to remain."

A large number of migratory blacks had definite claims on government support. Many had been slaves, freed by the advancing Union armies; many had been in the Union armies as soldiers, and still others had been in army employ. They had ceased to have local ties: where else were they to turn but to the Northern occupation authorities?

General Mitchel, Commander of the Department of the South, had his headquarters during the latter years of the war at Hilton Head, South Carolina, and organized, even during hostilities, the nearby village of Mitchelville, to be exclusively inhabited by freedmen. It had an elected council, free public schools with compulsory attendance, a sanitary code, and provisions for punishing drunkenness and failure to observe the Lord's Day. Its population was nearly a thousand, but having no economic base it survived only as long as rations were distributed by the federal army. James City, North Carolina, was another such all-black new town, established during the war and likewise dependent on army relief. Before it was converted into a national cemetery, the Lee estate of Arlington across the

river from Washington was briefly a freedmen's village. Visitors
thought the location peculiarly appropriate. "The little whitewashed village is the picture of neatness," one reported. "Children are playing in the hard, gravelled streets, and old men
sunning themselves on benches before the door." But prolonged government tutelage for freedmen was generally deplored, and in 1874 the land was dedicated as a cemetery.

The largest of the postwar black communities was probably
Hampton, Virginia. Immediately after the war black refugees
and freedmen established a makeshift community of their own
in the ruins of the town of Hampton, and were encouraged by
the army authorities at nearby Fort Monroe to farm the surrounding fields. Though the black town acquired a bad reputation and was soon destroyed by the returning white inhabitants
of Hampton, the community served as the basis of the Hampton
Normal and Agricultural Institute established "with special re-
gard to the wants of the colored race" in 1868.

Twenty years after the end of the war were to pass before
genuine black towns inhabited exclusively by blacks were
established in the South, though Illinois had one—Brooklyn—
in 1874, and other temporary ones had been set up in Ohio in
the days of the underground railroad. The first emergency past,
there was no great need or demand for them, especially with the
development of black settlements on the edge of town. And
in time many of the freedmen, tiring of city life perhaps, and
finding no jobs, drifted back to their native countryside and
even back to the plantations where they had formerly been
slaves. Often they were hired on a contract wage basis by their
former owners. Sometimes the plantation owners leased land to
groups of blacks—"squads," each squad farming a hundred or
more acres and paying so many bales of cotton. The squads
lived in their own villages where each worker had a half acre
of garden for himself and his family. But nothing seemed to
discourage the constant migration of blacks to the newer cot-
tonlands west of the Mississippi, to Texas and Arkansas and
even Missouri and Kansas, and many Southerners foresaw the
time when the great bulk of the black population would live
west of the river. For land of their own was what the blacks

were yearning for; a contract binding them to work for a year under strict supervision was a poor substitute in their eyes for the government land, given outright, that most of them had dreamt of. The eighty-acre homestead, the confiscated land divided and redistributed, the forty acres and a mule guaranteed (so it was widely thought) by Sherman—none of them materialized. Promises were broken, postponed, misunderstood, and eventually forgotten; speculators and Northern officials and even influential Southerners managed to get what public land was made available; much of it, moreover, was of such a nature that considerable money would have been needed to make it suitable for farming, nor did a single Southern state adopt an honest program of black landownership. The best that most of them could hope for was to be able to rent a farm—of a hundred acres or less—carved from a plantation. From tenant farmer with at least a minimum of responsibility and control over his fragment of land, to sharecropper was a short and inevitable step; not only for the vast majority of rural blacks but for thousands of impoverished and landless whites. Under this dispensation, the plantation owner provided food and shelter, in return for which he received one third of the crop. A tenant farmer, on the other hand, was usually a man who had some equipment and resources of his own, and who paid his rent either in cash or in a fixed number of bales of cotton. Little wonder that with this dividing up of the plantations the number of small farms increased by a sensational ratio after the war; in most states they more than doubled in twenty years. But few of them were owned by the men who worked them, and with the exception of Texas and Florida, both pioneer states, every Southern state had less land under cultivation in 1880 than before the war. Ignorant for the most part of how to organize their work, given no guidance or instruction, with only the most primitive of tools, compelled by their impoverished landlords to raise cotton, the one reliable cash crop, the average small Southern sharecropper farmer inevitably contributed to the further deterioration of the landscape.

The division of the plantations into a swarm of semi-independent units, each with its own dwelling, destroyed within a short time what had been one of the traditional community forms of the South: the plantation headquarters. Not only were the slave quarters, often the size of a compact village, entirely abandoned in favor of the isolated homestead cabin, the headquarters itself ceased to be the recognized center for sociability, for barter, for local administration. The dilapidated plantation house of Southern legend is less likely to be the product of Union vandalism than of this process of decentralization, and indeed not a few such houses were eventually occupied by tenant farmers.

This melancholy decay of mansion and grounds was in part compensated for by the growth of the crossroads settlement— a huddle of cabins irregularly grouped around a general store, one or two churches, and perhaps a cotton gin. Seldom very appealing in appearance and never prosperous, these nevertheless represented a new way of life to many country blacks. During slavery the men had been almost entirely confined during the day to the plantation, and unauthorized night travel had been strictly forbidden: few slaves had cash and none had credit. The country store was therefore a novel delight, and many Southern veterans found a livelihood in operating such an establishment at a likely rural crossroad. The energetic building of railroads in the South during the first years of Reconstruction, and the more systematic exploitation of the upland forests further increased the number of country stores. Some years later, the State Board of Agriculture of South Carolina declared, "Along the lines of railroads and everywhere in the rural districts there has been a remarkable increase in the number of establishments engaged in trade. The crossroads store has become an important factor in the organization of labor and in the distribution of wealth. Established in the first instance as an adjunct to other industries, as commissariat for farm hands, or those employed in sawmills . . . they have gained a foothold of their own, drawing around them small but growing communities. . . . The 33,000 plantations of 1860 are divided out among 93,000 small farmers in 1880. Wholly occupied by their struggle with the soil and seasons these small farmers of necessity entrust their trading interests to the care of the country storekeeper. And thus the crossroads store stands again . . . a pioneer in a new industrial departure. The blacksmith, the wheelright, and the trial justice settle near them, and when two or three stores are gathered together churches and schools are opened."

Bereft of wheelright and blacksmith, but now possessing an off-brand gas pump, they still stand, the dirty whitewashed porch still adorned with advertisements and notices; dark, fly-blown, but sociable and inviting combination post office, bus stop, gas station, and general store. Their appearance in the postwar Southern landscape seems to have attracted the favorable attention of Northern travelers, and there were even those who saw in the evolution of the crossroads village a prophecy of brighter, more democratic days. "Now that the large plantations of the South are being divided," a Northern scholar declared, "the mechanic and the artisan appear at the crossroads and form the nucleus of a village, instead of finding employment on the lands of wealthy planters; and with the village hamlet comes the first beginning of local self government." Perhaps; but it was not long before the color line was established, and the store with white patrons was duplicated by the store for blacks.

The same held true of the small churches which arose at the crossroads village and in the nearby woods: the custom of joint religious services, with the blacks segregated either in the gallery or in designated pews, was rapidly discarded after the war, and separate churches—often separate sects—became the rule. In *American Negro Slavery* Phillips describes the temporary mingling of races at country and plantation church services and at camp meetings before the war. Baptist and Methodist churches were the most popular with the blacks, and Methodist camp meetings were especially well attended. After the war the Methodist church in the North aligned itself strongly with the Republican party and its Reconstruction policies, and promptly undertook missionary work among the blacks in the South; black preachers were licensed, black church districts were organized, and by 1870 there was a Colored Methodist Episcopal Church. The blacks, however, in most cases wished to be entirely free from affiliation with white churches, and independent sects proliferated, first in the towns, then in the country. Largely lacking in social institutions and places for assembly, the country blacks in particular used their churches for festive as well as religious events and decorated them in a manner which shocked many whites; the whitewashed building, perched on brick piers, decorously named (according to Baptist or Methodist tradition) Pleasant Grove Independent Baptist Church or Mt. Zion African Methodist Church, resounded after dark with powerful singing, and whoever peered through a window was astonished by the bright garlands, the paper flowers, the color and glitter, the animation. The architecture of these modest churches, with small twin towers and an important window, has yet to be studied. Often precariously erect and half hidden in the pine woods, they are unmistakably places for celebration, profane as well as sacred.

3. REFORMS

It was the mere beginning of a landscape, not yet prosperous or beautiful, with its fragmented fields and scattering of shanties and crude little crossroads villages; red earth showing through the pine woods, sluggish streams bordered by a jungle of vines; with its scars of war and poverty; but to not a few Southerners it was the sketch of a better landscape and a better way of life in the future. The salvation of the region, many believed, lay in the small farm no longer in bondage to King Cotton but raising a diversity of crops; in a culture which a Georgia editor defined as based on "the spindle, the anvil and the loom, the vineyard, orchard, hay meadow, stock and grazing, and grainfields." A latter-day version of the agrarian dream undertook to exalt the small farmer over the planter. To give respectability to the new social order the son of General Lee made a point of driving his own wagon into Richmond with a load of hay, and less celebrated officers worked in their fields and abandoned their large houses for more modest quarters. "Smaller farms, more villages," was the solution proposed by one farm writer, "Less pride, more industry." The day of the large plantation (so it was hoped) had passed; a new kind of agriculture calling for less hard labor and more skill and knowledge would soon transform the South and restore its prosperity. Peanuts, before the war eaten only by blacks and children, had not been taken seriously as a crop; now they were extensively raised and sold throughout the country. Hampton Institute showed local farmers how to grow vegetables and ship them to New York and Boston. Peaches, hitherto largely wasted and fed to the hogs, became a profitable Georgia specialty; in Florida, Harriet Beecher Stowe among other Northerners started to grow oranges. Farmers in South Carolina reported (somewhat prematurely) spectacular success in the growing of tea. Novel ideas abounded: Why not raise sheep? Why not rival the North in dairying? Why not raise fish? On hundreds of Southern farms fishponds were built and stocked with imported German carp.

The Southern farmhouse, all too often bleak and dilapidated, was to be beautified. "We do not strive as we ought to," a Southern farm editor remarked in 1870, "to make our homes beautiful, and because we do not, other and more inviting localities make our children weary of a place that awakens little else than disgust." He recommended removing unnecessary fences and outhouses, plowing up the naked ground around the house and sowing it to grass. "Whitewash your fences, and by this little done the country must be very poor if your home will not become cheerful again." And a South Carolina farmer declared that "the nondescript buildings about our old homesteads are unsuited to our times. They were built for the days of slavery, when the owner had a man to look after the horses, another the cows, a third after the sheep. I believe," he added, "in adopting the Yankee plan of having a good barn with every animal housed with the necessary feed under one roof."

Many Northerners shared this vision of the future, interpreting Reconstruction as a kind of conversion to the yeoman philosophy. Among the first postwar visitors to recognize the importance of encouraging the small Southern farmer was a farmer from Minnesota (though a native of New England) by the name of Oliver Hudson Kelley. In 1866 he was sent by what was then called the Bureau of Agriculture to gather information about conditions in the South. He was soon convinced that one of the

needs of the new breed of Southern farmer was an organization
to help exchange information and experience and at the same time
mitigate country loneliness and isolation. As an enthusiastic
Mason, Kelly thought of a national secret society of farmers.
Accordingly, with two colleagues in Washington, he organized in
1867 the Patrons of Husbandry, better known as the Grange,
modeling it on the Masons, with degrees, signs, and passwords,
and formal meetings to be held in local Grange Halls. Blacks
were excluded, but women were not, and to the men's degrees of
Laborer, Cultivator, Harvester, and (highest) Husbandman,
there were corresponding degrees for the women: Maid, Shep-
herdess, Gleaner, and Matron. Though the movement got off to
a shaky start, by 1870 it had begun to spread throughout the
Union, with its greatest popularity in Minnesota and Wisconsin.
Soon there were chapters in the South as well, and at one time
the South had the highest proportion of Grange members among
the white farm population; one reason for its acceptance in that
region being that it was one of the few practical manifestations
of a desire for reconciliation between South and North.

The role of the Grange in national politics and in state legislation is a familiar chapter in our history during the first postwar decade, but it was also important and beneficent in innumerable rural communities, particularly in the impoverished South.
Basic to its policies was opposition to all monopolies, to high
rates of interest, and exorbitant profits for the middleman; but
what was perhaps of more immediate appeal to its Southern
membership was its emphasis on diversified farming, on rural
improvement and beautification, and on sociability. In the course
of its brief period of power, the Grange, or its state chapters,
established local cooperatives both for selling farm produce and
for providing farm and home supplies at reasonable prices to its
members. Montgomery Ward got its start as a Grange commission firm. Southern economy in the postwar years being what it
was, cooperative ventures in that part of the country were on a
small scale, and for the most part short-lived; but the Texas
cooperatives were held to be the most successful of any in
America, and throughout rural Georgia and Alabama and Kentucky and other states there were Grange gristmills, Grange

packinghouses, Grange retail outlets for fertilizer and farm machinery, and Grange life insurance companies. Naturally enough, all the enterprises were strongly opposed by the small town merchants and commission men.

What proved to be the undoing of most of these ventures was precisely that condition which the Grange had been established to combat: the isolation and lack of experience of the small Southern farmer. Nevertheless certain activities persisted and continued for many years to give something like variety to the existence of country people. The regular meetings in the Grange Halls—or where these were lacking, in schools or churches— relieved the monotony of life; Grange picnics, usually held in the local "grove" were important and festive events. Grange members relieved the victims of the Mississippi flood of 1874, and neighborhood cooperation did much to bring people together. The Grange diffused agricultural knowledge by subscribing to farm magazines, and it never ceased warning its members against the dangers of raising too much cotton.

Yet despite its earnest support of diversification and of a homespun way of life, it was the harbinger of a very different kind of economy. As the first national movement to involve farmers in problems of national politics or economic policy it was inevitably the opponent of an old-fashioned self-sufficiency. The Grange came into existence as a challenge to post-Civil War capitalism; it had hoped to give the farmer a new status; instead it briefly gave him power.

And it was the redistribution of power—mechanical or political—that accounted for the changes in the Southern landscape; not the shift in status from bond to free. The geographer Merle Prunty has made the point that the Southern plantation did not disappear after the Civil War, that it merely changed from an agricultural factory with a high degree of centralized control of cultivating power to one where the cultivating power was dispersed. Specifically, whereas the antebellum plantation manager had controlled the location of the hands and the equipment they used—such as hoes, mattocks, shovels, and the mules and mule-drawn implements—after the war the houses of the tenants or sharecroppers were dispersed, each on its own plot of farmland, and the equipment—including the mules—was likewise dispersed to the various households. "The compact plantation village has disappeared; it has 'exploded' into fragments, as it were. Settlement is more or less uniformly dispersed throughout the cropland at a ratio of about one housesite to each thirty or forty acres. The large fields of antebellum occupance are gone, broken up into cropper subunits. . . . Because housesites are dispersed and fields are smaller, far more roads and lanes are necessary. . . . Control of the mules [by the sharecroppers] meant personal mobility, the ability to go to town at will, to social gatherings, to church, to visit friends. . . . But dispersal of the mules among cropper-operated units meant that managerial control of the cultivating power was weakened. 'Patch' cultivation was the major result . . . Another result was unevenness in the kind and quality of cultivation."

The spatial organization of the postwar rural South, with its smaller fields and small individual holdings seems at first glance to go counter to the tendency observable in all the rest of the country to increase the size of fields and farms. But only briefly; only as a manifestation of the sharecropper's newly achieved independent political status. The plantation, however its management had altered, continued to be the operating, the coordinating unit, and indeed it eventually conformed to the national trend by increasing in size. Credit being everywhere short in the South, the raising of cash crops—cotton or tobacco—was essential. The continued growing of these crops impoverished the soil and reduced the yield, and thereby compelled the landowner—planter and small farmer alike—to plant more acres if he was to break even. Twenty years after the war Georgia had almost tripled its acreage planted to cotton, yet it had not even doubled the yield. "Diminishing fertility and ever increasing debts produced the tragedy of Southern agriculture," Paul Gates remarks; and the tragedy was compounded: King Cotton was once again enthroned, and his subjects, white as well as black, instead of being small farmers owning their own land, were little better than serfs.

4. NORTHERNERS

"The field is large," wrote a Northern clergyman after the war, "society is to be recast in a higher mold." Few of the many Northerners who moved during the first postwar years doubted their ability to improve in one way or another the condition of the South; but just how large and varied the region was, geographically as well as socially, did not become immediately apparent. The cities, few and small, were soon explored, and the cotton landscape, for all its importance, occupied less than 16 percent of the area; farther south and to the north and west of the old Confederacy lay regions with unsuspected problems and resources.

Florida, so primitive, so scantily populated that many questioned the propriety of its being a state, a flat and uninteresting mass of swamps and everglades, "resounding only to the cries of the wild animals that peopled them," attracted soon after the war a small but adventurous group of winter residents from the North. From her four-hundred-acre farm near Jacksonville, Harriet Beecher Stowe wrote informative essays about the Florida winter. She warned tourists that they would be exchanging the "comforts of well-established homes for the roughness and deficiencies and discomforts of a half-arranged Southern life." What Florida needed, she said, were "practical, hardworking farmers from the North and industrious artisans." She herself planned to produce some sixty thousand oranges from her newly planted groves. Despite its vacant lands Florida welcomed few homesteaders, black or white, and large-scale lumbering moved in to exploit the untouched forests of the west coast of the state, one firm acquiring no less than four hundred thousand acres. Another, owned by New England interests, bought some two hundred thousand acres near Pensacola, and built a company town for its workers, "where," according to an Englishman who visited the place in 1872, "liquor is forbidden to be sold by restrictive law . . . in this new Maine in the Southern wilderness."

All of the coastal plain from Virginia south to Louisiana, was rich in forests of yellow pine; the timber was not only strong and durable, well suited for building, but also provided most of the naval stores of the nation—the turpentine, rosin, and tar. Growing in easily accessible stands, the forests were first exploited by Southerners; little capital was needed to set up a small sawmill, and many veterans tried their hand at lumbering. The procedure was to cut all the trees in an area, ship the lumber by boat, then move the mill elsewhere. The denuded land was often set on fire to produce a better stand of grass for the cattle. Northern capital, better equipped and more closely integrated with the new railroads, eventually controlled the business, and exploited the pine as well as other Southern forests so effectively that large areas of the countryside of Georgia, Alabama, and Mississippi were all but stripped of their tree cover. Small towns sprang up along the new railroad lines. In the North, conservationists, farmers, foresters noted with alarm the changes being wrought in the Deep South; in 1873 an engineer who had been working on the reconstruction of the Alabama railroads reported to an Illinois gathering that within the space of little more than five years a wide stretch of country between southern Kentucky and the Gulf at Mobile—some five hundred miles—had entirely lost its magnificent forest; there was scarcely a "timber tree" left standing. "The old fields are washing into gullies, and getting into such a condition that it would be impossible to restore them. . . . Take the Southern yellow pine region; we know that it is being exhausted very rapidly, that mills have been torn down and moved, denuding one section after another until you can scarcely find any timber within a reasonable distance of any streams." The description suggests that lumbering procedures in the South a century ago resulted in total devastation, whereas in fact transportation difficulties limited the area of cutting to a mile or two on both sides of a river or rail line. Moreover, the mutilated landscape evidently had powers if not of recuperation at least of survival, for many of the lumbering towns continued, though greatly reduced in vitality, to serve as local trade centers. It was not until the end of the century that a more efficient and more ruthless type of lumbering evolved in the South.

Nevertheless such reports, no matter how inaccurate, served to excite a public already worried about a threatened shortage of wood and the silting up of rivers once navigable far upstream; and the theory was widely held, particularly after Hough's address to the AAAS that same year, that forests (and deforestation) had a direct bearing on climate. So at a time when many were proposing extensive programs of tree planting through the Midwest and the Great Plains it was exasperating to learn of wholesale deforestation in the South.

The South itself was not much perturbed by Northern outcries. Few parts of the world contained so extensive or luxuriant a forest as the mountainous region south of the Ohio and east of the Mississippi. In the older South along the Atlantic almost three centuries of settlement had not materially reduced the stands of wood, and across the mountains, where settlement had come later and was still sparse, the forest was essentially untouched. Even well after the Civil War, Tennessee was more than half covered by virgin forest, and could boast that "its forest acreage equalled the combined forest acreage of Maine, Minnesota, Wisconsin, and Michigan." For hundreds of miles, from the tip of West Virginia down to Alabama, amid the highest and remotest mountains east of the Rockies there stretched a forest unmatched in variety and beauty. Everywhere grew immensely tall and straight tulip trees, whiteoaks, chestnut and walnut and hickory trees; extensive groves of cedar and pine, maple and ash. In the spring banks of white and scarlet rhododendron gleamed among the great trunks; even the summits of the mountains were concealed by forest. Charles Dudley Warner traveled through some of the region on horseback in the eighties and as a loyal New Englander compared the Southern mountains to those nearer home. "In every direction the mountains were clear, and a view was obtained of the vast horizon and the hills and lowlands of several states—a continental prospect scarcely anywhere else equalled for variety or distance." But he added, "Magnificent and impressive as the spectacle was, we were obliged to contrast it unfavorably with that of the White [Mountains] . . . There is no limestone or granite. And all the hills are treecovered. To many," he generously conceded, "this clothing of verdure is most restful and pleasing." He also acknowledged that in North

Carolina alone there were more than twenty summits higher than Mt. Washington.

The term Appalachia was not in current usage a hundred years ago; it was the Cumberlands or the Blue Ridge or the Smokies; and the inhabitants of the great forest were simply referred to as Mountaineers. It was a later generation which began to study them as vestiges of an Anglo-Saxon or Elizabethan population; before the Civil War they were ridiculed for their primitive way of life or admired as children of nature, depending on the temperament of the observer.

The Mountaineers lived for the most part in scattered settlements along the floor of the twisting valleys, growing corn and wheat in nearby clearings; but even off in the remote forested mountains where the roads were little more than steep and rocky trails there were crudely built little churches, and lonely cabins which looked out across an immense hazy panorama of rounded peaks. There was a spinning wheel on the porch and when a traveler appeared he was offered hot corncake from the open fire, wild honey and milk; and invariably he was asked if he was looking for ore? Was he a rock hunter? For prospectors were everywhere searching for iron and gold and coal and copper and mica, and surveying for the narrow-gauge railroads which were soon to cross the mountains from the East. Suspicious and contemptuous of strangers, aware of their own different speech and way of life, the mountaineers nevertheless always provided overnight accommodations for travelers, and early nineteenth-century accounts praised "the true Western hospitality" of the Mountaineers of Tennessee. After supper the family "sang hymns . . . in quavering, high pitched voices, during which the hounds now and then joined in with their musical howl." Hunting bear and panther consumed most of the time the men did not spend visiting on the porch or looking for a stray horse; and going to the county seat for court sessions or elections was the chief diversion. But after the war, inspired by the example of the wandering prospectors the mountaineers started to collect mineral specimens on their own. "Many a farmer had caught the prevailing mica fever," a traveler reported in the 1870s, "and some had really found deposits of the valuable

mineral worth thousands of dollars. . . . There is no danger
of underestimating the mineral wealth of this mountain country."

Nor any danger of its remaining long undisturbed. Warner
mentioned a new mining enterprise in western North Carolina
"where a big company store, rows of tenement houses, heaps of
slag and refuse ore, interlacing tracks, denuded hillsides, and a
blackened landscape are the signs of a great devastating American enterprise." But once again the South was spared the severest
impact of industrialization for another twenty years; until coal
mining moved into Appalachia and with it the systematic destruction of much of its wonderful forest.

At first the confrontation was essentially between Southern
isolation and poverty, and Northern enterprise; between Yankees
and Mountaineers.

Whatever the Mountaineers thought of the Northern peace-
time invaders, they had to accept them; as for the invaders
themselves—and there were tens of thousands of them throughout the South—they seemed to fall in love with the country.
Many Northern soldiers were discharged in the South and instead of returning home stayed on. Those with money to invest
bought farms and plantations in Georgia and Alabama and
Mississippi; Southern rumors gave the number of Northerners
along the lower Mississippi, a few years after the war, as fifty
thousand. Many ventured into Texas and Arkansas. Plenty of
them no doubt were secretly convinced that with their superior
energy and education they could easily surpass their new
Southern neighbors and become important men in the community, and much of the journalistic enthusiasm for the South
derived from the untouched sources of wealth everywhere
apparent: any underpopulated countryside was seen as an invitation to immigration—hardworking Europeans or even Chinese; every river called for a factory or a dam, every somnolent
town was waiting for a brisk merchant or a railroad line. The
black population was hopeless; the white population almost as
bad. Comments on the backward ways of the Southern farmer
were almost always harsh. With amazement and disapproval
the Northern visitors noted that it was "customary to milk standing, with the right hand, the left hand holding a small vessel to

receive the scanty contents." Corn was allowed to stand five or six weeks after it was fit to be harvested; bad fences permitted the depredations of stock, feed was distributed in a shiftless, haphazard way; "In summer milk cows are driven half a mile or more from the city to break fences and devour crops; and in winter they are allowed to run at large in the streets and forage from wagons vending hay, oats, etc." The crude wagons were drawn by small shriveled oxen, sometimes by a team composed of an ox and a mule, "a man and an ox traveling eighteen miles [to the city] to sell a dozen small sticks of wood for twenty-five cents!"

People were not punctual, the food was atrocious; there was too much braggadocio and not enough performance; by all means let the society be recast in a "higher mold"! Yet in the meantime what an agreeable and lighthearted society it was! The war had hardly come to an end before the circus reappeared. Whitelaw Reid, passing through Montgomery in 1866, noted with astonishment the excitement caused by the advent of the first circus since 1860. The leading newspaper declared ("in double-leaded type") that "the circus has always been a favorite amusement in the South, and the Southern taste upon the subject has ever been so fastidious and demanded so much, that it is a well-known fact . . . a circus that would go down well on the European continent and elsewhere, would be criticized and ignored in the South." In small villages itinerant troupes of showmen with trained dogs and cats, traveling ventriloquists and "humorous lecturers" held the population spellbound. Akin to the circus in its appeal, but socially more exclusive, were the tournaments in medieval costume. Inspired by much reading of Walter Scott, they had been popular before the war, and now reappeared, either as special events or as part of an agricultural fair. The participants took such titles as "Knight of the Lost Cause" or "Lone Star" and in full armor performed feats of horsemanship before various queens and their ladies-in-waiting. Hearing of this frivolity, the *Nation* solemnly denounced the whole spectacle as "semi-civilized." Horse racing, despite the lack of good horses, was soon re-established, as popular as ever. State fairs resumed, but were attended more for their horse races and sideshows than for their agricultural importance. Mardi Gras continued to be celebrated in Mobile and New Orleans—less opulently than before the war, but no less joyously. "Entering a horsecar," a journalist wrote from New Orleans during the celebration of 1872, "you are confronted by a cynocephalus that would delight the soul of Darwin; he demands your fare, springs onto the roof, and thence disappears into the window of a passing coach." The carnival in Mobile featured "beautifully conceived *tableaux* of scenes from 'Conquest of Granada,' 'The Cave of Merlin,' 'The Reception of Columbus by Ferdinand and Ysabel.'"

The watering places of Virginia had long been fashionable with Northerners as well as Southerners before the war; they quickly regained their reputation, even though the most famous of them all, Greenbrier White Sulphur Springs, now was located in West Virginia. Its accessibility was increased by the construction of the first leg of the new Chesapeake and Ohio Railroad, Virginia's long delayed move to unite the Midwest to its ocean harbors. The former routine was resumed: drinking the waters, sitting on the hotel piazzas, or shooting in the nearby woods. Dancing sometimes began in the morning, and was continuous throughout the day. General Lee was a frequent visitor at Greenbrier and went out of his way (so we are told) to show attention to the guests from the North.

Watering places were scattered throughout the South, and their presence in other parts of the United States is pretty good evidence of Southern influence if not of Southern settlement. Many of them, particularly in North Carolina and Tennessee, were of a modest description, and the war had not improved their condition, but they retained their loyal public of planters and former officers. Warner stopped at such a spring in the mountains of North Carolina: "Colonels and politicians stand in groups and tell stories, which are followed by explosions of laughter; retire occasionally into the saloon, and come forth reminded of more stories, and all lift their hats elaborately and suspend the narratives when a lady goes past." Even the general run-down condition of the vast hotel had its charm. "There is a sense of abundance in the sight of fowls tiptoeing about the verandas, and to meet a chicken in the parlor was a sort of guarantee that we should meet him later on in the dining room."

The one contribution which the North made to the gaiety of the postwar South was the introduction and popularization of baseball. Entirely amateur during its first years, the game was enthusiastically played by all classes, and almost every town or city boasted of several rival clubs with such names as the "St. Elmo," the "Up and At 'Em," "The Up and Skump 'Em."

Southerners seem to have had a talent for inventing fancy titles for the groups to which they belonged; the rejection of conventional names underscored, as it were, the freshness of their sociability; they were imitating no one. Thus the Confederate units assigned to the defense of Charleston during the war had given themselves such names as "The Live Tigers," "The Marion Scorpions," "The Yankee Smashers." The organizations which produced the Mardi Gras pageants were variously known as the "Cowbellion de Rakin Society," "The Strykers," and of course "The Mystick Krewe of Comus." The blacks appear to have been particularly imaginative in the matter of group nomenclature; among the first benevolent societies established in the postwar South were "The Knights of Wise Men," "The Sisters of Sympathy," and "The Young Men Never Lies Society." Certainly the names of many of the smaller black sects indicated the same desire to achieve a new kind of definition, to create new forms to accommodate new ways of worshiping.

During those bewildering years immediately after the war, when countless institutions and relationships fell apart and vanished, there seems to have taken place in the South a resurgence of pageantry, of public festivities only remotely related to the past, a flourishing of community and ritual. But there was not only resurgence, there was also the creation of fresh social forms, from the crossroad hamlet to the new evangelical sect; and one wonders whether the workaday South was not even then beginning to give shape to that vernacular American culture which we only now recognize for what it is: neo-Southern. For more than a century we have been taught to believe that the greatest contribution of the South was its tradition of aristocratic conservatism. No doubt it once was, but has it not been succeeded by something much more universal and vigorous? For decades a distinct way of life persisted in Backwoods Appalachia, in the slums of Memphis and New Orleans, among the poorest and most obscure of Southern blacks and whites; quite suddenly it has emerged to lend a new style to our speech, our dress, our music, our sports, our ways of enjoying ourselves and of coming together. Every highway, every place of amusement, every popular spectacle or pageant is an extension of the South—but of the South which begins beyond the Piedmont.

CHAPTER SIX

The Plains

1. BUFFALO

In those days there must have been at least seven or eight million buffalo grazing across the vacant land between the Rocky Mountains and the Missouri. Once there had been several times that number, and the range had stretched all the way to the Blue Ridge Mountains; it was near the Potomac, in 1607, that Englishmen saw their first buffalo. But at the rate of about ten miles a year the herds had been pushed westward across the Mississippi, and with the coming of the nineteenth century buffalo were being hunted and killed in increasing numbers. The broad path or series of routes across the continent, made by Americans on their way to the Pacific—on horseback, in wagons, and finally by rail—had divided the great mass into two distinct herds: one centered in the South in the Texas Panhandle, the other far to the north in the Dakotas and Montana.

Buffalo did not migrate from one part of the continent to another, as many early explorers thought; they merely wandered far afield in the spring when the new grass came up. In droves of thousands they moved slowly across the open plains, eating the short buffalo grass, and the tall grass in the valleys, and gathering for water at the infrequent streams. They were nearsighted animals and panicked easily; when this happened a whole herd would gallop cross-country at an amazing speed, trampling one another and sometimes hurtling headlong to their death down a sudden embankment or into a river. Every year countless buffalo were frozen in blizzards, killed by wolves and coyotes and bears, smothered by quicksand. There were places where their bones lay thick. In the mating season they fought with a red-eyed fury among themselves. But each spring their numbers were replenished by tens of thousands of honey-colored calves that gamboled around their mothers as they grazed in the warm prairie sunshine.

The sight of these immense herds, darkening the plains like the shadow of a cloud, filled every traveler with wonder. "Of all the quadupeds that have lived upon the earth," an American naturalist wrote almost a hundred years ago, "probably no other species has ever marshaled such innumerable hosts as those of the American bison." Hunters who had never even seen a good-sized town confidently told of seeing herds numbering in the millions. They were a mass phenomenon; the individual with his own unique characteristics, endearing or otherwise, was never perceived; merely the species. It was only toward the end—and then it was too late—that settlers on the plains caught a glimpse of the buffalo as a solitary creature. In her *Autobiography of a Prairie Girl,* Eleanor Gates tells of a prairie fire near her homestead in Nebraska in the 1880s. She and her small brothers were racing to escape the flames: in a brief clearing in the smoke she saw a dark bulky form. "It was a bison, evidently one of those lonely bachelors that, exiled from their kind, were the first hermits of the plains. . . . He galloped blindly, as if he was failing in strength. Even as they looked he tumbled to his knees and let the antelope pass over him, meeting an ignoble death beneath a hundred sharp hoofs and in the embrace of the fire."

They lived in multitudes and perished in multitudes; it seemed that nothing could diminish their numbers. Indians hunted them on horseback or afoot, with bow and arrow as well as with rifles, more expertly than any white man. They found a use for almost every part of the beast—hair, hide, flesh, innards, and bones. Even the droppings, known as buffalo chips to white settlers, served as a fuel. If we are to believe Sir Richard Burton, who crossed the plains in 1860, in one year Indians killed at least two hundred thousand of them.

But when white American hunters began to take part in the chase, then the yearly toll went up by 1870 to two and a half million. The hunters worked for pay, usually not much more than a dollar a day. They hunted independently, or for the large fur-trading companies; until the Civil War, buffalo robes were highly prized. The railroad lines hired hunters to eliminate the buffalo in the areas where track was being laid, and also to provide fresh meat for the construction workers. Even after the construction was finished the herds of buffalo sometimes held up trains for hours. "The bison has a strange and entirely unaccountable instinct or habit," a writer observed in 1872, "which leads it to attempt crossing in front of any moving object near it." He told of how crowds of animals raced next to the train. "Car windows are opened, and numerous breechloaders fling hundreds of bullets among the densely crowded and flying masses. Many of the poor animals fall, and more go off to die in ravines . . . All over the plains, lying in disgusting masses of putrefaction along valley and hill, are strewn immense carcasses of wantonly slain buffalo. They line the Kansas Pacific Railroad for two hundred miles."

Commercial hunters eventually did away with this particular hazard to train travel, and their accomplishments also earned the gratitude of more than one government official. Columbus Delano, Secretary of the Interior under Grant, declared that the disappearance of the buffalo would hasten the Indians' sense of dependence on agriculture and a sedentary way of life; and General Phil Sheridan told the Texas legislature that instead of stopping the hunters, they ought to give them a unanimous vote of thanks. "These men have done . . . more to settle the vexed Indian question than the entire regular Army has done in the last thirty years. They are destroying the Indians' commissary . . . For the sake of lasting peace let them kill, skin and sell until the buffaloes are exterminated."

How much of the slaughter, each year more extravagant, was inspired by greed it is of course impossible to guess; but a love of sport, of a barbaric kind, certainly played its part. Accounts of buffalo hunting strangely resemble those of deep-sea fishing:

there is the same absence of choosing a particular quarry and in consequence the same absence of any emotional bond between quarry and hunter; the same absence of ethical constraints which make traditional hunting something else than butchery; and the same minimal dangers. Yet many of the earlier buffalo hunters had a brave and adventurous style, and were proud of the hard life they led. Thousands of buffalo were killed in the name of sport, killed without thought of profit by men who called themselves sportsmen, and for many years public opinion sanctioned and even admired their actions. The railroad companies did what they could to cash in on the current passion; excursion trains as early as 1868 ran from Kansas City out into the plains, and for $10 the tourist was all but guaranteed a dead buffalo of his own. The most elaborate buffalo hunt occurred in 1872 when General Sheridan invited Grand Duke Alexis, son of the Czar, to his headquarters in Nebraska. General Custer and Buffalo Bill were of the party. The Grand Duke killed two head, and in the evening a group of Sioux Indians performed a war dance for his benefit.

The wholesale and frequently wanton killing of buffalo eventually gave rise to protests. In 1870 a delegation of Sioux Indians visited the Secretary of the Interior to beg for his intervention; senators and representatives from Arizona, California, Massachusetts introduced bills to restrict the slaughter of buffalo; army officers, stationed on the Plains, urged some sort of control of the hunters. "All reports about fine sport and good shooting," said one of them, "are mere gammon. It would be equally good sport, and equally dangerous to ride into a herd of tame cattle and butcher them indiscriminately." The redoubtable Henry Bergh, founder of the Society for the Prevention of Cruelty to Animals, added his voice, and newspaper editors, particularly in the Mountain West, denounced buffalo hunting as wasteful and inhumane. Some states tried, without effect, to impose legal restrictions on out-of-season hunting. From many points of view—from that of the Indian deprived of his main source of sustenance, from that of future sportsmen, from that of the buffalo themselves—the commercialized buffalo hunt was widely and loudly condemned.

Yet in the East and in the city press the interests of one important element were generally overlooked: those of the settlers who had begun to invade the domain of the buffalo in the Great Plains. There is perhaps some significance in the fact that those states most immediately interested in attracting a population of farmers were halfhearted and perfunctory in their moves to protect the buffalo by legislation. Texas refused altogether to legislate on the matter; Nebraska passed a bill in 1875 when it was already too late; in Kansas a bill "to prevent the wanton destruction of buffalo" was vetoed by the governor. And in fact Congress, largely because of the protests of representatives from Texas, allowed a bill forbidding the killing of buffalo in the territories to die in committee in 1876. But by that year the last of the great herds had been decimated, and the wholesale slaughter was at an end.

2. KANSAS

It was in Kansas, in the years just after the war, that the great buffalo hunts took place, that being first of all where many of the buffalo were; then the building of the Kansas and Pacific Railroad (which was to reach across to Colorado by 1870) brought hunters to clear away the herds and provide fresh meat.

It also brought, directly or indirectly, an influx of settlers. Out there on the edge of the Great Plains they confronted the farmers' version of the buffalo problem—something they had not met before. Buffalo, they found out, could easily trample and destroy a field of corn or oats—especially since fences on that treeless frontier were all but unknown—and buffalo in any number had a way of devouring the prairie grass, leaving none of it for the settlers' livestock. Indians entered the picture too; never happy to see white settlers and white hunters in a region where the last herds of buffalo were still to be found.

Plenty of signs indicated to the newcomers that they had moved into a part of the world they knew nothing about and had no feeling for. Kansas, before the war, had meant the narrow eastern fringe of the state: in terms of recent history the violent and bloody ground of John Brown and Quantrell, but in terms of geography an extension of the placid Midwest, well suited to established ways of farming. New England (which boasted with some reason of having invented Kansas) had helped provide that

eastern quarter with a distinctly Eastern (or Midwestern) landscape of neat villages and small farms scattered across wooded
valleys and green hills; hedges of osage orange reminded the
traveler of an Old World ordering of the land. When Kansas was
thought of, this was what mid-nineteenth-century America visualized: something essentially familiar, no matter how remote.

But west of the well-watered region bordering on Missouri the
landscape began to undergo a change, and roughly a third of the
way across the state became something altogether new. Not
merely because in the late sixties there were few settlers there,
strung out along the river valleys; the difference lay in the topography and the climate. The true Prairie had already begun; to the
north and west and south it stretched with only the slightest of
variations for hundreds of miles—immense, wide open to the sky,
faintly undulating, creased by infrequent valleys where groves
of cottonwood and willow crowded the banks of shallow streams.
The unprotected, featureless uplands were swept by constant
winds and bleached by the sun. It was a vacant world of short
rippling grass. Great expanses of brilliantly colored wild flowers
often suddenly appeared in the spring; there were deer and
coyote and antelope. The singing of meadowlarks was always
inseparable from the prairie, and so were the mourning doves in
the groves of the cottonwood trees. At certain seasons, certain
hours it was an extraordinarily beautiful landscape, easily producing a kind of invincible optimism and sense of purpose. Here
(the first settlers exclaimed), the buffalo roamed, the deer and the
antelope played; and not infrequently was heard the discouraging
word "drought" as the sky remained cloudless sometimes for
weeks on end.

But *was* it drought? Or was the prolonged failure of rain to
come when it was needed the normal order of things in the
Great Plains? Was dryness and the storms of dust that always
ensued merely part of what an earlier generation had called the
Great American Desert—an area totally and forever unfit for
permanent habitation by men? No one knew the answer; even
to this day no one does. The first descriptions of the arid bleak-
ness of the Great Plains by explorers who barely escaped dying
of thirst were largely discounted by the better-informed Ameri-

cans of the mid-nineteenth century; but still there was no final
assurance that farmers could survive there. Government reports
and the reports of army officers stationed for far too many
months at some windy post in the midst of monotonous grass
dwelt on the shortages and hazards of the whole region between
the Missouri and the Rockies; on the other hand, according to
the accounts of disinterested travelers and of far from disinterested promoters of land sales, the Great Plains were emphatically
the empire of the future. A succession of years with generous
rainfall in the early seventies seemed to bear out every enthusiastic forecast, and those who had claimed that the strategic planting of trees would alter the climate for the better stood vindicated,
or so it seemed.

But in any case it was always a matter of waiting a decade or
so for confirmation of the verdict; and in the meantime the
individual settler on his own individual piece of land had only
his day-by-day experience to guide him; each seasonal variation
brought home the fact that he was still almost entirely ignorant
of the environment he had come to live in; eventually he would
have to choose between accepting it as it was, adjusting as best
he could to its vagaries, or else adopting some sort of strategy for
outwitting it and even controlling it. If it can ever be said that
there are critical moments in the evolution of a man-made landscape, when decisions are taken which in the long run prove to
be fateful, then that postwar decade when Americans confronted
the High Plains and debated what next to do was surely one of
them. In itself, the settlement of the area was no very spectacular
or dramatic event; the taking possession of the vacant land, the
extinction of the buffalo and the driving out of the last Indians
were by way of being epilogues to already accomplished acts.
Nevertheless we then began what proved to be a new chapter
in our history. We faced a new environment and we faced it
(after a period of doubt and apprehension) in a new way; and
we cannot yet be sure if it was the right way.

The shift was slow in coming, even in the brand-new country.
The first wave of settlers in Kansas after the war seems to have
been of the old breed: adventurous when it came to pulling up
stakes and pioneering, but content to live as before, in a make-

shift cabin near some stream where the ground was easy to
turn over, raising a field of corn, a patch of vegetables, owning
a few head of wandering livestock; not overly fond of work, too
poor to improve the land they were homesteading or to launch
any kind of experiment. When the spirit moved them, they sold
out and went even farther west. Subsequent settlers (most of
whom arrived, belongings and all, by train) looked down on
these pioneers who came in covered wagons or on foot; the
distinction seemed a significant one. Poor whites fleeing conditions in the South were no small element in that wave, and there
may have been something in their background of Appalachian
fundamentalism that accounted for their aversion to energetic
farming and their consequent love of migratory cattle raising.
Stuart Henry, who grew up in Abilene, Kansas in the seventies,
saw a close connection between the Old Testament beliefs of the
small landowners and their distrust of the plow: "Did not everything show to such zealots how clearly Jehovah meant the
Plains to be a cattle instead of an agricultural country?" he
asked. "He favored, as claimed from reading the Bible, people
with herds. He dealt directly with humanity in such a poor kind
of region as Judea instead of rich Egypt or rich Babylonia. . . .
No farmers nor businessmen entered into this divine discourse.
The Holy Ghost understood and preferred the livestock operation and He liked the sort carried on in arid, non-irrigated Pales-
tine and on the arid, non-irrigated American Plains. Hence the
latter was bound to thrive as a cattle realm under the direct
guidance of Heaven."

This prejudice and the way of life that went with it in pioneer
Kansas received powerful reinforcement from the cattle industry
—appropriately enough the cattle industry of Texas, in those
days still very much part of the South. At the end of the war
the ranchers and landowners of southern Texas found themselves
—thanks to their four years' isolation from Northern markets—
with an enormous number of cattle on their hands; according to
some accounts, more than five million head of longhorns were
roaming about the brush and mesquite country between the
Nueces and the Rio Grande. Texas at that time had no rail connections with the rest of the country; the solution to the prob-

lem of the surplus was therefore to drive herds north to the nearest railroad where they would then be shipped to the Northern and Eastern cities.

In the spring and summer of 1868 the first of such cattle drives took place. From a point on the Red River on the Texas-Oklahoma line, some thirty-five thousand longhorn steers were driven up through what is now Oklahoma to Abilene, Kansas, a small way station on the Kansas and Pacific Railroad. Here a shipping yard, complete with barns, corrals, scales, as well as a nearby hotel for the accommodation of the cattlemen and the prospective buyers, had been built; and here the cattle were loaded on freight cars and shipped to Kansas City or Chicago. The trail was more than eight hundred miles long.

Abilene thus became the first of the cow towns that western fiction and western movies have made so familiar. It was the first but not the only one; in the course of the next decade a number of other cow towns—each one a little farther west—rose to handle what was known as the Texas Cattle Trade: Wichita, Caldwell, Ellsworth, Dodge City, and—most remote of them all— Ogalalla, Nebraska. These small towns competed with one another for the business of shipping the cattle back East by rail, but in many respects—economic, social—they resembled one another. As the first, Abilene received the most attention from contemporary journalists; it was Abilene that the cowboy first appeared in public view, and Abilene was the first of the cow towns to break away from the cattle trade and to revert to its original country status.

The trail that led from Texas to Abilene was known as the Chisholm Trail; and while there is still heated debate among western historians as to the origins of the trail, its correct name, and even as to its location in certain stretches, there is general agreement that it was the setting of the largest mass movement of animals directed by man that ever took place in America; more than three million steers are supposed to have moved its length during the five years when it was most used. Today almost all traces of the trail have vanished, though no doubt aerial photography could easily discern its path. In its heyday it was in some places a mile wide, but for most of its length it consisted of a dozen or more smooth parallel paths across the Oklahoma or Kansas range. In herds of fifteen hundred or more, guided by a dozen cowboys, the steers ambled northward at the rate of about ten miles a day. After the first confusion the three months' journey was usually uneventful, and when all went well there were hours of inexplicable silence when the men ceased talking and the cattle uttered not a sound. But some emergency always arose—a sudden wind to panic part of the herd, a sudden late spring blizzard, a river in flood to push the reluctant cattle across—and in the early days there were Indian raiding parties to cope with, and the buffalo. For the men it was a long, rough, frequently monotonous but always profitable job, and there was no lack of would-be cowboys who wanted to be able to say that they had ridden the Chisolm Trail all the way to Abilene. Though the cattle grazed as they moved across country they were lean and weary by the time Abilene came in view. Once over the last rise from where they could see and smell the water and fresh grass around the small town, the steers broke into a trot, and the trail fanned out into a score of small paths where the animals separated from the herd to graze and rest. From the town itself the appearance of each herd as it scattered was an exciting spectacle. The variegated colors of the steers—brown, buff, black, mottled white and red—the sound of their bawling—gave movement and brilliance to the prairie.

At the beginning of the cattle trade Abilene was a dusty, half-dead little settlement of log cabins with dirt-covered roofs, one short street, and of course the depot. At the end of the first season of shipping it had already acquired a number of saloons, gambling houses, brothels, and hardware stores, and the population had grown to more than two hundred. Whenever a new herd came in the population was increased, if only temporarily, by the presence of a number of drovers, buyers, and cowboys, and Abilene, despite its size, became a lively and dissipated place. It did not take long for the Eastern newspapers to discover this new and incongruous aspect of rural Kansas; what particularly fascinated the visiting journalists were the cowboys. Weary from riding the trail, dirty, unshaven, with long hair and filthy dungarees, they were far from picturesque. It was only when they had been paid, when they had been to a barber to have their mustache dyed and "set" and to the clothing store to buy a new wardrobe that they revealed their style.

There was nothing of the colorful conventionality of the modern cowboy or rancher about their dress. A recognized "Western garb" seems not to have existed. Descriptions of the Abilene cowboys in their new clothes consequently mention a bewildering assortment of many-buttoned corduroy suits, suits of fringed buckskin; sombreros, derbies, skintight high kid boots with high heels and enormous spurs; canes, kid gloves, and an occasional white clerical tie. But always the finery included a large lone star, symbol of Texas. "The cowboy," one reporter observed, "never forgets to be a Texan, and never spends his money or lends his appearance to a concern that does not in some way recognize the emblem of his native state: so you see . . . a general pandering to this sentiment, and lone stars abound of all sizes and hues, from the big disfiguring white one painted on the hotel front down to the little pink one stitched in silk on the cowboy's shilling handkerchief."

Did this attachment to the Lone Star signify loyalty to Texas only, or to some more inclusive concept: loyalty to the South, and a kind of defiance of Puritan Kansas? Though most of the cowboys were very young, in the first years of the drives many were Confederate veterans, and Confederate military titles were common, so we are told, among the drovers and cattlemen. And certainly it is tempting to interpret the holiday cowboy costume, that lighthearted collection of expensive finery, no item even remotely related to the occasion or to any of the others, as a very early indication of the neo-Southern style. The Western cowboy while he flourished kept alive many traits of popular Southern culture that middle-class society deplored: its dress, its vocabulary, its weakness for violent and dangerous pleasures, its weakness for gambling, and for every kind of pageant or show. If he has now vanished from the scene it is only in the one capacity as a special kind of worker; as an element in a youthful way of life, as a figure of unconventional vitality and joy, the cowboy is still as refreshing a spectacle as he was in Abilene a hundred years ago.

In none of the cow towns was the relationship between the townspeople and the cowboys cordial, and Henry in *Conquering the Great American Plains* told how Abilene became a divided community and repeated on a miniature scale the fragmentation characteristic of most American cities. The "civilians," the population of clerks and storekeepers and part-time farmers, withdrew from the gaudy violence of Texas Street to live in respectability on the right side of the tracks; and Abilene may well have been the first town where that phrase had a definite spatial connotation. Off among the empty lots they built their frame houses, painted them lead gray, planted trees and hedges; went to church to sing hymns and hear about eternal damnation. Few of the men in the town dared so much as visit the Texas Street bars; for entertainment they loafed around the depot. "The hot, hot summertime! In dog days the men sweat profusely while figuring in their little stores or offices. Between sales or trades you beheld them idling there, longing for something to occur. A bunch of Indians skirting through, a string of prairie 'schooners' passing, a train an hour late, even a change in the wind, afforded subjects of extended interest. Godsends in the way of news were a dogfight, a swearing quarrel between two residents, the broken limb of a neighbor tumbling off a new roof."

And all the while Texas Street with its borders of brightly painted false fronts, the rattle of dice, the cracking of the cowboy quirts, the yells and laughter lay within earshot. The two elements declined all lasting contact. "Our houses," Henry wrote, "stood between the jaws of Texas Street, and no cowboy ever entered the yard nor paid the slightest heed there to members of our household. Crazily drunk, they raced past, filling the air with shots and curses, while our doors stood always open or unlocked."

Still, the coolness between the two sides of the tracks, between Texan ruffians and well-behaved civilians came from something more mundane than a difference between moral codes. Misbehavior was tolerated if not condoned only so long as it was a necessary feature of a profitable partnership, and the partnership as the years passed seemed less and less of a blessing. Farmers and homesteaders continued to come and settle in the surrounding countryside. Not always models of energy or enterprise, more than willing, it sometimes appeared, to sell out to some later arrival—nevertheless owners of land, owners of their own kind of livestock—they plowed after a shallow inefficient fashion, and put up fences when they had to. With these settlers came a more substantial type of townsmen, agents, and small officials and professional men whose work impinged little if at all on the noisy business of shipping cattle. The Elks Lodge, the Odd Fellows Hall, the Masonic Temple became centers totally removed from Texas Street.

In the intervals between cowboy saturnalias and the turmoil of shipping, the cattlemen and the buyers uneasily watched the plowing up of more land and the erection of more fences; they correctly foresaw in them a threat to their continued use of the open range. The immigrant farmers were seen as potential enemies, and echoes of the Old Testament doctrine were heard with greater frequency, spiced now with scientific or ecological complaints: the farmers (so the cattlemen declared) were plowing up land which God had meant for grazing; plowing in this region of deficient rain produced only weeds and flying dust; small farmers could never survive; it was better by far to keep the land in large acreage, open to periodic grazing. To which objections the farmers replied by urging the passage of stricter herd laws, by investing in machinery for deeper plowing, by experimenting with crops which could survive the dry years. Chance, inscrutable luck, the god of the gambler and herdsman, was no longer the god of the small farmer, and the more prosperous, better educated breed of farmer who was starting to appear, preached its version of a scientific agriculture.

The break came when the farm population began to outweigh in economic importance the drifting population of cattlemen and cowboys. But it assumed the form of a conflict between two codes of conduct. In the winter of 1872, when cowboys and cattlemen, barkeeps and prostitutes and gamblers had all withdrawn until the first herds were to appear in the spring—when Abilene, that is to say, had reverted to its normal somnolent self —a group of its citizens produced a circular and sent it throughout Texas and the cattle West. "We, the undersigned [four fifths of the male population of the town] . . . most respectfully request all who have contemplated driving Texas cattle to Abilene the coming season to seek some other point of shipment, as the inhabitants . . . will no longer submit to the evils of the trade."

That was all, but it was enough to destroy Abilene as a cow town. The cattlemen, as far as one can learn, made no protest, and soon found another terminus for the drive. Abilene never recovered its brief prosperity, and its sudden decline was sensational enough to bring out a second contingent of journalists. The towns which took its place went through much the same evolution, as cowboy rowdyism, lawlessness met the opposition of a growing farmer element. By the end of the decade the last of the Kansas cow towns had entered its final decline, and the cattlemen and their cowboys, like their Bible prototypes, were once more on the move—this time into Colorado and Wyoming and Montana. As for Kansas, it settled down to the raising of winter wheat.

The conflict between the virtuous townspeople and the wicked cowboys had much to do with the disappearance of the Texas cattle trade; the conflict between farmers and cattlemen even more; most important of all, however, was the conversion of the whole rural community from a passive acceptance of a traditional environmental order to a determination to try new crops, new techniques, new ideas.

To some there was no doubt great irony in the circumstance that no sooner had the farmers rejected the Old Testament dispensation than they were overwhelmed by one natural disaster after another. In 1874 there was a plague of grasshoppers unparalleled in its extent, a plague which ate everything green from the Rockies through Kansas. A year later there came a drought, and then an infestation of chinch bugs, and as a result of these misfortunes almost total destitution in county after county, so that private charities in the East, as well as government funds, were all that kept many alive. But the irony was only apparent; the lesson learned was not that the Old Testament was right, but that there were still obstacles to overcome before the environment could be finally subdued.

CHAPTER SEVEN

California

1. THE COUNTRYSIDE

When they went back East, often without having made the fortune they had dreamt of, the Forty-niners remembered California with affection. For all its disappointments it was still God's country. But "the strong expression," Henry George explained, "loses half its irreverence as, coming over the sage-brush plains, from the still frost-bound East, the traveler winds in the early spring down the slope of the Sierra, through the interminable ranks of evergreen giants . . . and sees under their cloudless sky the vast fertile valleys stretching out to the dark blue Coastal Range in the distance."

The long descent into the Sacramento Valley served to dramatize the remoteness and self-sufficiency of California, its lavishness of scale, its beauty. There in the open country reaching out of sight into the mountains north and south was a great flood of wheat fields, towns and ranches rising out of it like tree-grown islands, with a great river bordered by lagoons and greenery wandering across it. In the fall of the year fleets of sailing vessels carried the grain down the river to the Bay, out through the Golden Gate onto the ocean—a procession lasting weeks. The gold of California in the seventies was the gold of wheat;

California which a San Francisco clergyman described as "the beloved Benjamin of American States, whose autumn sack is filled with grain, while the mouth of it contains a cup of gold." Wheat grew in the hot and treeless plains of the Central Valley, grew among the scattering of oaks on the hills, grew in the farms of the Bay Region. Near Santa Cruz wheat grew to the edge of the sea, drenched by fog and mist. Long after wheat had been replaced by plowed fields and orchards its imprint on the landscape and the rural way of life persisted.

There were other regions, equally beautiful. Within a hundred-mile radius of San Francisco a transplanted East had evolved. "Substantial private dwellings, well-fenced fields, broad patches of vineyard and fruit orchards," a contemporary Californian wrote, "alternate with grainfields, extending as far as the eye can reach." Frame houses with broad verandas and green shutters resembled their contemporaries in Ohio and Illinois, though their bright gardens with palm trees and exotic vines brought from Asia or Australia lent them a luxurious, almost tropical air. Registered cows were milked in white barns; the owners experimented with new seeds, new techniques, devised ingenious sprinkler systems to produce lawns as soft as those in the East; read agricultural journals and won prizes at fairs. There were neat schools and churches; well kept roads, planted with trees, led to the nearby town. Occasionally there were picnics off in the mountains within sight of the ocean. There was botanizing, and to the parklike landscape of venerable live oaks growing on the sides of bright green hills the excursionists responded appropriately by citing Olmsted and Downing and Weidenmann. Whatever educated circles in the East thought and did, educated circles in the Bay Region were prompt to think and do. Tree planting was an Eastern fashion; eucalyptus trees suddenly became the rage in California, and an Oakland nursery sold one hundred thousand in a year—as windbreaks, as ornaments, as potential fuel. Did forests affect climate? Then the redwoods must at all costs be saved from destruction. A peculiarity of the species, said the author of *The Natural Wealth of California,* "is the great power it possesses in condensing fogs and mists; . . . hence springs situated in or near the redwoods are seldom in want of a good supply, while crops on the Coastal Range are not liable to fail. It will surely happen," he warned, "that if the redwoods are destroyed . . . certain portions of California, now fruitful, will become comparatively a desert."

So there could be no such thing as too much vegetation; more and more foreign plants appeared in gardens, until a member of the California Academy in 1868 complained that the growth in the prosperous suburbs along the peninsula was more Australian than native. Much the same complaint was made of the new campus at Berkeley: too much Australian material. To the delight of all, F. L. Olmsted in 1864 had offered suggestions as to how to design the campus. He also laid out a beautifully romantic cemetery for Oakland.

There was more to California, of course, than the Bay Region. There was a south which began somewhere near Santa Barbara, a town whose harbor was "often covered with an iridescent film of oil, which finds its way to the surface over an extent of at least twenty miles." Perhaps the day was not far off when California would be self-sufficient in the matter of kerosene, for in the south there were many such seeps and springs of oil. But it was more than geology that set the region off from the north: the population of Los Angeles County was predominantly Spanish-speaking for one thing, and somewhat lacking in enterprise. Fruit raising occupied much of the land: groves of orange trees and large vineyards. Los Angeles was a picturesque town; the old Mexican houses, roofed with the local tar, flanked the two principal streets paralleling the river, and here and there a tall palm rose from a courtyard or from behind a hedge of cactus. When the rains came the surrounding countryside was quickly covered with waving grass.

There were days, especially in the fall, when the air in Los Angeles was unaccountably hazy, and the eyes of its inhabitants smarted; back in the thirties Dana had told of the phenomenon. But for most of the year the region enjoyed brilliant sunshine. The background of steep brown mountains, the green of the vineyards and groves, the bright blue sky and far away to the west the bright blue sea gave an almost Mediterranean quality to the landscape.

A peculiar element in the population, most noticeable during and immediately after the war, were the poor whites from the southern states. Rough in manner and speech, seldom engaged in work, they lived with their families in wagons, and seemed to think nothing of traveling across the continent in the same slow and primitive vehicles.

The California which most Californians knew was thus largely limited to the prosperous and variegated region around the Bay, for it was there, after all, where almost half the population lived. They were familiar with the expanding wheatlands of the Sacramento Valley, and with the western slopes of the Sierra which until recently had been the scene of much mining activity, and the coast as far north as Eureka was part of their world. When the railroad across the continent was completed in 1869 it was not long before tourists appeared, and what might be called the perceived landscape grew to include the Yosemite Valley, more than two hundred miles south and east of San Francisco.

First seen by white men in 1850, the valley was opened to the public seven years later, and in 1864 it was designated a park. The variety and magnificence of its mountain and forest scenery offered something to every taste, but in the earlier years its great appeal was perhaps less the wild grandeur of the scenery or the opportunity to explore and study an untouched wilderness environment than the parklike beauty of the valley floor. Olmsted (who in 1864 had urged the preservation of the area) is said to have preferred the valley when the surrounding mountain walls were hidden by clouds and only the idyllic foreground of trees and meadows and river was visible. If the early literary effusions inspired by Yosemite are reliable testimony, the usual response to the spectacle was to see it as a kind of confrontation with the Sublime, if not with God. Few seemed to have felt the need of a closer relationship with nature, which could be admired and contemplated at a respectful distance. Nordhoff, writing for tourists in 1874, probably expressed a popular point of view when he suggested that the valley install some improvements: more and better hotels, better roads, and baths. And who other than Olmsted should be engaged to do the improving?

Yet tourists were not the only ones to come to California; there were other interests to serve, notably those of would-be settlers and farmers. The westward moving tide of Americans had surged over the desert and mountains to invade the state. The fame of California as a land of infinite promise, first expounded by the returning miners, was now being spread even more effectively by the railroads and the land promoters. If the choice lands around the Bay and in the Sacramento Valley were already taken, there were many other areas ideal for settlement. With a few rudimentary improvements—an irrigation system, a railroad, a dam, a canal—there was not a corner of California, however forbidding it might at first appear, which could not become a small paradise.

The postwar influx of settlers coincided with, and perhaps furthered, a radical shift in the economy of the state: a shift from cattle ranching to the large-scale raising of wheat. There had been a period immediately before the war when the raising of cattle and sheep had been the most important occupation for the great landowners of California, and though the American ranchers introduced better stock—some of it driven all the way from Texas and Missouri—their philosophy differed little from that of their Mexican predecessors. Theirs was the same unthinking reliance on the natural resources of the environment—resources extensive enough to make them wealthy without any great effort on their part. The ranchers accordingly raised no feed, provided no shelter, drilled no wells, built no fences; their immense herds were allowed to graze for months on end across the open landscape—valley and plain and hillside. Once a year a "rodeo" or roundup was held, and if the stock had increased (and it usually had) then the rancher saw the operation as a successful gamble.

It was a romantic and agreeable way of life, and with it went prestige and considerable political power. The great cattle spreads left little desirable land for the small farmer, and whoever tried to cultivate a field or two soon discovered that the antagonism between stockman and farmer, horseman and plowman, was as acute in California as in Kansas and the Great Plains. Ranchers and their cowboys (according to reports) made a practice of "purposely herding their enormous droves so as to trample down some poor man's little grain patch, his solitary hope of the year for the maintenance of his wife and children." Fences, in the treeless range country, were costly for the farmer to build, but the legislature, dominated by the cattlemen, refused to pass any fence law for the protection of the farmer.

The natural order which the cattlemen complacently assumed was on their side abruptly revealed its less cooperative aspects. In 1861 a great flood suddenly swept into the San Joaquin Valley, the center of much ranching, and transformed it for several weeks into a sea almost as large as Lake Michigan—two to three hundred miles long and from twenty to sixty miles wide; and some two hundred thousand head of cattle were drowned. Scarcely had the waters subsided than California was hit by a two-year drought, and tens of thousands of the surviving animals died of starvation. The range cattle industry never completely recovered from the disasters.

It bequeathed to the community a wide and empty area of overgrazed range, totally unimproved, and an isolated remnant of ranch culture which even today is visible in the California landscape.

The early nineteenth century had a word for Missourians who left their home state to make a living elsewhere: they were called Pukes. Polite usage softened the term to Pikes, and devised a spurious etymology (based on Pike County, Missouri) to justify it. Pukes invaded California long before the Gold Rush days, trailing livestock over the mountains. In time the word was applied to all migrant Southerners; there were Texas Pukes and Arkansas Pukes. Whatever their origin they had certain characteristics in common: a dislike of steady employment, a dislike of farming, and a strong dislike of any racial minority—in California the Chinese; and a corresponding partiality to cattle raising and the social values which went with it. When, after the accumulation of setbacks in the early sixties, ranching ceased to be a profitable occupation in California, the Pukes declined to give it up. They remained loyal to their traditional way of life, and established themselves in the hot and relatively barren region in the lower San Joaquin Valley around Visalia—a town which later gave its name to the well-known stock saddle. Nordhoff described the typical rancher of the Visalia area: "His cattle wandered over a million acres hereabout, his will was law; his *vacqueros* (cowboys) were the ministers of his will, and his voice was public opinion." And then in the seventies came the railroad. The Pukes prophesied that it would bring with it a host of small farmers, and that the farmers would fence in their land, and ruin the open range. The railroad, Nordhoff happily concluded, was the great civilizer, for it would drive off the Pukes, who had already begun to sell out and move to Arizona. Scornful jokes were told about the illiterate Pukes: how one of them refused to allow telegraph wires across his land because "he didn't want the whole country to know every time he whipped his children"; how others disapproved of public schools because the school bell scared off the deer. They had brought their diet of pork and cornbread and greens to the San Joaquin Valley, and lived in the same kind of dogtrot house their forebears had developed in Appalachia. Yet somehow they succeeded in leaving an indelible mark on California; today the southern end of the San Joaquin Valley is the bastion of neo-Southern culture in the state. Bakersfield is not merely an important center of cotton growing, it is a center of drag racing and country music, and of religious revivalism; and if the original Pukes in time departed, the Depression, by bringing in thousands of itinerant Okies, added a powerful new infusion of Southern manners.

Those who believed that the elimination of the cattlemen and their arrogant ways promised a bright future for the small farmer in the now vacant rangelands were soon undeceived. It is true that when the railroads were built in the Central Valley in the seventies agriculture in California had at its disposal an immense new domain—extraordinarily fertile, easily cultivated and controlled, with a wonderfully predictable climate. It was also a domain almost entirely void of the grace and variety and human association of the older region around the Bay. But the raising of wheat in commercial quantities soon proved to be well beyond the means of the small farmer, for the procedure adopted resembled a Western version of the bonanza wheat farming of Minnesota and the Dakotas, entailing large investments in money and machinery and land. The California wheatfields were if anything larger than those of the Red River Valley, dustier, more monotonous, more overpoweringly hot, and the equipment more complicated. The invention of the Stockton gang plow—a combination of three or four plows in a single span, drawn by as many as eight horses or mules—did much to speed up the plowing process. The fresno, or horse-drawn scoop, was another local invention. A steam tractor was tried out at an early date. The wheat farmers experimented tirelessly with machines and techniques to shorten the work of raising and harvesting wheat and disposing of it—new plows, new harrows, new threshers and combines. Plowing, seeding, harvesting, sacking, and shipping were done on contract; storage, whether of the crop or the machinery, was reduced to a minimum. Once the harvesting was through with, the farmer left the farm to retire to town until the next season. The contractors were paid off, and the hired labor sent on its way, the landscape stripped and empty of life. In 1873, W. N. R. French, the partner of the Chicago landscape architect Horace Cleveland, prophesied the advent of the "agricultural engineer," the man who would transform farmland by "applied machinery . . . improved tools and mechanical contrivances of all kinds to the purposes of agriculture"—a bold prophecy for the Midwest of those times, but in the wheatfields of central California a prophecy immediately fulfilled.

Those were the years when California acquired the reputation which Texas has only recently inherited: the "California Style" in the last decades of the nineteenth century meant a style of living, a style of work which was lavish, ruthless, uncouth, and boastful; and because it *was* ruthless and sure of itself it produced its own landscape, a spatial organization of hitherto unheard of dimensions that took full advantage of environmental characteristics— notably the hot, rainless summers and mild wet winters—and laid heavy emphasis on specialization of every kind.

Immense though it was, exciting and spectacular, the wheat landscape was not well known. The artists and writers of the Bay Area either ignored it, or in their eagerness to show how civilized they were outdid one another in expressing their revulsion. Yet despite its dust and heat and the appalling monotony of its land forms and weather, the wheat country had a beauty which could not be entirely denied. A traveler in 1875 praised the huge and treeless hills which seemed "clad in deerskin, soft and smooth as velvet, or a rich cold brown; or when they stand beneath the sun they take on a damson purple. . . . Nowhere else on earth . . . have I seen the light of the sun rest on this beautiful world so tenderly as it streams down through this white-lilac autumn haze of California." But in human terms the environment was hideous. The typical dwelling or ranchhouse was little more than a shanty. "Unfenced, unshaded, unplaned, unpainted, it looms stark and rigid across the tawny plains. . . . Ten thousand acres of splendid golden wheat may wave around it, but not one tree within eyeshot."

Nor was the social atmosphere any more enlightened. "California," said Henry George in 1871, "is not a country of farms but a country of plantations and estates. . . . The farmer raises wheat, he buys his meat, his flour, his butter, his vegetables and frequently even his eggs. He has too much land to spare time for such little things or beautifying his home, or he is merely a renter, or an occupant of land menaced by some adverse title. . . . He hires labor for his planting and reaping, and his hands shift for themselves at other seasons of the year. . . . And over our ill-kept shadeless, dusty roads, where a house is an unwonted landmark, and which run frequently for miles through the same man's land, plod the tramps, with blankets on back—the laborers of the California farmer—looking for work in its seasons, or toiling back to the city when the plowing is ended or the wheat crop gathered."

The tramps or itinerant farm workers differed little in their need from the migrants who invaded the Red River Valley, but in California they were more numerous: miners who had given up looking for gold; Chinese no longer working on railroad construction projects; Indians alienated from their communities; city jobless, recent immigrants, small farmers ruined by drought. All of them were paying the price of an agricultural system which defined the landscape in terms of specialized environments. "Such specialization," wrote a historian of California agriculture, "inevitably gives rise to a demand for labor that varies greatly in the course of the year. Casual labor has usually been on call, however, and has not been the employer's responsibility in off seasons. Hence the farmer has had little economic incentive to adjust his farming so as to regularize employment. . . . What adjustment would the Midwest have made, had the labor demand of its crops been as rigid and as uneven as in California? Would that region too have built up a special labor group? Might it perhaps have welcomed and retained Negro slavery?. . . Certainly it would not have developed its present farm sizes and labor pattern."

The steady, unending flow of abundance out of the wheatlands hypnotized more than one beholder into acquiescence with the system, just as its remoteness and ugliness dulled the awareness of the educated class. But there were those who, like T. F. Cronise, clung to the hope of more traditional family-sized farms. "Many holders of Spanish Grants," he wrote in 1868, "which embrace some of the most extensive and fertile districts, could greatly benefit the State . . . by dividing these estates into small farms and selling them to actual settlers at a fair price. It will be a grand day for California when the word 'ranch', like the idea and system it represents, has only a historical meaning, and when small farms, well tilled, dot the lovely plains."

2. TOWNS

A Methodist minister by the name of William Taylor was for seven years during the Gold Rush a street preacher of the Gospel along the docks of San Francisco. His audiences were tough and sometimes unruly, but he was an eloquent man and (according to the book which he later wrote about his missionary work) he converted not a few of his hearers.

In Taylor's considered opinion California was the hardest country in the world in which to make conversions. He gave several reasons: first (he explained) "the migratory character of our population. The Christian does not settle down long enough to get acquainted with his neighbors." Second, "the *isolated* condition of society. In all old-settled communities, each member, however humble, is a link in a chain of association, which runs through the whole community. . . . But here the links are nearly all separated. . . . Social ties and relationships, and ties of blood, are very important 'conductors' for Gospel 'electricity.' California differs too from all other *new* countries in this respect. Our other western states were settled up by a gradual emigration of families. Every family was a nucleus of social life. . . . But here we have in the space of a very few years a population of three hundred thousand souls. A state vieing with the great states of our Union in the development of its physical resources, while even the foundations of its social life have not been permanently laid to this day."

Taylor was writing of social conditions during an unusually confused period of California history, but the obstacles he enumerated to the spread of religious fervor were much the same as those which prevented the formation of communities of the traditional American sort. If the riotous and spendthrift miners had almost entirely vanished after the war, they had been replaced after a fashion by the regular ebb and flow of farm workers, city unemployed, and recently arrived settlers. Almost all of these were single men, usually without money, without local ties, ready to move on whenever the prospect of work presented itself. Furthermore they were strangers to one another, differing in background, in race or nationality, yet competitors for the same jobs.

In keeping with the established American procedure, the towns which came into existence in the sixties and seventies were usually laid out by a small-time speculator hoping to take advantage of some nearby installation: a railroad stop, a ferry, a mill. A grid was the inevitable pattern of house lots and streets, and the first arrivals—pioneers to a later generation—came less with the intent of establishing permanent homes than to cash in on the future prosperity of the town as a real estate venture. In the meanwhile they provided themselves with houses and without much zeal undertook to exchange goods and services with the migratory population and with one another; becoming blacksmiths, barkeeps, proprietors of rooming houses. Scattered across the otherwise empty grid, like counters in a parlor game, prefabricated houses, shipped in by rail from the East, began to appear. Most of them were humble, one-story affairs, easily moved elsewhere, but there were others adorned with prefabricated gingerbread and stained glass.

The unassembled building arrived by rail, and the purchaser erected it himself. "The 'package' included all the building components, all necessary pins and dowels, and an erection diagram complete with instructions. The diagram showed stakes as foundations and a dead air space as insulation between house and ground. Sills were placed on top of the foundations and the floor laid on top of the sills." Horace Bushnell, the Connecticut theologian fresh from solidly built Hartford, described this building procedure with uncomprehending amazement. "Set up some wooden legs on bits of plank that rest on top of the ground; on the legs rest the timbers for a floor, and lay on the floor. Then take some rough boards, and nail them on upright around the outside timbers of the floor platform. . . . Then nail on, inside, a slat to support the timbers of the next floor. . . . *Presto,* it is done—a house, a church, a hotel, an Oakland college, whatever you will."

Near the railroad tracks and often parallel to them developed the town's business section, a more substantially built assembly of "blocks," warehouses, stores, banks, and hotels. What invariably bewildered the Eastern traveler was the extraordinary number of hotels, lodging and rooming houses, restaurants, and saloons. Accustomed to associating these establishments with a high degree of urban culture, he was at a loss as to how to account for their presence not only in the small railroad towns but even in crossroad hamlets. Out along a dusty highway the traveler often discovered a hotel large enough to accommodate the entire local population. The explanation was simple enough: these businesses existed to serve the *transient* population. The numerous lodges of fraternal orders had the same origin; their symbols and insignias decorated the upper floors of the buildings and "blocks" in the center of town. Wherever solitary men congregate and think of growing old and dying far from their family, fraternal orders flourish and multiply; and the commercial farmlands of mid-nineteenth-century California counted them by the score. When Sacramento was a town with less than fifteen thousand in the sixties, it contained organizations of Good

Templars, Druids, Knights of Honor, Knights of Pythias, United Workmen, Red Men, Janissaries of Light, Champions of the Red Cross—as well as hundreds of Masons and Odd Fellows. Founded as mutual benefit and social societies, the fraternal orders provided companionship and, what was scarcely less important, impressive funeral services. Not a few of them reflected the social tensions of mid-century California: the touchy ethnic awareness of some groups, the economic discontent of others and (a trait common to almost all of them) a fear and resentment of the Chinese.

The miners with their bursts of temporary wealth had given a picturesque vitality to many of the country towns, but farm workers, even though more numerous, had little money to spend on celebration and little to celebrate. Their month-long periods of idleness were passed in the rooming houses and hotels near the tracks, or on the sidewalk. Across the town in their own well-defined neighborhood, lived the Chinese; and somewhere on the fringe of the community, in the borderland between town and open country, were the shanties and tents of the itinerant Indian and Mexican population.

The real nucleus of the town consisted of the well-to-do farmers and landowners, the contractors and shippers and bankers and railroad officials who made the place a small but effective center of economic and political power. Their contacts with the more modest element in the population were few. Their ornate houses stood on the tree-grown streets in the most desirable part of town, surrounded by fenced gardens and lawns kept green by dint of incessant watering. The eminent California geologist Hilgard denounced the practice as requiring "an inordinate cost of money and labor, and sometimes of health. . . . The hose and lawn sprinkler are probably in more general use here than in any other country, and innumerable attacks of rheumatism and malarious fever are traceable to their intemperate use."

But the fashions of the wealthy had to be followed, for local traditions did not exist. "All through the state, until you penetrate to the remote, lonely cattle ranches, and the habitations of the Pikes," a traveler in the mid-seventies remarked, "there is a suggestion of city life, of city atmosphere." All around in the immense, unsmiling, dusty landscape of stripped wheatfields enormous fires of burning straw in the fall filled the valley with a haze of pale smoke. But in the towns, richer by another bumper harvest, "young men drive spanking teams to spick-and-span new sulkies or buggies with elegant cashmere or wolfskin afghans. Their talk is the talk of the town; it has gold in it, and stocks, and horse races."

California had in fact produced one more environmental wonder. Along with its record-breaking yields of wheat, in 1874 the largest in the nation, it was evolving a new kind of country town, half slum, half service and administrative center: a town which was more and more the exclusive location of management, while the countryside was demoted to be the location of labor. In the East this new division of functions was apparent only in the larger and more advanced industrial establishments—and had not yet begun to affect the relationship between the rural and urban landscapes and their respective inhabitants. In the Central Valley of California, however, the fateful break between office and plant, white collar and blue collar, brain and hand, had been accomplished a full century ago. Disdain for the dull workaday utilitarian countryside (and for the newly rich men who exploited it so effectively) became characteristic of a peculiarly California environmental philosophy: a philosophy which to this day persists in seeing two, and only two, significant aspects of the world: the city and the wilderness.

It was perhaps the miniature scale of those rural centers that made their citified character so unwelcome. Aspects of daily existence that in Merced, for instance, or in Salinas seemed restrictive and inhuman appeared in quite a different light in the setting of San Francisco. The monotony of the streets, the jerry-built houses, the fragmentation of society and the contrast between ostentatious wealth and dejected poverty—above all the visible symbols of power concentrated in the hands of a few— these were characteristic of the city as well as of the country town. Even so, their greater complexity in San Francisco made them essential elements in the city's fascination and charm.

Thus the grid layout, universally condemned by the postwar generation for its unfeeling rigidity, somehow managed in San

Francisco to produce a wonderful juxtaposition of contrasting neighborhoods. The original alignment of streets had been notorious for its complete disregard of the hilly and often precipitous terrain. The sudden steepness of some of the streets rendered them impassable for heavy wagons, with the result that commerce was confined to the more level parts of town. The nearby hillsides became desirable residential quarters, favored with fine views, clean air, little disturbed by through traffic yet conveniently near downtown. Subsequent attempts to remedy the situation by reducing the grade of the steeper streets only produced deep cuts through the hills, and did nothing to modify the sharp boundaries between place of residence and place of work. It was much as Morris Copeland with his topographically determined city would have wanted it: people lived in their own houses on the heights, and worked down in the vicinity of the waterfront.

Topography came to the rescue of the city in another instance. Had San Francisco been less hilly it undoubtedly would have followed the general American procedure and placed its railroad station (with its attendant swarm of warehouses and factories) in the very middle of town. But the station was relegated to the flat southern margin, and a lively and diversified downtown area came into being.

There it was that rows of pompous masonry buildings (locally considered the equivalent of anything Europe had to offer by way of architecture) housed the banks and mining companies which still controlled the wealth of the state. There it was, along Kearney and Montgomery and Market Streets that the best of the city's three hundred restaurants were to be found, as well as the most luxurious hotels. It was there that the daily "promenade" took place—the American equivalent of the Mexican corso. This was one of those public gatherings which served to attract all classes, and to bring together the sedentary hillside element and the transients from out of town—an event which made the afternoon street scene of downtown San Francisco unique in the country.

The more demanding of the transients stayed in such hotels as the Baldwin, or the Palace—at the time of its completion in

1875 the largest and most expensive in the world. The far more numerous transients from the mines and farms and ranches, and from the ships in port contented themselves with rooming houses and primitive lodgings near the harbor, spending much time in the ornate saloons of the district. Beginning in 1867 the water-front had been improved and extended; earth from the steeper hills being used to fill in the obsolete slips. It was still a dis-orderly and sometimes dangerous part of town. The floating population had greatly changed in character since the days when Taylor had preached to the Forty-niners; instead of predom-inantly American sailors the men were now from China, Russia, South America, and Europe, and when San Francisco called it-self the second most cosmopolitan city in the United States it was this element of foreign workers that largely justified the boast.

The Chinese were of course the largest group; in 1868 some four thousand of them lived in a well-defined Chinatown on Sacramento Street, a sordid labyrinth of sunless alleys and pas-sages, leading to crowded workships, eating places, tenements. Bitterly resented by the numerous unemployed, disliked because of their foreign ways, the Chinese were subject to various sorts of harassment. The police hit upon the ingenious idea of passing an ordinance which prescribed a minimum of five hundred cubic feet of air for every occupant of a tenement. The move was in keeping with the then fashionable concern for sanitation, and allowed the arrest of many Chinese violators and their confine-ment in jails where the allowance of air was far below that minimum. Under police escort tourists visited the Chinese the-aters and temples and explored the opium dens. They too learned to dislike the Chinese of Chinatown.

It was however at the hands of hoodlums that the Chinese suffered their greatest humiliations. First identified and given a name in the postwar years, the hoodlum seems to have originated in San Francisco. "This sudden efflorescence of a sharply defined criminal class among boys," said a visitor in the seventies, "is somewhat alarming. It shows there is a screw loose somewhere in our social mechanism. . . . The Hoodlum drinks, gambles, steals, runs after lewd women, rifles the pockets of inebriated citizens

going home in the small hours, parades the streets at night singing obscene songs. . . . One of his chief diversions, when he is
in a more pleasant mood and at peace with the world at large,
is stoning Chinamen. This he has reduced to a science."

How was one to account for this violent and lawless breed?
The trade unions, according to the writer, with their policy of
virtually excluding apprentices, were largely to blame; but no
doubt an important cause for the prevalence of young hoodlums
was the lack of parental supervision. "A large portion of the
people have no homes. They live, or rather they exist, in hotels,
in boarding houses, in lodging houses, eat at restaurants, spend
their days at their place of business, and their evenings at resorts of amusement."

The cabarets and theaters of San Francisco seem not to have
played so important a role in the social and cultural life as is
sometimes supposed. If the city was visited by many celebrated
artists it was less because of the discriminating taste of its audiences than because it was a logical end to a nationwide tour.
Despite its amiable illusions on the matter San Francisco in the
mid-nineteenth century was neither a generous patron of the
arts nor an inspiration to more than a handful of artists. Its
pleasures in fact were of a commonplace sort: the Cliff House,
overlooking the surf and the seals lounging and splashing and
roaring, was a favorite haunt. There were Mr. Woodward's Gardens, a private park open to the public and containing a botanical
garden, a zoo with several grizzly bears, a Museum of Curiosities
and a collection of copies of old masters. When the craze for
roller skating hit San Francisco, Woodward's installed a rink.
The ferryboats provided excursions to Alameda with its extensive nurseries, and farther afield there were various hot springs.
Hunting seals off the rocks near Monterey was not only a pleasant
sport but a profitable one, for the Chinese were said to pay a
handsome price for the whiskers.

What was missing was a large public park. Olmsted had offered
suggestions for one, and the site was chosen: an eleven-hundred-
acre tract of sand and scrub reaching down to the beach. A dis-
agreeable feature of the San Francisco afternoon were the clouds
of sand that blew in from the ocean; and since the city was

beginning to expand to the west, a park in that vicinity would on every account be desirable. It was not Olmsted's plan which was executed but that of the engineer William H. Hall. Aided by local botanists and gardeners Hall eventually produced in Golden Gate Park one of the handsomest public pleasure grounds in the United States; and the stabilization of the drifting sand, the laborious search for trees which would grow in it, were in themselves remarkable accomplishments. The city soon began to surround the park.

Pleasure seekers or not, most San Franciscans wanted homes. In 1868 there were no less than thirty Homestead Associations —associations whose members pooled their savings to buy sizable pieces of land for division into house lots. Subsequently the members borrowed from the Association to build their houses. The Homestead Associations were the Pacific Coast equivalent of those workers' organizations which in the sixties made Philadelphia a city of small homes. The San Francisco houses were almost all two-story frame structures, tightly wedged together on the steep streets south and west of the central part of town. Whether they possessed in their earlier days a neighborhood identity it would be hard at this distance in time to say. Their basic design appears to have been inexpensive and convenient: well adapted to the needs of the workers' families who occupied them, and derived for the most part from the books and manuals of reputable builders. They were conspicuously adorned with quantities of turned and carved wood gingerbread on gable, porch and door and window trim. These "building adjuncts"— the expression used by the manufacturers—were bought separately from catalogues and local distributors; California and San Francisco in particular proved to be an eager market for this kind of applied decoration. Chicago, chastened by the fire of 1871, foreswore all gingerbread and adopted a more severe style for the frame dwellings it subsequently built. But San Francisco had had no such lesson, and if the earthquake of 1868 had any influence on architectural design it was to discourage the decorative use of brick, which tumbled from chimneys and cornices, and rarely withstood a serious tremor.

The gingerbread exuberance in San Francisco was more than

anything an attempt to "customize" a mass-produced house, to give individuality to a dwelling which was essentially identical with its neighbors. At a time when the larger Eastern cities had given up building low-cost family dwellings and were erecting either multi-family tenements or expensive row houses, San Francisco (and probably other medium-size cities) was producing houses specifically designed for the taste and pocketbook of workmen—specialized forms to suit a specialized market. They often embodied still another prefabricated element—the bay window. A San Francisco publication in 1876 attempted to outline the architectural evolution of the previous decades by showing how the amount of window had increased. "One can tell the age of any dwelling in San Francisco within five years by the amount and quality of glass in it. The convex [bay] window is still very characteristic of the city."

The invention of the cable car in 1873 had the effect of opening to residential development the heights of Russian and Nob Hills. Despite the magnificent views obtainable there, and despite the fact that architects were responsible for their design, few if any of the pretentious mansions built on the heights surrounding the Bay show any recognition of their site. The evolution of an architectural idiom related to the scenery and climate of the Bay Region had to wait a good half century.

Where beauty has to be sought out and extracted from a reluctant environment the arts often seem to flourish best; wherever it exists in profusion and variety it is likely to be accepted as a condition of daily existence, a kind of birthright calling for no special acknowledgment. There are in fact certain natural landscapes whose beauty is so manifest that no analysis of the relationship between the world around us and ourselves seems needed; nor artist to interpret or intensify the experience. Much time can pass before a dialog is finally entered upon. A hundred years ago when the hills surrounding it were still covered by fields of wild grass and when the Bay itself was like a small sea, the Bay Area must have been one of those rare landscapes. Perhaps that is why the people of San Francisco were slow to feel the urge to establish any formal esthetic interaction with their environment. Almost any style of building sufficed, almost every

open space, every street revealed to them the marvelous light
and the incomparable view. Now the relationship between the
city and its setting has changed, and a dialog—not always ami-
cable—between the two is underway; but the cheerfully tasteless
quality of mid-nineteenth century San Francisco was like the
expression of a belief widely held among Americans: that a gen-
uinely urban civilization derived not so much from works of art
or enlightened social institutions as from a healthy and inspiring
natural environment.

CHAPTER EIGHT

New York

1. NEW YORK AS AN ENVIRONMENT

To the immigrant coming from Europe in the years immediately following the Civil War the first sign that he was at last near his goal was when, off Sandy Hook, the ocean water turned a paler green. Then came the passage through the Narrows, between the wooded heights of Long Island to the north, and Staten Island with its green hills and villages and scattering of white farms. The immense bay was alive with steamers and sailing vessels and tugs and oyster boats. It glittered in the sun; the shadows of smoke and steam and small broken clouds, rapidly passing, mottled its surface. To the north and west there was a hint of tree-clad country, fading into blue, and directly ahead lay the city. Even at the brightest of times it was hidden by a haze, and all that the newcomer saw, as his ship waited offshore, was a mass of roofs and chimneys and spires, punctuated by the glint of windows. Very indistinct in the northeast rose the two immense towers of the incomplete Brooklyn Bridge. Two great rivers embraced the city, whose waterfront was fringed by a tall black hedge of masts. The sky was like an Italian sky.

No nation ever had a more splendid gateway. It was not merely a city that lay within it, but a new world of light and water and movement, and the city itself was more than a city: it was a man-made environment. Already in 1873 its profile, seen from the harbor, had begun to display a strange irregularity, and in 1875 two tall structures—the Tribune Building of 260 feet, and the Western Union Building of 230 feet—had abruptly emerged out of their slate and brick surroundings; the incomplete bulk of the monstrous Post Office Building added a third vertical accent. New York was proud of all three, and when in the fall of that year Thomas Huxley arrived on his way to deliver the inaugural address at Johns Hopkins University, shipside reporters eagerly asked the question repeated countless times in subsequent years: What did he think of the New York skyline? Huxley answered in effect that in a democracy it was fitting that the most impressive buildings be dedicated to the spread of information.

An ingenious reply; but many New Yorkers continued to lament the paucity of imposing public architecture. New York (which at that time did not include Brooklyn) was a city of nine hundred thousand souls, yet where were the public buildings worthy of its size and importance? There was indeed a beautiful City Hall with a celebrated clock tower, but it lay remote from where most New Yorkers now lived, and its park with the immense trees had been half destroyed for the new Post Office. The Tombs was a cheerless edifice and the Custom House was not much better. St. Patrick's Cathedral, begun in 1858, was nowhere near completion, and Trinity Church, once celebrated for the extensive panorama visible from its steeple, was now overshadowed. There existed no museum, no art gallery, not a monument or statue worth a second glance; no great public square. Other than this handful of buildings there was little else than Castle Garden in the midst of the recently landscaped Battery Park, and there the real spectacles were the recently arrived immigrants and the drama of their bewilderment.

Time and again the press deplored the destruction of the few remaining antiquities and clamored for better public architecture. Its continued absence was usually blamed on the elected officials of the city—"notoriously unfaithful, extravagant and incompetent." But New Yorkers themselves were peculiar; unlike the inhabitants of other cities they demanded monumental buildings not as symbols of civic status or as an inspiration for civic virtue, but simply as curiosities. "Whatever ornaments this city," declared the *Ledger,* "or makes it a place of marvels, is another eddy added to its maelstrom power to draw the country to it, as a centre. . . . All hail to each new warehouse that inspires public talk on behalf of its size and splendor; hail all palatial residences, that widen the renown of our squares and avenues."

It accordingly devolved upon the private sector to furnish the appropriate metropolitan setting, and it responded in a grandiose manner. After the war, when New York began to expand and grow still more prosperous, the principal streets and avenues were rapidly transformed by new hotels, expensive stores and elaborate residences, and in a ceaseless procession, by night as well as by day, New Yorkers, seeking perhaps a substitute for civic grandeur, walked their length. Broadway, particularly the stretch between City Hall and Union Square, gaudy and extrovert, was the favorite spectacle. "Seen from one of the hotel balconies," wrote a commentator in 1873, "the effect is very fine. The long line of the magnificent thoroughfare stretches away into the far distance. The street is thronged with a dense and rapidly moving mass of men, animals and vehicles of every description. . . . Toward evening the crowd is more leisurely, for the promenaders and loungers are out. Then Broadway is in its glory. . . . At night the scene is different, but still brilliant. The vehicles in the street consist almost entirely of carriages and omnibuses, each with its lamps of different colors. They go dancing down the long vista like so many fireflies. The shop windows are brilliantly lighted, and the monster hotels pour out a flood of radiance from their myriad of lamps."

Here were to be found the most popular theaters and restaurants, and near at hand was a wide variety of places of entertainment—"sinks of iniquity," according to an indignant contemporary, "where every crime denounced in the decalogue, and many that Moses never dreamed of, are plotted and committed." But Broadway itself was the chief source of entertainment. Crowded with sailors, beggars, pedlars, street musicians, sightseers, and office workers, festooned with advertising banners and streamers, every exterior space a mass of lettering, with painted transparencies glowing after dark at the entrances to bars and dance halls, it fascinated every visitor. The heavy traffic of carriages, wagons, carts, horse-drawn buses gradually compacted itself into furious immobility until the police intervened. The side streets, perspectives of new brownstone or marble or cast-iron facades, often terminating in a web of ships' rigging, were scarcely less lively. Everywhere there were deep excavations where the older three-story brick houses had stood, and where some marble building would arise.

Only those who could recall a more modest New York regretted the change. G. W. Curtis, the editor of *Harper's,* wrote in the late sixties of how it had not been "many years since every noted man was known to all Broadway"; now it was crowded with strangers. "Among all the costly and colossal buildings that have been erected how few show any real taste or grace; how little but stone and iron and space have been bought for the money! . . . Great wholesale stores stand where the pretty shops stood, and if you go below Canal Street of an evening there is something ghostly in the gloom of the closed warehouses." He might have been foreseeing the near future of Boston or of Chicago after the fire, the remoter future of a dozen American cities.

The old families had of course long since fled the lower end of the island, retreating first to the leafy neighborhood of Washington Square, then to Fifth Avenue. In the early seventies the fashionable quarter lay between Eighth and Fortieth streets and Fourth and Sixth avenues. Most of the black population of New York—at the end of the war some ten thousand—lived in Greenwich Village, a location formerly conveniently near the houses of their wealthy employers and patrons. Perhaps to maintain the relationship, the blacks had started to move north along the East Side, and pressures from other minority groups encouraged them to do so. Another consequence of fashion establishing itself along Fifth Avenue was the presence on East Twenty-fourth Street of a horse market, reputed by some to be the most important in America if not in the world. Housed in a double row of dingy stables reaching from the East River to Madison Square the horse market—or "the street" as it was called by initiates—was controlled by a small group of wealthy and influential dealers. All kinds of horses were bought and sold: coach and streetcar horses; brewers' teams; running, trotting, and saddle horses from Kentucky, polo ponies from the cattle ranches of Kansas and Texas, race horses from New Jersey and Long Island. Buyers came from all over America and even from Europe, but the most profitable customers were the residents of nearby Fifth Avenue; it was they who sought out the handsomest animals for their coaches and carts and the coupés of their wives. Despite the dictum of the *New York Times* that it was vulgar to drive a pair of horses and that the only "genteel way" to take the air was on horseback, driving horses remained in demand, and brought as much as $1200 a pair. The resort of jockeys, English grooms, trainers, and young men of fashion, animated by expertise and animal grace, East Twenty-fourth Street in those days must have had style of its own.

The twin rows of solid, expensive houses, all much alike as to furnishings and appearance, continued up to Fifty-ninth Street, and a straggling few even confronted Central Park. New houses were rising everywhere on the East Side; whole blocks of them on Madison Avenue; isolated specimens, or clusters of two and three, on otherwise empty streets. Outsiders thought that the monotony of the facades, together with the dreary predictability of the street numbers, presaged a city without variety or color, but those familiar with New York knew better; for despite the grid of uniform streets and avenues, the leveling of every hill, despite even the sameness of brownstone fronts, New York, as never before, was becoming diverse, evolving innumerable specialized areas, some no larger than a block or two, others the size of a small town. Each had a sharp identity. There had been a time, not long before, when artists and sculptors and actors lived and worked in the busiest part of town, rubbing shoulders with every citizen; the center of artistic life had been a picture framer's store on Fulton Street. But by the sixties Bleeker Street had become a well-defined and recognized Bohemia. Sightseers made a point of visiting it to marvel at the long-haired young men and the eccentrically dressed young women going in and out of the dilapidated mansions. There were Jewish quarters, each with its synagogue; a German quarter, a French quarter, with their own newspapers, their own restaurants, their own holidays. There was a quarter where Italian organ-grinders lived, and even a small Chinatown whose inhabitants peddled candy and cigars. To visit these exotic neighborhoods, hear a foreign language, eat foreign food, was almost as good as going to Europe. Poverty and degradation likewise had its own part of town—an arrangement which many New Yorkers found satisfactory enough, since it made police supervision of the "dangerous classes" easier. Five Points, however, was a risky section to explore, and a glimpse of notorious Mulberry Street usually had to suffice. The Bowery was rough and loud, but less menacing, and its colorful street life gave a brief but adequate picture of how the lower orders lived.

A fragmented society necessarily offered fragmented experiences which in the end added up to a new concept of the urban community; and there were those who were beginning to see New York as a city different from any other the world had hitherto known. "What a marvelous place is this our city of New York!" the editor of the *Ledger* exclaimed. "Other cities have growths and homogeneities! This is extemporized as regards its greatest proportions, and is composed of diversities of nations and customs, of thoughts and acts." London, he said, remained intensely English, Paris intensely French; "The foreign element does not touch even the epidermis, much less the interior, vital qualities of the body." And a long-established homogeneity in Europe had produced a rigid social structure, with little or no upward mobility. "But how different this our New York! O, rural cousins! O, men and women who live in it! Have you ever seriously analyzed the wonderful—unique—unparalleled city in which you live?" It was Fanny Fern, the indefatigable columnist of the *Ledger,* who first analyzed it, not seriously to be sure, but in a number of instantaneous impressions, brief and casual snapshots: the pleasant flower gardens on Murray Hill as seen from a passing horsecar; the sounds of early morning in the city streets, the informality of New York in summer, celebrities smoking cigars outside the Astor House. She loved it all. "New York," she wrote, "seems to spoil one for living elsewhere. [Here] it is emphatically living, real *live* living." Hers was a New York where popular landmarks took the place of monuments, anecdote substituted for history; the play of light and shadow was the true aspect of the city.

If the readers of the *Ledger* enjoyed Fanny Fern's animated pieces it was probably because she expressed a point of view which they shared; but the new perception of the urban environment, most noticeable after the Civil War, was undoubtedly strengthened by two technological developments. One of these, though not the first in point of time, was the building of the New York Elevated Railway. The congestion of traffic on Broadway had become a serious problem, and office workers in downtown New York preferred living in Brooklyn or New Jersey to living in upper Manhattan with its slow and infrequent horsecars. There were those who advocated an underground railway, after the model of London, which could accommodate freight as well as passengers, and in fact a trial length of a Pneumatic Transit System was built under Broadway in 1870. "The men are at work like moles or gophers, slowly digging a hole eight feet in diameter," the editor of the *American Agriculturist* explained to his youthful readers. "They are making a big blow gun! I suppose every boy has blown peas through a tube. This underground channel . . . is the tube, and an immense fan driven by a steam engine does the blowing. . . . *The peas!* . . . Oh, they are the cars that are blown from one end to the other." But the Elevated started first; a stretch between the Battery and Courtlandt Street was completed in 1868, and by 1876 forty trains a day were running between the Battery and Fifty-ninth Street. Strong objections to the Elevated were promptly voiced. The smoke and soot of the steam engines were hard to tolerate, and landowners and residents of the affected streets brought suit against the company for the damage it did not only to real estate values but to domestic quiet. The New York papers pointed out that in London the building of the underground had been costly but that once built it inconvenienced no one, whereas in New York the expense of the Elevated was immediately passed on to neighboring property owners.

The impact of the Elevated on the growth of the city and especially on the development of uptown Manhattan was spectacular: far from finding its presence a nuisance, speculators in real estate dreamt of developing "respectable colonies in the neighborhood of elevated stations." Some suggested moving houses back and planting trees to prevent cinders from coming into the windows. No less impressive was the impact of the Elevated on its passengers: in addition to conveying them up and down town at a rate often exceeding twenty miles an hour, it afforded them an entirely new perspective of New York: at a height of twenty-five feet above the street they could enjoy for the first time an extensive view of the city, combined with fleeting glimpses into the windows of nearby houses. The eye became a camera instantaneously registering wide distances and intimate detail, registering New York as a novel spectacle always on the move.

The second development was the increased use of the camera as a device for recording instant occurrences. The popularization of the stereograph or stereopticon view owed much to enthusiastic articles by Oliver Wendell Holmes in the *Atlantic Monthly*. In 1861 he described his impressions of what he called Sun Painting and Sun Sculpture, noting that "there is a strange indifference to [stereography] even up to the present moment, among many people of cultivation and taste." But the stereograph, with its three-dimensional quality, was not to be compared with the ordinary photograph, he pointed out; it was, for one thing, absolutely truthful; it could not be tampered with; and it was instantaneous. Telling of his first view of the stereograph he reported that "it produced a dreamlike exaltation of the faculties, a kind of clairvoyance. . . . It is wonderful to see how nearly the effect of motion is produced by the slight difference of light on the water or on the leaves of trees as seen by the two eyes in the double picture." He then described "a miraculous instantaneous view" of Broadway: "Notice the caution with which the man driving the dapple gray horse in a cart loaded with barrels holds his reins—far apart, one in each hand. See the shopboys with their bundles, the young fellow with the lighted cigar in his hand, as you see by the way he keeps it off from his body. . . . All is still in this picture of universal movement. Take ten thousand instantaneous photographs of the great thoroughfare in a day: everyone of them will be as still as the tableau in 'Enchanted Beauty.' Yet the hurried day's life on Broadway will have been made up of just such stillnesses. Motion is as rigid as marble, if you only take a wink's work of it at a time."

The instant was captured in still another manner: by the perfection of the process of wood engraving for magazine illustrations in the early seventies. Previously all pictures for reproduction had to be drawn in reverse on the woodblock—a tedious and demanding job; but with the invention of a method of transferring a photograph—already reversed—of the artist's drawing onto the block it became possible to reproduce the original technique—charcoal, pen and ink, wash, crayon. "Men drew, or painted, their designs with freedom, of any size," the editor of *Scribner's Magazine* explained, "and often direct from nature, and the photograph, preserving this freedom and its results, reduced everything to the proper size . . ." The result was a type of illustration which immediately conveyed the artist's technique and intention: his first rapidly sketched impressions of the world were faithfully reproduced on paper. The fresh perception, the spontaneous response became part of the illustration. It was then that the carefully objective, detailed engraving went out of fashion; and the wood engraving emphasized those aspects of the environment that the writer had previously monopolized. The title of McCabe's popular book about New York, published in 1873, was *Lights and Shadows; or, Sights and Sensations of the Great City*—a title equally suited to a collection of contemporary wood engravings with their partiality for tumultous skies, splashes of sun, the flare of gas lamps, the steam of locomotives.

It was along the waterfront that the spectacle of New York as a man-made environment was best observed. Here as elsewhere in the city there were specialized areas; steamers from Europe and from Boston docked along the North River. Hunters with their dogs rode the ferries to New Jersey, to spend the day in the meadows, shooting waterfowl and relaxing in the many German beerhouses; coming from New Jersey the ferries brought a stream of wagons loaded with hay, and herds of cattle which were driven bawling through the streets, dogs at their heels, to the slaughterhouses.

The East River, on the other hand, was where the sailing ships docked. Here were anchored the hay barges from up the Sound and New England; vagrants and "bummers" slept in them and in the summer afternoons men and boys dived naked from the barges and wharves into the cool river. There were lumberyards and shipyards and foundries along the east waterfront, and bars and lodginghouses frequented by sailors. Near Fulton Street there was always activity. Ten ferry lines plied between Brooklyn and Fulton Street, every five minutes, day and night. There were days when the fog was so thick that passing ships could hardly be seen, and there were stormy dangerous days of high seas; but even then there were sightseers along the waterfront, and much movement. Shortly before dawn long lines of farm wagons waited on the Brooklyn side to cross over to the markets, and around five in the morning the first commuters—most of them manual laborers—started to crowd the boats. Throughout the evening hours when the last of them had returned to Brooklyn where each night, as a historian phrased it, a million virtuous beds were honestly and healthfully occupied, there were always passengers seeking the fresh air from off the bay, or enjoying the spectacle of the lights in the two cities, in the ships at anchor, flaring lights from the foundries and shipyards: each ferryboat had many colored lanterns; and all of these were reflected on the rough surface of the river.

The river was a useful metaphor for the city: the water sparkling and splashing, the cool breeze, the shifting lights, and the descending darkness all lent themselves to comparison with the turbulence and flow of life on the island, and its transitory nature. "What oceanic currents, eddies, underneath," Whitman wrote in his later years, "—the great tides of humanity also, with evershifting movements. Indeed, I have always had a passion for ferries; to me they afford inimitable streaming, never-failing living poems." Whenever he visualized the city there seemed to be a foreground of river and light. It was on the river that he achieved what he called his "general subjective view of New

York and Brooklyn: Broadway, the ferries, the west side of the
city, the democratic Bowery—human appearances and manners
as seen in all these, and along the wharves, and in the perpetual
travel of the horsecars, or in the crowded excursion steamers, or
in Wall and Nassau streets by day—in places of amusement at
night—bubbling and whirling and moving like its own environment of waters."

2. CENTRAL PARK

During the mid-century the subject of monuments in New York
was frequently discussed in the daily press and magazines. No
one denied that they were poor and few; but was there perhaps
some meritorious reason for their lack; could the situation be explained in some manner which reflected credit on the people of
the city? *Harper's Magazine* seemed to think so: in 1870 it declared, "Hitherto in this country, with that distaste of profuse
and symbolic expression which is characteristic of our race . . .
there have been few statues of famous persons in our galleries
and public buildings." There was a certain depth and sincerity
of feeling among Americans that avoided lavish public expres-
sions.

Civic pomp, however, was one thing; monuments and statues
designed to quicken a love of beauty and enrich the inner life
of the individual belonged in a different class, and in the years
after the Civil War when Central Park was nearing completion
and had already become popular with New Yorkers, many citizens, especially those with an educated taste, believed that nothing could be more appropriate than to adorn the park with
the statues of famous men. *Harper's* comments were in fact inspired by the recent unveiling of a statue to Walter Scott. William
Cullen Bryant had delivered the dedicatory oration; after men-
tioning that the new park had of necessity possessed "no human
associations, historical or poetic, connected with its shades, its
lawns, its rocks, and its waters," he rejoiced in believing that
from then on "the airs that stir the branches of the trees will
whisper of feats of chivalry to the visitor," and he enumerated
several of the characters created by Scott that would presumably

haunt Central Park. There could not be too many such edifying monuments. "Fill the park with figures of really noble men only," said *Harper's,* "and it will be an inspiring Valhalla."

With the passage of years and a gradual change of taste, enthusiasm for statues in the park began to wane, and there were suggestions that a committee of art experts be formed to pass on the design and appropriateness of any proposed monument. Yet the notion persisted among an influential element that one of the purposes of the park was to be a Valhalla—or as some expressed it, a Pantheon or Westminster Abbey—and whether statues were desirable or not depended less on their artistic worth than on the way a park was defined.

What was its essential function? That it was meant to give pleasure to all the people of the city and not merely to one class was generally agreed; and in fact it was this democratic quality which made it of greatest value. The generation active before and during the Civil War years was inclined to describe America and its culture in terms of how it differed from the culture of Europe, particularly of England. To be sure, the park designed for public enjoyment was of European origin; but it was certainly particularly appropriate to the cities of the United States, for it was the democratic equivalent of the royal gardens and parks of Europe—amenities which the enfranchised Europeans were inheriting, but which a free and democratic society like that of the United States would create for itself. The splendor of the European prototypes derived in large part from the works of art, the historical monuments, which adorned them. Thus Andrew Jackson Downing, among the first proponents of a large park for New York, envisaged it not only as a beautifully landscaped area, but as containing art galleries, museums; a place where the refining influences of music and sculpture and architecture would be available to all.

The park, in short, was thought of as a means of inculcating traditional cultural values and acceptable modes of public behavior. "We knew," wrote a commentator on Central Park in 1861, when it was beginning to acquire its final form, "that when the people truly realized their sovereignty, that they would claim not only the utilitarian, but the artistic and munificent attributes of their throne—and that all the splendors and decorations, all the provisions for leisure, taste, and recreation, which kings and courts have made, would be found to be mere preludes and rehearsals to the grander arrangements and achievements of the vastly richer and more legitimate sovereign, The People." The natural setting, the landscaped background of this cultural display, might conform to current fashions and be picturesque; but the true purpose of the park was to provide the inhabitants of the city with a refined and edifying contact with art.

The culturally alert element in New York consequently thought of the park as a kind of open air museum. As early as 1859 a group of prominent citizens suggested that at least a hundred acres be set aside for a zoological garden—"an area many times larger than that of any Zoological Garden in Europe." James Jackson Jarves, the art critic, proposed a nondenominational cathedral. An arboretum and a botanical garden were included in the original design submitted by Olmsted and Vaux. In 1871 the state legislature authorized the erection of two buildings in the park—one to serve as a Museum of Natural History, the other as a Museum of Art. Countless other cultural installations were urged during the first decades—and rejected. And though Central Park, like most other metropolitan parks in the country, has been continuously menaced by this sort of intrusion, it is worth noting that whereas within the last half century the proposals have usually been for schools, playgrounds, maintenance facilities, etc.—invasions pure and simple—in earlier times they were offered as adornments entirely suitable to the cultural definition of the park.

That early didactic definition appeared to many to be vindicated by the response of the public. Observers were gratified to see that visitors, regardless of class, behaved beautifully. Drunks were remarkably scarce, and those who walked on the grass were taken care of without trouble. "It has been observed," said one writer in 1869, "that rude, noisy fellows, after entering the more advanced or finished parts of the Park, become hushed, moderate, and careful."

It is possible that their subdued conduct derived as much

from disappointment and frustration as from awe. When the park was still in its formative stages and its purpose open to debate, there was more than one suggestion in the popular press that it would make an ideal setting for athletic competitions and mass spectacles. The proposed parade ground (later eliminated) stirred many hopes, and there was happy speculation as to where the best views of the military evolutions could be had: from the Terrace? from the slopes near the Mall? A cricket ground was of course essential, and it was agreed that the Elysian Fields of Hoboken (in the sixties the largest public space available for sports) would be deserted, once Central Park was open. "A footrace a week," one paper suggested, "entries limited to residents of Fifth Avenue, would do something toward the physical improvement of the race; and a wholesome game of baseball would not be deserving of contempt." Genial advice came from all directions: alpine gardens among the rocks, more sparrows (only recently introduced to America and still a popular bird), more gray squirrels; a grove of chestnut trees where boys and no one else would be allowed to climb after the nuts. "Let us not restrict the privilege with any miserable rules about breaking a twig or grazing the bark." A most desirable feature would be a track for trotting horses, after the example of the Bloomingdale Road.

Vain hopes! The only playgrounds provided were those for children—and by no means all children; only those who could present a certificate "from his or her teacher of punctual attendance at school, and of good character." For these little paragons the playgrounds were open three days a week. Still wanting to play games themselves, adults begged for the same privileges, but were refused. "By the method adopted of confining the use of the playgrounds to school children," the 1868 Annual Report of The Park Commissioners explained, "the practice of adult clubs of match games, and the objectionable features that have become the frequent attendant of those games, have been effectually prevented." One of the objectionable features referred to appears to have been betting.

Thus a century ago two distinct and conflicting definitions of the park threatened to meet head-on: the upper-class definition with its emphasis on cultural enlightenment and greater refinement of manners, and a lower-class definition emphasizing fun and games. Had either one of them got the upper hand the subsequent history of public parks in this country would have been a very different one: in Central Park we might have had a landscape dotted with shrines and statues and museums, or a landscape devoted to tracks and fields for forms of sport which by now would be either unpopular or obsolete.

That neither of these fates befell Central Park is due almost entirely to the influence of Frederick Law Olmsted, and his persistent efforts to see his own vision of the park materialize. It is scarcely necessary to review the career of a man who spent much energy successfully promoting his own public reputation. The son of a prosperous Hartford merchant, Olmsted, without professional training, developed an early interest in farming that led to a trip to England and the purchase of a farm on Staten Island. In 1857, thanks to influential connections, he was appointed superintendent of the new (and as yet undesigned) Central Park in New York City.

The following year he and his partner Calvert Vaux—formerly associated with A. J. Downing—won the competition for the plan of the park, and Olmsted was appointed chief landscape architect. Although he took a leave of absence for two years during the Civil War to serve as secretary to the Sanitary Commission—the equivalent of the Red Cross in those days—and in 1863 went to California to superintend the lands of a large mining company, he kept in touch with the development of Central Park. In 1865 he was back in New York as Landscape Architect to the Board, a position he kept, despite frequent disagreements with its members, until 1873. In 1868 he and Vaux started the design of Prospect Park in Brooklyn; in subsequent years Olmsted —usually with Vaux—designed public parks in Buffalo, Albany, Newark, Providence, Fall River, Hartford, and New Britain. He became the best-known and most influential landscape architect in the United States, an eminence he maintained until his death in 1903.

It would be inaccurate to call Central Park the first designed public park in the country. As early as 1853, Hartford, Connecticut, Olmsted's native town, created a fifty-acre park in the center of the city where there had previously been a slum. It was later named Bushnell Park in honor of the man who first proposed it, fought for it, and was responsible for its attractively romantic design. Central Park, however, with its more than eight hundred acres of unredeemed rock and scrub, was a far larger, far more ambitious project. In terms of engineering, designing, planting, maintenance, and administration it was on an unprecedented scale. All of these phases in the creation of Central Park Olmsted supervised with great efficiency. We have been taught to see the park as Olmsted's exclusive accomplishment, and it was certainly he who provided the organizing capacity needed for the execution of the design; without that talent Central Park would never have achieved its final form. He was, however, greatly assisted by several men who have never been properly recognized. George Waring, Jr., in his capacity of soil engineer provided the complex and much altered topography with a new and model system of drainage. Jacob Weidenmann, a Swiss-born landscape architect and engineer educated in Geneva and Munich, became Olmsted's landscaping assistant. He later redesigned several New York parks—Gramercy Park among them—and became superintendent of parks in Hartford. The Austrian landscape architect and botanist Ignaz Pilat was largely responsible for the planting in the park. He had already had a distinguished career as director of the Botanical Gardens in Vienna when he was engaged by the commissioners of Central Park as Chief Landscape Gardener—the title of Landscape Architect being reserved for Olmsted and Vaux. Pilat it was who made what we would now call the first ecological studies of the area and compiled a complete catalog of its plants. "For many years the most important person upon the Park," an obituary noted at the time of his death in 1870, "was less known and received less credit than almost anyone connected with the enterprise." As for Vaux's contribution, we hear very little about it; it seems in fact to have been largely confined to the structures in the park. Olmsted was no doubt justified in assuming that his own work—the general design and the vision of its future development—was the more important.

Yet in the long run, even more significant was Olmsted's definition of the public park and its uncritical acceptance by a whole generation. To him the park was an example of natural scenery which acted "in a directly remedial way to enable men to better resist the harmful influences of ordinary town life and to recover what they lose from them," and throughout his career he remained loyal to the definition. The "scenery" (as he liked to call it), natural or modified, was thus the most essential feature, and anything which reduced its restful quality or its beauty threatened the integrity of the park itself. Facilities for games and sports, museums and galleries and monuments were all equally unwelcome, for the city park was a work of art appealing to the eye, a kind of three-dimensional landscape painting. In Olmsted's opinion the landscape painter was more likely to appreciate the beauty of park scenery than was the architect, for the painter knew that a landscape in its natural condition was not always beautiful and often had to be "arranged" before it could be considered a satisfactory composition, whereas the architect looked upon scenery merely as a convenient background against which to show off his handiwork. Those architects who dared to invade his parks, whether in New York in the 1870s or in Chicago at the time of the World's Fair were denounced as "Cockneys," influenced by the French—two almost unforgivable characteristics.

There were of course other public pleasure grounds; he frequently enumerated them: the plaza or tree-lined promenade, the children's playground, the athletic field, the public flower garden. Each of these was necessary and each had its special quality and purpose. But the loftiest purpose of all was that of the city park, where rural scenery served to refresh the town dweller exhausted by the confusion and strain of modern urban existence.

What, precisely, was this rural scenery so essential to the well-being of the urban citizen? Did Olmsted have any particular landscape in mind? Certainly it was not the everyday scenery of the rural East: plowed fields, row crops, orchards, and muddy roads; nor was it the half-tamed scenery of the pioneer West. His was an idealized landscape, compounded of the English

deer park and of pastoral New England; an underinhabited landscape of undulating lawns, groves of trees cleared of undergrowth, massive rocks, clear streams, wide and placid views; one
that conformed to Winckelmann's definition of the Classic as
possessing a noble simplicity and quiet grandeur. It eliminated
the bric-a-brac beloved by the early nineteenth-century gardeners: the ruins and rustic shelters and tombs, and the historical
allusions which Bryant and others had hoped to see introduced
had no place in Olmsted's work. Aside from a weakness for a
kind of Olde Englishe nomenclature—"Greensward," "Nether-
mead," "Lullwater," "Fens," "Playstead"—he betrayed no sympathy for historical reminiscence.

Olmsted in fact shared little of the nature Romanticism of the
prewar generation. He expressed no anti-urban bias, nor any
great love of the wilderness experience. And while he was persuaded that the contemplation of rural scenery had a therapeutic
effect, he did not ascribe to the experience any religious value;
it gave pleasure and relaxation, and nothing more.

Though the purpose of the park—repeatedly stated—was to
refresh the city dweller by providing the contemplation of rural
scenery, neither Olmsted nor his numerous disciples ever explained how the cure operated; and in Olmsted's writings there
is so little evidence of familiarity with crowd behavior, or with
the inhabitants of industrial centers, that one is tempted to con-
clude that the frequently mentioned "exhausted townsman" was
simply a convenient lay figure, necessary for the composition of
the picture—much like the shepherd who reclines on his elbow
in the foreground of eighteenth-century landscape paintings,
gazing at the ruins and providing scale.

The variety and magnitude of Olmsted's work, its calm perfection, and the indignant manner in which he defended it against
criticism or misuse not only discouraged all doubts as to its
merits, but established it as the standard for all other city parks
regardless of the needs of the local population. But Olmsted's
fame must eventually rest upon his work as one of the great
American artists of the nineteenth century. He created a uniform
style where previously there had only been diversity; he per-

fected a medium, and taught a new appreciation of natural beauty.

These are substantial accomplishments; must we admire him as a social prophet as well? There was nothing new in his belief that environments could and should be designed to produce health and a sense of well-being; countless environmental reformers had already reached that conclusion. His insistence that parks serve one purpose only was entirely in keeping with the widespread contemporary emphasis on spaces with specialized functions. Though he wrote voluminously and with much assurance on problems of urbanism, his field of reference was limited, and what he said was all too often commonplace. On the rare occasions when he tried his hand at designing communities he showed little understanding of how landscape architecture could improve the way people worked and lived; his talents showed themselves at their best when it was a question of designing places of recreation or estates for the rich.

We are now in the midst of redefining that recreational environment. The city dweller is still exhausted, to be sure, by city existence, and he still relishes a glimpse of rural scenery. But weariness is no longer his chief complaint, and participation rather than passive contemplation is what he is asking.

3. SLUMS AND TENEMENTS

If we suppose that Americans a hundred years ago were indifferent to the slums we do them an injustice; they were better acquainted with them than we are. Cities were smaller and easier to explore, whether in a slow-moving streetcar or on foot; and journalists looking for sensational copy wrote much about the slums and their lurid existence, thereby feeding a taste for dramatic contrasts, the juxtaposition of sunlight and shadow, squalor and wealth. Few guidebooks to American cities failed to mention the more notorious streets and rookeries. Early accounts of the Five Points in New York were detailed; insensitive to ethnic picturesqueness, unburdened by sociological theory, they bluntly described the section as a "nauseous sink of filthy poverty and beastly crime. . . . A great plague spot of moral pollution and death," and to drive their point home there were illustrations showing the crumbling houses, the gin shops, the unpaved streets swarming with drunks and beggars and prostitutes and vagrant children. The public reacted with predictable indignation: at all costs the slum must be destroyed. One of the differences between the first half of the nineteenth century and the second was in the method chosen. The shift from one to the other marks an important change in American attitudes toward the urban environment.

In the early days it was not always easy to identify the slum; was it not merely a part of town that had been allowed by its inhabitants to deteriorate? Until the great influx of foreigners into New York directly after the Civil War, few dwellings or tenements were specifically built to accommodate the poor. Fifty years previously the Five Points had been a region of comfortable single-family brick houses, with not a few houses of some distinction—all of them American versions of the average English middle-class dwelling. The New York version was wider and more elaborate than the Boston version, but it lacked the Boston service alley in the rear, and the penalty was eventually paid; back-to-back building became the curse of New York. It was not until the 1830s that indoor plumbing was introduced to most New York houses, and by that time the original owners of the Five Points dwellings had moved out, to live where there was more space and less business. The majority of the houses had merely one water outlet, and the backyard was where the privies stood.

When the first owners withdrew, they were replaced by a poorer and more numerous group; the houses became lodging houses or were divided (and redivided in the course of time) into flats with airless, windowless bedrooms, a community faucet in what had once been the kitchen, and privies in the yard. Later, with increasing pressure, more flats were built in the backyard, or in the attic and cellar.

Yet the exterior aspect of the houses—indeed of the whole neighborhood—remained much the same. It was shabbier, dirtier, noisier, more crowded, but to the passerby all that was evident was a sad deterioration. Clearly the new tenants had lower standards than their predecessors; the general sloppiness indicated either foreign origin or deficient upbringing. So in the 1850s it seemed logical to define the slum (though the word was little used in polite circles) as that part of town inhabited by the poor and shiftless and criminal. The man-made environment of substantial brick houses had once been extremely pleasant; it could be so again, given a better type of resident.

As it was, trash and garbage overflowed the sidewalks into the mud and stagnant water of the alleys. Ashes contributed to the litter. In the more prosperous parts of the city gas was piped in, and coal was burned, but the slum still depended on wood. Vendors of firewood came down in their wagons from Connecticut; they drove through the poorer streets, stopping from time to time to yell out "Wud!" After dark when cookstoves were lighted the area was wrapped in a haze of wood smoke. The air was redolent of horses; a century ago New York counted more than a hundred thousand. At the end of the day the teamsters and drivers usually parked their wagons along any convenient curb near home—creating traffic hazards and (according to contemporary complaints) invitations to crime and immorality. As for the animals themselves, they were lodged in yards or in public stables —filthy firetraps, sometimes five stories tall. Manure was heaped in back alleys and vacant lots, rarely if ever carried away. A constant element in the street life of the congested districts was the spectacle of sick or exhausted horses floundering and slipping on the wet streets, and the sounds of brutality and fury. Cows were less conspicuous, but they were there; more than ten thousand of them were kept in various underground stables in New York until well into the seventies. "In some of these stables," Paul Gates tells us, "milk dealers rented stalls, paying five dollars a year, while in other cases nearby residents bought slops from brewers or distillers for seven to nine cents a barrel. The milk from cows fed this 'smoking hot' distillery mash was bluish, watery and insipid." The cows did not survive for long; and it was in the Five Points that most of the tanneries, rendering plants, and glue factories were located.

The filth and overcrowding and general misery of this way of life did not go unnoticed. As early as 1840 there had been detailed surveys of the housing situation in New York; thousands of families were discovered living in wet cellars or in makeshift flats in the backyards; many thousands more were packed together in dark rooms. In the 1850s so-called model tenements were built. Gotham Court was one of the earliest; the brainchild of a benevolent Quaker, it was five stories high and accommodated five hundred people without plumbing or heat. A row of privies was built in the cellar. In 1865 it was labeled "about an average specimen . . . in respect to salubrity." The Big Flat, also built in the 1850s, was likewise a model tenement for one hundred families. It soon acquired the reputation of being a hangout for thieves; an attempt to convert it into a home for working women was a sensational failure.

What was wrong with these and similar efforts? Public opinion viewed them with scepticism. If, as was generally agreed, a slum was that part of town where antisocial behavior prevailed, then the sensible course was to reform the behavior of its inhabitants; and in fact that was the method most in favor for solving the problem of the slum. Sanctimonious criticism of the way of life of the poor was as general then as it is now, but along with it went recognition that slum dwellers could not be held entirely responsible for their degraded state: certain benign influences had been kept from them. They were victims of poor schooling or no schooling at all; of faulty religious and moral instruction in the home; of the lack of jobs. In 1858, one hundred thousand New Yorkers were members of families with no wage earner. When in the fifties the Children's Aid Society was founded, to operate chiefly in the Five Points, it gave as its objectives "to promote the *education,* the *employment,* and the permanent change of character of the children of the poor."

The list of the Society's activities in that worst of all slums was impressive: trade schools, employment agencies, subsidized emigration of orphaned children in new homes in the Midwest, dormitories for homeless children, and the rescuing of children from jails. But changes of the environment were not included; the Society had no playgrounds, no clinics, no cleanup campaigns, no games, no excursions to the country, no model flats or tenements. Though it was well acquainted with the menaces, physical as well as moral, of the slum it appears to have worked on the assumption that if the children of the neighborhood could be taught to be industrious, law-abiding, self-supporting adults, the problems of the slum would automatically disappear.

It was in the decades after the war that a radical change in this point of view began to take place. The causes were several, but perhaps it can be said that for a variety of reasons the slum, instead of being popularly defined by the kind of people who lived in it, was redefined by the kind of houses to be found there, by the environment. For that was a time when the house, the dwelling, began to lose its old traditional aspect and assume a number of new forms. As the city grew, the speculator-built tenement for the immigrant population became general; in the emerging streetcar suburbs of New York and Brooklyn, free-standing frame cottages or houses were built for wage earners, and on the East Side row after row of brownstone mansions were bought by prosperous professional and business men. None of these resembled the others; and none of them resembled the old New York dwellings, now chiefly surviving in the slums.

The prestige of the brownstone house in New York harked back to the early 1850s; the stone, actually a sandstone, was favored by builders not only because it was cheap, and easy to work, but because it was undeniably elegant. A severely Classical or Italianate facade with a flat roof hidden by the cornice became almost universal, and one of the signs of a change in taste after the war was the increasingly condescending references to the monotony of New York facades in architectural journals; something with more of a play of light and shadow was what the seventies demanded. Anticipating Lewis Mumford's term, "The Brown Decades," a writer complained, "What is there in this dismal hue that so endears it to the sons of Manhattan? Brown stone would be well enough if the rage for brown stopped there. As a basis, brown is good. But observe the costly and magnificent streets inhabited by our men of wealth, and see to what length and height brown has been carried. Brown are the houses, from basement to roof; the railings are brown, and brown the blinds and shutters. . . . The eye roams over the house fronts, tall, solemn and monotonous, and wanders up and down the street, longing to rest upon some object that is not brown."

As far as exterior went, the brownstone house of the sixties was in the main loyal to the New York tradition: flat-roofed, narrow, with a stoop leading up to an ornate front door; the sunken basement area was likewise retained. But the interior was different: instead of the dining room being in the basement next to the kitchen, it was now upstairs, back of a greatly enlarged living room—an arrangement more in keeping with stylish forms of entertaining. Moreover the dining room jutted out into the yard in the back—a space from which the privy had been banished, and where laundry was no longer hung. Each of the bedrooms had an interior dressing room and bath, the downstairs hall was more spacious; and whereas the old New York dwelling had three stories, the brownstone house had four. It was true, as critics remarked, that the New York house was designed and built by a contractor or speculator, and that there was little individual variation, inside or out; whereas the contemporaneous Boston house was designed by an architect in the employ of the owner. But the very uniformity of the brownstone houses served to indicate the cost of the individual specimen within a few thousand dollars; they were easy to read as symbols of wealth and position.

And if a handsome prefabricated setting conferred status on the rich, could it not also be said that the poor likewise derived their status (or lack of it) from *their* environment? In the old days there had been a dramatic contrast between the former respectability of the old New York houses and the poverty of their tenants—a contrast unfavorable to the tenants. But there was no such contrast between tenants and the new tenements being rapidly built to accommodate the thousands of impoverished immigrants arriving in New York every month: to live badly and unhappily in these monstrous barracks, many of them five or six stories high, was no indication of being uncivilized. These new dwellings rising everywhere below Fourteenth Street and even farther north repudiated the old traditions of domestic architecture—in appearance, in floor plan, in construction, and in amenities. They were tall stacks of identical flats, four to a floor; they occupied up to three quarters of the narrow lot, with a dozen dark and airless rooms surrounding an interior stairwell. There were no private toilets, and only a communal water supply. Despite public outcries, denunciations in the press, and city ordinances, the new speculative tenements lacked elementary fire protection or adequate sewerage, and many were so flimsily and dishonestly built that they soon collapsed. "Our American cities," an editor wrote at the time of the first tenement boom, "unlike any other cities in the world, are shells of architecture, thrown up and together with such speed as may well be suggested by capital in hot haste on the one side, and crafty contract, greedy of profit, on the other." Architects urged the adoption of floor plans allowing both of privacy and of air.

The strongest reason for objecting to the existence of tenements—and after the war almost a third of the city's population was living in them—was their filthy, crowded, unsanitary condition. "Disease," said the Report of the Metropolitan Police in 1866, "is certainly working in them. They are the plague spots, both of disease and crime threatening the community." *Harper's Weekly* published a series of articles on "Water and Health," "Light and Health." There were, it wrote in 1867, "over four thousand dwellings constructed for the purpose of tenement houses in which dwell one hundred thousand men, women, and children, in which four thousand persons die annually from diseases generated by the filth and the imperfect ventilation in which they are forced to exist." The paper also noted that flats in many old family mansions were subdivided and sublet by their impoverished tenants: as for the new tenements, most of them "are five and six stories high throughout, are built on lots 25 x 100 feet without courtyards, and each is occupied often by as many as four or five hundred tenants. It is simply impossible that houses thus constructed can be properly ventilated or kept clean."

Proposals for improving tenement house design or remodeling existing tenement houses therefore dwelt almost entirely on the sanitary problem, and the need for social amenities—privacy, space for play and recreation, even space for hanging out wash— was given little thought. The Tenement House Act of 1867—the first of its kind—was meant to reduce the density of population in the most overcrowded sections, to improve natural lighting, and ventilation. Every room was to have a proper "ventilating passage" communicating with the outdoors; there were to be sewer connections, and mortality was to be further reduced by an annual whitewashing of all walls and ceilings.

The law, such as it was, never was properly enforced; but for all its limitations it marked the dawn of a realization that there was such a thing as an urban environment which could be planned or modified to foster health—an environment with its own artificial system of light and water and air. It contained little more than that, to be sure; and in addition to its social short-comings it was restricted by being confined to the conventional dimensions of the city lot, or at most the city block. This limita-tion had at least two unhappy consequences: no housing com-plexes, no embryonic communities occupying more than a block could be built; the service alley and the street remained the chief sources of light and air, and no court or open yard was feasible. The other consequence was a hideous interior plan: an ever-increasing emphasis in the interior arrangement on corri-dors or exterior balconies as means of access. The traditional provision of rooms for a family in the old converted mansions had been crowded and unwholesome, but it at least created a group of related domestic spaces. With the coming of the long dark corridor (or what was in many respects even worse, the outside balcony) the time-honored organization of space for family living became obsolete—at least for the poor. A linear arrangement of rooms, reached by one or two flights of stairs, became the standard plan in the newer tenements. It is more than likely that the layout was in part inspired by that of the contemporary office building; for the office building, just begin-ning to evolve in the seventies, was a sensational example of an environment skillfully designed in terms of maximum rent per square foot.

"The right which every citizen has to have a cleanly neighbor-hood around him has never been fully recognized," was the italicized complaint of a New York paper in 1867. By that it no doubt meant the right of every citizen to be protected from disease emanating from the slums; for the obsession with sanitation had the effect of expanding the individual's environment from the house to the neighborhood and ultimately to the city. This was one of the results of the outbreak of cholera in New York in the spring of 1866.

It made its appearance in October 1865 when an English steamer reported on its arrival that there were sixty cases of cholera on board.

The passengers were promptly quarantined, but the citizens of New York, already acutely conscious of the need to control disease, demanded that a more active sanitary board be created to cope with this and other menaces to health, and in the winter of 1866 the State of New York authorized a Metropolitan Board of Health to supervise a Metropolitan Sanitary District. For the first time Americans organized themselves into a body to deal with a problem of health and sanitation; and the Metropolitan District itself represented a very early example of an administrative territory that ignored existing political boundaries.

The Board of Health was by good fortune composed of energetic and experienced men, converts to the relatively new theory that cholera was usually transmitted by a contaminated water supply. It therefore set to work organizing the gigantic task of cleaning up the city, of disinfecting dangerous areas, and quarantining the victims. The streets of New York, few of them paved, had been buried under layers of mud and filth, sometimes more than a foot deep. Backyards and vacant lots were heaped high with rotting garbage, the manure of cows and horses, the overflow of privies. In the poorer and more congested parts of the city, goats and pigs still foraged in back alleys. In the course of the first months of the campaign more than 160,000 tons of manure were removed, thousands of backyards and privies were disinfected, and hundreds of cisterns were ordered emptied. The bedding and clothing of cholera victims were burned, and (often in the face of opposition) quarantine centers were set up. There seems to have been no mood of panic in New York, and by November 1866 there had been only 591 deaths from the disease. The effectiveness of the measures taken by the Board of Health was generally acknowledged, and the notion, hitherto widespread in all classes, that cholera was the result of intemperate and vicious habits, was replaced by the notion that its origins were to be found in the environment.

In his remarkable book *The Cholera Years*, C. E. Rosenberg gives an account of the epidemic of 1866, as well as of the two previous ones in 1832 and 1849. But the great value of the work lies in its discussion and analysis of the ways in which physicians and the public responded to the disease during each outbreak; of how cholera, "a scourge to the sinful to many Americans in 1832 had by 1866 become the consequence of remediable faults in sanitation." Whereas (Rosenberg observes) "ministers in 1832 urged morality upon their congregation as a guarantee of health, their forward-looking counterparts in 1866 endorsed sanitary reform as a necessary prerequisite to moral improvement."

As a result of the health crisis of 1866 and the successful strategy of the Board of Health, a series of long overdue sanitary reforms were instituted in one American city after another—a movement known in its time as the Sanitary Awakening.

The alacrity with which health reforms were legislated strongly suggests that the American public had for some time been unconsciously waiting for an excuse to adopt a kind of naive environmentalism as a basis for redefining the city. The sudden awareness of sanitation and public health produced a redefinition of urban space. The city ceased to be the domain of a society neatly divided into the indigent poor, the deserving poor, the middle class, and the rich; it was now seen as an environment, governed by natural laws and with natural boundaries. It took time for the new definition to be officially accepted. It was not until 1887 that the Small Parks Law permitted the demolition of obsolete buildings and the creation of public areas of air and sunlight, and the cutting through of streets to improve sanitary conditions. It was at that period that George Waring played an important part in the ordering of New York's health and sanitation. And it was many years later still that the social and human aspects of the urban environment were taken into account. In the postwar decades all that mattered was the environment designed for physical health.

How indiscriminating the acceptance of the new environmental definition could be is indicated by a quotation by Rosenberg from the Health Officer of Cincinnati in 1866: "Before erecting statues, building opera houses and art galleries and buying expensive pictures, towns should be relieved of bad odours and fermenting pestilence. Good privies are far higher signs of civilization than grand palaces and fine art galleries."

The new faith, less extravagantly expressed, was espoused by social reformers, architects, teachers, and clergymen. It represented enlightened opinion; it was a polite and indirect way of rebelling against the arbitrary forms imposed on society—and on the landscape—by an earlier generation of classically educated Americans. The war on the slum could be resumed, now that more effective weapons were at hand. The determination to produce more sanitary living conditions in the tenements was reinforced, and the old moralistic solution to the slum was put to one side. A New York editor declared that if the Five Points was ever to be cleaned up it would not be done by sermons and Bible classes. "The remedy of all evils in the city," he declared, "must be topographical."

In other words, the solution lay in acquiring a greater knowledge of the natural order and in controlling it more effectively.

CHAPTER NINE

The Centennial

At dawn on the tenth of May, 1876, the bell in the tower of Independence Hall began to ring. It rang for a full half hour and one by one all the chimes and church bells in Philadelphia joined in the clamor. They were proclaiming the opening of the Centennial Exhibition to celebrate a hundred years of American Independence.

For some years the city had been preparing for the event, asking itself how it could best play the role of host to millions of visitors from all over the world. Historically its qualifications were impeccable, despite the rival claims of Boston and New York and Washington, but it had the reputation for being a quiet, somewhat provincial city, loyal to old-fashioned ways. Travelers marvelled at the repeated vistas of neat brick houses along quiet streets, but for all the private devotion to white doorsteps and sparkling window panes Philadelphia a hundred years ago was neither clean nor attractive. Its unpaved, poorly lighted streets were strewn with garbage never collected, muddy from the waste water of nearby kitchens. The old section of the city by comparison with that of New York or Boston had an almost medieval aspect; blocks of one-story houses sheltered a growing slum population; wealthy families were moving away, either to the western sections of the city or out to the new communities along the main line of the Pennsylvania Railroad. The port no longer flourished, and the growth of the city was haphazard and diffuse.

To many Philadelphians these traits were not in themselves intolerable; they reflected, though in no very flattering light, the modesty and conservatism of the Quaker philosophy. But there were restless spirits advocating change; was this a city that could compete with New York? Was this a suitable background for a World's Fair? A commission sent to Europe to study the organization of international exhibitions brought back sobering information on the work and expense involved, and also reported on the impact of such events on the local economy. Whereas world cities like London and Paris and Vienna were little affected, socially or economically, smaller cities could either be ruined or transformed. Philadelphia, though the second largest city in the United States with a population of some seven hundred thousand thought of itself as belonging in that second group.

So the approaching fair served to vitalize many vague plans for improvement. Penn Square, a park in the very center of the older Philadelphia, became the site of a new and extremely pretentious city hall which, when once completed, ranked as the largest building in the nation. One-story houses were no longer to be allowed. A new market was built, and there were proposals —never carried out—for beautifying the waterfront. The system of horsecar lines was so greatly extended that Philadelphia earned the name of having the best mass transportation network of any American city. Impressive new buildings began to rise, and there was a project for making Broad Street "a far more imposing avenue than the Champs Elysées."

All of these proposals were designed to change Philadelphia from what was called "a mere aggregation of townships" into a full-fledged metropolis. But the most auspicious step had been the acquisition shortly after the war of some three thousand acres of open country, along the Schuylkill and Wissahickon rivers. It was a beautiful and varied landscape of fields and forests, named Fairmont Park after an estate included in the area. Though the original reason for buying the land had been to protect the water supply of the city, it was soon evident that the park could be made into a vast pleasure ground for the people of Philadelphia. It was accordingly landscaped by the architect H. J. Schwarzmann. The pleasant scenery which he produced in a surprisingly brief length of time was not to everyone's taste. Unlike Central Park, Fairmont Park in its original form had been rich in associations, containing areas of true farmland. "The dells are converted into gentle slopes," a visitor complained, "The wild flowers and ferns which beautified them have given place to greensward. . . . Primness and stableness is now the rule. Art has sought to improve nature, and has almost obliterated it, instead." But this was not the point of view of the leading citizens: many of them, as in New York, banded together to foster the cultural role of the new park; to provide it with inspiring statues, busts, and commemorative fountains. When it was proposed to set aside some 340 acres of the most accessible section for an International Exhibition the idea was enthusiastically received, especially as two of the projected buildings were to be preserved, one to be an art gallery, the other a horticultural hall. These two institutions, along with the celebrated zoological gardens, would permanently fix the educational character of the park.

Whatever objections purists of the Olmsted school may have raised to this high-handed appropriation of scenery for festive purposes, as far as the fair itself was concerned a more favorable location could hardly have been found. The park environment became one of its greatest assets, for the fair was the first example of an exhibition designed to take advantage of its natural setting. This distinction was not lost on the public. Philadelphia proudly reminded visitors that it possessed a new kind of designed environment: architecture and landscape architecture blended into a harmonious whole. The poet Bayard Taylor pointed out that whereas the first World's Fair in London had had exterior space but no landscaping, and Paris had had neither space *nor* landscaping, and Vienna in 1873 had had space *and* landscaping, but no topographical variety, the Centennial Exhibition could boast of all three. "Fairmont Park," he wrote, "offers a solution which could hardly be improved upon. With its old trees, its slopes of mellow turf, its high breezy plateau, it seems designed by nature for just such an occasion."

The grounds were laid out on a generous and imaginative scale, taking advantage of the uneven terrain. One of the innovations of the Centennial Fair was the great number of small pavilions; these were informally sited on curving parklike roads to produce an almost suburban atmosphere, while the larger, more imposing buildings were related to the two great axes, crossing at right angles and dividing the grounds into four parts.

Appropriately enough, architect and landscape architect were the same man: Schwarzmann, the creator of Fairmont Park. The son of a noted German painter, brought up in Munich at a period when that city was experimenting with parks and urban design, he showed himself capable of doing what few of his American contemporaries could do: producing competent (if uninspired) designs in two separate fields. His conscientiously monumental art gallery—in "Modern Renaissance"—and his conscientiously fantastic Horticultural Hall with Moorish ornamentation were coolly received by contemporary critics, and subsequent critics have been severe on his lack of structural innovation. But Schwarzmann's buildings were utilitarian containers well adapted to their contents; for the innumerable cluttered displays and showcases he provided a spacious and dignified background.

There was not much to be said for the design of the smaller buildings—the pavilions put up by the states, the participating nations, and various private industries and organizations. The English building, a large half-timbered structure with an interior of medieval gloom, was extremely popular. The Japanese pavilion excited curiosity from the very beginning when the laughable methods of the Japanese workers could be observed; later when the building had been assembled and furnished the public was full of admiration for the simplicity of the construction and design, the flexible partitions between the rooms, and the chaste ornamentation. In subsequent years American architects had no difficulty in combining what they considered the best features of the English and Japanese pavilions in their own version of the Queen Anne style. As for the pavilions of the states, they were obviously not meant to be taken seriously as architecture. Most of them were of frame, lavishly adorned with verandas, turrets, dormer windows, ingenious interlocking gables, painted in lurid colors. Critics were moderately pleased with the New Jersey building—"though perhaps a trifle overdone;" the Connecticut building was the most popular. A quality which they all shared was their almost total indifference to any formal architectural idiom. It might be supposed that the occasion for the very existence of the Centennial Exhibition would have inspired some reference to the Revolutionary period; yet there were no replicas of eighteenth-century buildings, no adaptations of the Colonial style. Massachusetts produced a pavilion hailed as "a specimen of Colonial architecture, quaint-looking, derived partly from the English and partly from the French." It had a large central tower with a pointed roof; wide verandas surrounded it, and it was painted brown with stripes of chrome green.

Indeed, aside from one small building, "a New England Log House" purported to be an exact imitation of a Revolutionary dwelling where divers Colonial antiquities were displayed, the absence of any attempt to recall American history or the evolution of American civilization was one of the remarkable features of the Centennial Exhibition. There had been a proposal for a demonstration of Colonial farming techniques, contrasting them with those of 1876, but nothing came of it. As can be imagined, there was no lack of full-blown oratory both at the opening and at the closing of the fair; yet references to history were perfunctory and few. The past was prologue; interesting enough, but not to be compared with the marvels of the present and the promise of the future. A remarkable exhibit was the "Centennial Safe." In it were deposited not only the autographs of all the fair notables, and photographs of the fair itself, but the autograph of anyone who cared to pay five dollars to be included. The safe (so all contributors were told) would remain unopened until the next Centennial in 1976.

Surely no great public event in American history has ever been treated with such condescension. Few modern American history books give the Centennial Exhibition more than a passing reference, and it has fared especially ill at the hands of the art and social historians who have discussed it in some detail, usually to condemn it as a tasteless display of mid-nineteenth-century materialism. Criticisms of the sort were uttered in 1876; a prominent lecturer sarcastically inquired why the fair did not include, among typical American products, a New York tenement house, an abandoned farm, a corrupt politician.

Certainly the artistic component was less than brilliant. Although all participating countries were requested to exhibit works of art "of a high order of merit," with the exception of Great Britain no nation bothered to send any important examples of contemporary painting or sculpture, and the American examples were poorly chosen, though the display of Rogers groups was popular. All visitors to the fair remarked on the large numbers who were interested in the art collections, and the photographic display—mostly of landscapes—surprised many by its variety; here again the English contributions were judged the best. The display techniques of the commercial exhibits—show cases containing formal arrangements of stuffed birds, sewing machines, inkwells, gatling guns, pumps, etc.—appear to have been strikingly successful; Howells mentioned the "finest of the pavilions," that of an Oswego starch manufacturer, "where an artistic use of the corn and its stalk had been made into the carved ornamentation of the structure. But there were many and many cases and pavilions which were tasteful and original in high degree," and he particularly liked the display of agricultural machinery. The absence of any overall esthetic coordination of the exhibits produced a bewildering impression: Mrs. Brooks of Arkansas created an *alto relievo* of the "Sleeping Iolanthe" in butter, weighing fourteen pounds. Mr. Schlich of New York exhibited an automatic bottle-washing machine. A pair of moccasins, made of tanned human skin, was displayed by the Department of the Interior.

It was how things worked that had the widest appeal. Among the marvels to be seen was the newly invented typewriter, the rotary press, the safety bicycle, the electric lamp, the telephone. The atmosphere in the large Main Building and in the Agricultural Building was that of a county fair: samples and leaflets were distributed, demonstrations given, and children were presented with souvenir hats and allowed to walk through the latest model sleeping cars. There was a continuous background of music.

No history, no art; education of a very fleeting kind; nevertheless the crowds enjoyed themselves wherever they strolled through the grounds. There were popcorn stands and ornate dispensers of soda water; band concerts, the smallest steam engine in the world; the largest cigar in the world, the largest opal in the world; an indoor waterfall fifty feet high. At night there were torchlight processions, and magnificent displays of fireworks. "Magnesium balloons were let off. A simultaneous flight of shells of turquoise and ruby stars followed, and then came an ascent of 100 brilliant tourbillons, followed by a flight of rockets and the discharge of a battery of saucissons." Each state had its special day, and the governor appeared to make a speech and shake hands. Parades were almost continuous: Knights Templar, Knights of Pythias, Odd Fellows, all in their respective uniforms, with music. Outside the fairgrounds was something hitherto unknown: an amusement sector, "Shantyville," the predecessor of many midways. From the opening of the fair until its closing in November, more than nine million visitors came out to Fairmont Park, complained about the inadequate signs, the ignorance of the guards, the high price of food, the errors in the catalog; admired the beauty of the site and the splendid flower beds, the quality of the items displayed, and above all the punctuality, the ease of movement, the quiet efficiency of the whole operation.

President Grant, accompanied by Mrs. Grant and the Emperor and Empress of Brazil, inaugurated the Exhibition on that May morning in a lengthy but impressive outdoor ceremony. While a crowd of a hundred thousand patiently watched, some perched on the two gigantic gilt winged horses—"Pegasus being led by the Muses"—others on the nearby roofs, speech after speech was made. Wagner's "Centennial March"—commissioned for the occasion—was played, and Whittier's "Centennial Hymn" was sung. Then the President reached into his tailcoat pocket, produced a manuscript, and read his speech in a mild, almost inaudible voice. He then declared the Exhibition open; at a given signal the American flag was run up the highest staff on the Main Building.

The Presidential party then went to the center of the Main Building where stood the immense Corliss machine, 30 feet high, weighing over 700 tons, capable of producing 1400 horsepower, which was to provide power for all the exhibits throughout the fair. George Corliss, the engineer and inventor, stood next to it, bareheaded. "Are you both ready?" he said to the President and the Emperor; "Then Your Majesty will turn that handle." There ensued a sound of rushing steam. "Now, Mr. President, yours." The sound of steam became much louder as the other engine joined in. Then the Corliss machine rapidly assumed its normal rate, and the subdued din of planing, stamping, turning, and the whirl of wheels throughout the exhibits in the building made a chorus to the murmur of the underground shafting.

True to its love for the biological simile, the nineteenth-century public compared the Corliss machine to a great heart whose steady beating kept the entire exhibition alive and moving. But the Corliss machine had another more contemporary significance. The reason why the Corliss machine as a type was called the greatest advance in the use of steam power since the day of Watt was its unique ability to regulate its own speed and its own consumption of energy, depending on the load imposed upon it. Corliss had developed the machine many years earlier in response to the insistent demand among New England textile manufacturers for regularity of speed in the looms. The machine therefore did much more than produce power: it produced it in a steady, uninterrupted flow.

Steady uninterrupted flow was becoming the universal American requirement, not merely in industry, but in every field of production of goods and wealth; even in the control of movement. The city sought in countless ways to achieve it in the flow of traffic, in public utilities, in economic activity. It was therefore appropriate that the Centennial Exhibition itself provide illustrations of the control of flow of movement. The entrances to the grounds were provided with a novel apparatus: an automatic, self-registering turnstile. It proved to be remarkably efficient in regulating the flow of visitors; so much so that the public was often bewildered by the absence of waiting lines on the most popular days. Movement to the fair from the city was handled with equal efficiency. Perhaps for the first time in history traffic flow was planned: temporary streetcar lines were laid down, and were able to discharge 12,000 passengers an hour; special railroad tracks and temporary stations were built for the same purpose, and these took care of an added 24,000 an hour. Within the grounds themselves a narrow-gauge railroad, circumscribing the entire four hundred acres, provided for movement, and there was in addition a small elevated railroad crossing Belmont Ravine; its wheels had rubber tires to reduce noise and vibration. Previous to the opening of the fair, tracks had been laid directly to the site of the buildings, for the uninterrupted transportation of building materials and displays. When visitors commented on the smoothness of movement, the absence of jams, they were therefore acknowledging the efficiency of the new techniques of regulated flow.

Enterprises on such a vast and complex scale have always had a way of obscuring and transcending their original purpose. Whether the Centennial was a commercial or a patriotic display, whether it enlightened the public or merely entertained it were questions debated even during its four months of existence. There were those who saw it justified as a stimulus to the national economy, still recovering from the panic of three years before; and there were those who welcomed it as an encouragement to immigration from Europe. To innumerable orators it marked the triumphant end of a century of nationhood, and the beginning of even greater accomplishments. To its contemporaries, in short, the Centennial was a sign of growth.

In a more distant retrospect it becomes an event in its own right. With great clarity and sureness it manifested the spirit which in the decades to come was to remake the national environment. Here in Fairmont Park, within topographically defined limits, was a characteristically American organization of space: the interaction between landscape and architecture, the areas with specialized functions, the emphasis on the linear process; here also was displayed the principle of regulated flow —of energy, of materials, of people. The whole world could see and wonder at the qualities of Americans: their indifference to history, their delight in organizing space and time and labor, their eagerness to acquire new ideas, their abundant creativity. It is from this event, all but forgotten by most of us, that we can well date the birth of a new relationship between the American people and their landscape.

In the late afternoon of November 10, 1876, President Grant and his cabinet, accompanied by a distinguished group of citizens, arrived in the fairgrounds. After several speeches the President motioned to the operator of a telegraph instrument near at hand, who tapped out the signal "7-6." The same current gave a signal to the Corliss engine to stop. It did so, and all the shafts and belts, all the hammers and presses and wheels fell motionless and silent, and the Centennial Exhibition had come to an end.

Reading List

CHAPTER ONE

Lewis Atherton *Main Street on the Middle Border* Bloomington, 1954, University of Indiana Press

Dee Brown *The Year of the Century: 1876* New York, Charles Scribner's Sons, 1966

J. C. Furnas *The Americans: A Social History of the United States* New York, G. P. Putnam's Sons, 1969

Paul Gates *Agriculture and the Civil War* New York, Alfred A. Knopf, 1965

C. N. Glaab and A. T. Brown *A History of Urban America* New York, The MacMillan Co., 1967

H. M. Jones *The Age of Energy* New York, The Viking Press, 1970

E. C. Kirkland *Industry Comes of Age* New York, Holt, Rinehart and Winston, Inc., 1961

Arthur Mann *Yankee Reformers in the Urban Age* Cambridge, Belknap Press of the Harvard University Press, 1954

Lewis Mumford *The Brown Decades* New York, Dover Publications, 1955

Norman Newton *Design on the Land* Cambridge, Belknap Press of the Harvard University Press, 1971

J. W. Powell *Report on the Arid Region of the United States* Wallace Stegner, editor. Cambridge, Belknap Press of the Harvard University Press, 1962

John Reps *The Making of Urban America* Princeton, Princeton University Press, 1965

A. M. Schlesinger *The Rise of the City* Chicago, Quadrangle Books, 1971

C. Tunnard *The City of Man* New York, Charles Scribner's Sons, 1953

Statistical Atlas of the United States, based on the results of the Ninth Census, 1870, 1874

CHAPTER TWO

Theodore C. Blegen *Minnesota: A History of the State* Minneapolis, University of Minnesota Press, 1963

Ralph H. Brown *Historical Geography of the United States* New York, Harcourt, Brace and World, Inc., 1948

Gilbert C. Fite *The Farmers' Frontier* New York, Holt, Rinehart and Winston, 1966

Hamlin Garland *Boy Life on the Prairie* Lincoln, University of Nebraska Press, 1961

Stanley N. Murray *The Valley Comes of Age* Fargo, North Dakota Institute for Regional Studies, 1967

Herbert S. Schell *History of South Dakota* Lincoln, University of Nebraska Press, 1968

CHAPTER THREE

Allan G. Bogue *From Prairie to Corn Belt* Chicago, University of Chicago Press, 1963

H. W. S. Cleveland *Landscape Architecture as Applied to the Wants of the West;* Roy Lubove, editor. Pittsburgh, University of Pittsburgh Press, 1965

Carl Condit *American Building Art* Chicago, University of Chicago Press, 1960

Clarence H. Danhof *Change in Agriculture: The Northern United States 1820–1870* Cambridge, Harvard University Press, 1969

Siegfried Giedeon *Mechanization Takes Command* New York, W. W. Norton and Co., 1969

Harold Mayer and Richard Wade *Chicago: Growth of a Metropolis* Chicago, University of Chicago Press, 1969

Henry D. and Frances T. McCallum *The Wire that Fenced the West* Norman, University of Oklahoma Press, 1965

CHAPTER FOUR

Bainbridge Bunting *Houses of Boston's Back Bay* Cambridge, Belknap Press of the Harvard University Press, 1967

Oscar Handlin *Boston's Immigrants* Cambridge, Harvard University Press, 1959

Stewart Holbrook *The Yankee Exodus* Seattle, University of Washington Press, 1968

G. P. Marsh *Man and Nature* David Lowenthal, editor. Cambridge, The Belknap Press of the Harvard University Press, 1967

W. H. H. Murray *Adventures in the Wilderness* W. K. Verner, editor, The Adirondack Museum, Syracuse University Press, 1970

Sherry H. Olson *The Depletion Myth* Cambridge, Harvard University Press, 1971

Vincent Scully *The Shingle Style* New Haven, Yale University Press, 1955

J. C. Vance, Jr. "Housing the Worker" in *Economic Geography* 1966, 67

S. B. Warner *Streetcar Suburbs* Cambridge, Joint Center for Urban Studies, 1962

W. M. Whitehill *Boston: A Topographical History* Cambridge, The Belknap Press of Harvard University Press, 1968

A. B. Wolfe *The Lodging House Problem in Boston* Boston, Houghton, Mifflin and Co., 1906

R. Woods and A. J. Kennedy *The Zone of Emergence* Cambridge, The M. I. T. Press, 1969

CHAPTER FIVE

Robert L. Brandfon *Cotton Kingdom of the New South* Cambridge, Harvard University Press, 1967

E. M. Coulter *The South during Reconstruction:1865–1877* Baton Rouge, Louisiana State University Press, 1947

U. P. Phillips *American Negro Slavery* Baton Rouge, Louisiana State University Press, 1966

U. P. Phillips *Life and Labor in the Old South* Boston, Little, Brown and Co., 1929

Whitelaw Reid *After the War* C. Vann Woodward, editor. New York, Harper and Row, 1965

T. Saloutos *Farm Movements in the South* Lincoln, University of Nebraska Press, 1966

W. W. Sweet *The Story of Religion in America* New York, Harper and Brothers, 1950

R. C. Ward *Slavery in the Cities* New York, Oxford University Press, 1964

CHAPTER SIX

W. B. Bracke *Wheat Country* New York, Duell, Sloane and Pearce, 1950

Everett Dick *The Sod-house Frontier* Lincoln, Johnsen Publishing Co., 1954

H. S. Drago *Great American Cattle Trails* New York, Dodd, Mead and Co., 1965

R. R. Dykstra *The Cattle Towns* New York, Alfred A. Knopf, 1968

W. Gard *The Great Buffalo Hunt* Lincoln, University of Nebraska Press, 1968

E. S. Osgood *The Day of the Cattleman* Chicago, University of Chicago Press, 1953

Nash Smith *Virgin Land* New York, Vintage Books, 1957

W. P. Webb *The Great Plains* New York, Ginn and Co., 1931

CHAPTER SEVEN

California Heritage J. and L. Caughey, editors Los Angeles, Ward Ritchie Press, 1962

R. F. Dasmann *The Destruction of California* New York, Collier Books, 1966

Paul W. Gates *California Ranches and Farms* Madison, The State Historical Society of Wisconsin, 1967

Henry George *Our Land and Land Policy* San Francisco, 1871

California Agriculture C. B. Hutchinson, editor. Berkeley, University of California Press, 1946

Charles Nordhoff *California, a Book for Travelers and Settlers* New York, Harper and Brothers, 1874

Earl Pomeroy *In Search of the Golden West* New York, Alfred A. Knopf, 1957

A. F. Rolle and J. Gaines *The Golden State* New York, Thomas Y. Crowell Co., 1965

CHAPTER EIGHT

Constance Green *American Cities in the Growth of the Nation* New York, John De Graff, 1957

This Was America Oscar Handlin, editor Cambridge, Harvard University Press, 1949

W. D. Howells *A Hazard of New Fortunes* 1895

The Rise of an American Architecture Edgar Kaufmann, Jr. editor New York, Praeger Publishers, 1970

J. D. McCabe, Jr. *Lights and Shadows of New York Life* facsimile edition, New York, Farrar, Straus and Giroux, 1970

Lewis Mumford *Sticks and Stones* New York, Boni and Liveright, 1924

Allan R. Pred *The Spatial Dynamics of United States Urban Industrial Growth* Cambridge, MIT Press, 1966

C. F. Rosenberg *The Cholera Years* Chicago, University of Chicago Press, 1962

Walt Whitman *Democratic Vistas* 1871

Index